POLITICAL ISSUES
IN
LUKE-ACTS

Prayers for
St. Luke's Day

Almighty God, who inspired your servant Luke the physician to set forth in the Gospel the love and healing power of your Son: Graciously continue in your Church this love and power to heal, to the praise and glory of your Name; through Jesus Christ our Lord, who lives and reigns with you, in the unity of the Holy Spirit, one God, now and for ever. *Amen.*

Collect for St. Luke's Day
The Book of Common Prayer

Father,
you chose Luke the evangelist to reveal
by preaching and writing
the mystery of your love for the poor.
Unite in one heart and spirit
all who glory in your name,
and let all nations come to see your salvation.
Grant this through our Lord Jesus Christ, your Son,
who lives and reigns with you and the Holy Spirit,
one God, for ever and ever.

Opening Prayer for Feast of St. Luke
The Sacramentary of the Roman Missal

POLITICAL ISSUES
IN
LUKE-ACTS

EDITED BY
RICHARD J. CASSIDY
AND
PHILIP J. SCHARPER

ORBIS BOOKS

Maryknoll, New York 10545

With the principal exceptions of the essays by Professors Danker and Derrett, the Bible translations in this volume are from the Revised Standard Version of the Bible copyright 1946, 1952 & 1971, 1973 by the Division of Christian Education of the National Council of the Churches of Christ in the U.S.A. and are used by permission.

Library of Congress Cataloging in Publication Data

Main entry under title:

Political issues in Luke-Acts.

   Includes bibliographical references and index.
   Contents: Luke's position on politics and society
in Luke-Acts / Robert O'Toole—The women at Luke's
supper / Quentin Quesnell—Politics and peace (eirēnē)
in Luke's Gospel / Willard M. Swartley—[etc.]
   1. Bible. N.T. Luke—Criticism, interpretation,
etc.—Addresses, essays, lectures. 2. Bible.
N.T. Acts—Criticism, interpretation, etc.—
Addresses, essays, lectures. 3. Christianity and
politics—Biblical teaching—Addresses, essays,
lectures. 4. Sociology, Biblical—Addresses,
essays, lectures. I. Cassidy, Richard J.
II. Scharper, Philip J.
BS2589.P64   1983   226'.406   82-19060
ISBN 0-88344-390-2
ISBN 0-88344-385-6 (pbk.)

Table of Contents

Preface

Four years ago, when the editors at Orbis Books began to contact scholars at various universities and seminaries to solicit pre-publication comments for *Jesus, Politics, and Society,* they were encouraged by the positive sentiments expressed regarding the book. In giving their endorsements, many of these scholars emphasized that the book had identified important, hitherto largely overlooked, themes in Luke's Gospel.

This trend of favorable responses continued as the book was reviewed in various publications. Many reviewers included their own personal comments and assessments concerning Luke's presentation of Jesus' social stance. As additional reviews continued to appear, it became clear that there was a considerable amount of interest regarding these aspects of Luke's writing and that many scholars wished to have further attention given to them.

As a consequence, Dr. Scharper from Orbis Books and Fr. Cassidy began to explore the feasibility of a book that would provide the opportunity for other scholars to contribute their insights on these subjects. It was decided to begin the venture by contacting those scholars whose interpretations had been treated in the first book as well as those who had written extended reviews about it.

Understandably, many of those contacted could not free themselves from other obligations and commitments in order to contribute. However many of those contacted did respond affirmatively, some of them making suggestions regarding other scholars who might be contacted. In such a fashion the book gradually took on its present form as a collection of ten essays each dealing with one or more of the social and political themes in the Lukan writings.

As the table of contents reveals, several different subjects are treated and, in some instances, there are different treatments of the same subject. It almost goes without saying that the arguments advanced by the respective writers are their own and would not necessarily be accepted by other authors represented in the book or by the editors themselves.

It has been a rewarding experience to see the book take shape over these last two years. The editors wish to express their appreciation to all of the contributors for their essays. Gratitude is also due to Sr. Claudia Carlen, IHM, of St. John's Provincial Seminary and to Mr. John Eagleson of Orbis

Books for their help in bringing the book through its final stages. It is to be hoped that the essays in this volume will foster a deepened appreciation for the complex, rich descriptions which the evangelist Luke has bequeathed to us.

—Richard J. Cassidy
Philip J. Scharper

October 18, 1982

Abbreviations

BAG	Wm. Bauer, W. F. Arndt, and F. W. Gingrich, *Greek-English Lexicon of the NT*
BETL	Bibliotheca ephemeridum theologicarum lovaniensium
Bib	*Biblica*
BTB	*Biblical Theology Bulletin*
BWANT	Beiträge zur Wissenschaft vom Alten und Neuen Testament
BZ	*Biblische Zeitschrift*
CBQ	*Catholic Biblical Quarterly*
ETL	*Ephemerides theologicae lovanienses*
EvQ	*Evangelical Quarterly*
HNT	Handbuch zum Neuen Testament
ICC	International Critical Commentary
Int	*Interpretation*
JBC	R. E. Brown et al. (eds.), *The Jerome Biblical Commentary*
JBL	*Journal of Biblical Literature*
JQR	*Jewish Quarterly Review*
JTS	*Journal of Theological Studies*
NovT	*Novum Testamentum*
NTAbh	Neutestamentliche Abhandlungen
NTS	*New Testament Studies*
RE	*Realencyklopädie für protestantische Theologie und Kirche*
SBT	Studies in Biblical Theology
SNT	Studien zum Neuen Testament
SNTSMS	Society for New Testament Studies Monograph Series
STANT	Studien zum Alten und Neuen Testament
TAPA	*Transactions of the American Philological Association*
TDNT	G. Kittel and G. Friedrich (eds.), *Theological Dictionary of the New Testament*
TF	*Theologische Forschung*
WMANT	Wissenschaftliche Monographien zum Alten und Neuen Testament
ZNW	*Zeitschrift für die neutestamentliche Wissenschaft*

1

Luke's Position on Politics and Society in Luke-Acts

ROBERT F. O'TOOLE, S.J.

This article addresses the topic of Luke's position on politics and society in Luke-Acts. First it lists the precautions which such a study requires. Then it summarizes and analyzes Luke's position on politics and society.

PRELIMINARY CONSIDERATIONS REGARDING METHODOLOGY

A number of considerations govern and limit any study in Luke-Acts. What methodology should be used? Certainly, historical criticism has its defenders.[1] Even if historical criticism could establish that Jesus was executed as a political prisoner, little would be gained. Admittedly, Jesus was not a criminal, so very likely he was executed for political reasons.[2] The real question remains what was the validity of the political charges made against Jesus. In spite of considerable efforts to prove that Jesus was a political activist, little convincing evidence has turned up.[3]

Most authorities agree with the theory that for his Gospel Luke used Mark's Gospel, the Quelle, and a source of his own. Since we have Mark's Gospel and can get a reasonably good idea of the nature of the Quelle from the Gospels of Matthew and Luke, redaction criticism appears to be the best methodology for discovering Luke's theological concerns. Luke's use of his sources can be analyzed and interpreted.

Attempts to delineate clearly Luke's sources in Acts have all failed.[4] This is not to say that such attempts have been abandoned but only that they have had little actual success. Here, Dibelius proved correct; Acts has to be approached differently from Luke's Gospel. In Luke the author had extensive sources; in Acts his sources were less extensive so he had to rely more on his own considerable literary ability.[5] Consequently, in Acts too, redaction criticism appears to be the best method of investigation, although some might prefer the term, "composition" criticism.[6] Whether one prefers the term "redaction criticism" or that of "composition criticism," our question properly stated will be what does Luke, the author of Luke-Acts, hold on political and social topics. We are not asking what Jesus himself held on these topics.

Finally, the terms, "political" and "social" call for some observations. To an extent Luke holds for a notion of the people of God as opposed to the world. For the people of God Luke proposes political and social directives; he has minimal interest in the "world." But the Lukan conviction that God is the God of all history and his theme of universality weaken any rigid distinction between the people of God and the world. Everyone is to do God's will. The doing of God's will among the people of God and in the world means ultimately not two things but one. For instance, the parable of the good Samaritan looks beyond membership in the people of God. Moreover, the readers of this article are Christians, members of the people of God, and for them Luke provides a self-image and directions on political and social topics. By "political topics" this article means Luke's attitude toward any governing official; "social topics" report his instruction to the Christians on how to live together and in the world.

TWO SPECIFIC CAUTIONS

Luke's Gospel and Acts must be studied together. No scholar has ever succeeded in establishing a separate authorship of Luke as distinguished from that of Acts. On the contrary, the vocabulary, grammar, style, and theological concerns of both Luke and Acts demonstrate their common authorship.[7] Therefore, any statement about Luke's portrayal of Jesus' attitudes toward politics and society must find support in both Luke and Acts. At least, any interpretation of data in one of these works should not be contradicted by data in the other.[8]

The history of the study of Luke's *Sitz im Leben* calls for precaution in interpreting Luke. Most likely, Luke, who wrote from a Pauline community, was an accomplished author who had had considerable experience in Christian communities. Unlike the other New Testament writers who addressed given communities, he addressed himself to the Christian world at large. Actually, no one has been able to reduce Luke's *Sitz im Leben* to one sociological setting.[9] Therefore, in this study no one Lukan concern dominates although some concerns seem more important for him than others.

THE NEED TO RESPECT LUKE'S THEOLOGICAL CONCERNS

Luke had deeper theological concerns which call for precaution in any interpretation of his attitudes toward politics and society. These deeper concerns can be arranged under three headings: faith and baptism, God as the God of history, and the imitation of Christ.

Luke calls for a belief in Christ and baptism in his name. This faith in Christ constitutes the starting point of a Christian life. Primarily Luke calls for faith in Christ who became man and died but was raised for us. Christ's incarnation and resurrection give human nature a radical dignity and an eternal hope. Consequently, Luke claims that something radically new has entered history. The Christian has a new self-image and a new life to live.

Is Luke a historian? In view of Luke 1:1–4 and Acts 1:1 an affirmative answer to this question seems the only response. True, Luke follows the Hellenistic model of a historian,[10] but the Old Testament influence dominates.[11]

The major influence of the Old Testament on Luke was that God was the God of history; this is what makes Luke a historian of *Heilsgeschichte*. Perhaps one should speak of promise-fulfillment with Luke.[12] Luke's primary referent is the God who has worked in Israel's history and presently works in that of Christianity (cf. Acts 13:16–43). This statement can help one explain many of the other themes suggested for Luke-Acts. The word grows because this God of history makes it grow; human effort cannot achieve such marvelous growth. The delay of the Parousia rests on this same truth, "It is not for you to know times or seasons which the Father has fixed by his own authority" (Acts 1:7). The Holy Spirit manifests God's will to the Christians: "Can anyone forbid water for baptizing these people who have received the Holy Spirit just as we have?" (Acts 10:47). The mission to the Gentiles, stressed by Luke through his universal framework (Luke 3:6; 24:47; Acts 1:8; 28:28), happens because of the will of God. Peter explains the Cornelius event: "If then God gave the same gift to them as he gave to us when we believed in the Lord Jesus Christ, who was I that I could withstand God?" (Acts 11:17; cf. 15:8–9). Later, at the Jerusalem Council, Peter asserts, "Brethren, you know that in the early days God made choice among you, that by my mouth the Gentiles should hear the word of God and believe" (Acts 15:7). The apostles and early Christians encounter hardships; but they enjoy ultimate victory. The cause of this victory is the God of history.

Ultimately, this victory consists in the resurrection. Certainly, the resurrection does not stem from mankind. Nor does one easily demonstrate that Luke saw a connection between Christ's resurrection and our own.[13] For Luke, our resurrection ultimately comes from the God of history. The Lukan Paul summarizes the hope in the promise made by God to our fathers with the rhetorical question: "Why is it thought incredible by any of you that God raises the dead?" (Acts 26:8). Before Felix, Paul admits:

> . . . that according to the Way, which they call a sect, I worship the God of our fathers, believing everything laid down by the law or written in the prophets, having a hope in God which these themselves accept that there will be a resurrection of both the just and the unjust [Acts 24:14–15].

Luke's conviction that God was the God of history means that political situations will serve God's purposes (cf. Acts 4:27–28). No politician will succeed in overcoming God's plan. In spite of this, we will see that Luke extended considerable effort to indicate that Roman political authority dealt fairly with Christians.

The final precaution concerns Luke's call for the imitation of Christ by the Christians. Christians are to be like the Father:

> But love your enemies, and do good, and lend, expecting nothing in return; and your reward will be great, and you will be sons of the Most High; for he is kind to the ungrateful and the selfish. Be merciful, even as your Father is merciful [Luke 6:35–36; cf. 6:27–34; 11:4; 17:3–4].

Recent research has revealed that the apostles and disciples in Acts have the same experiences and do the same things that Jesus did.[14] Several conclusions follow from this similarity. Luke stresses a continuity between Luke-Acts and between Jesus and his followers. Or, as W. C. Van Unnik phrases it, Acts confirms the Gospel.[15] At the same time, Luke reveals his conviction that Christians will be like Christ; Christians imitate Christ.[16]

Under this imitation of Christ come a number of considerations that will be seen to bear directly on the topic of Jesus and Christians in politics and society in Luke-Acts. For Luke Christ is the savior of the weak, downtrodden, despised, and sinners; and his followers care for the same type of people. They are to be the Good Samaritan to all their neighbors (Luke 10:25–37). This Lukan theme of the imitation of Jesus also embraces Luke's concern for the rich and poor.[17] Jesus and his followers are prophets[18] who are mighty in word and work but will suffer and be rejected; finally, Luke patterns the experiences and sufferings of the apostles and disciples after his earlier descriptions of Jesus and his passion.

LUKE'S ATTITUDES ON POLITICAL TOPICS

Mention of the suffering of Jesus and his followers introduces the topic of Luke's attitude toward politics. What was Jesus' attitude toward violence? Jesus acts violently in the cleansing of the temple (Luke 19:45–48). According to Luke, Jesus reacts to the greed of the merchants who have turned God's house of prayer into a den of thieves. But Luke abbreviates and tones down Mark's account; he leaves out the buyers, the overturning of tables and chairs, and the preventing of anyone carrying things through the temple (cf. Mark 11:15–16). Luke 22:36–38, 49–52 do not advocate violence. Luke 22:36–38, proper to Luke, fulfills scripture. Jesus' exhortation, "let him who has no sword sell his mantle and buy one" fulfills the scripture, "And he was reckoned with transgressors." For this fulfillment two swords suffice; they hardly establish the apostles as revolutionaries. The violence in Luke 22:49–52 belongs to one of Jesus' disciples; Jesus (only in Luke) heals the injured ear. Jesus' enemies have the swords and clubs. Consequently, Luke has downplayed Jesus' violence in the temple; but he does not leave the event out of his Gospel. His report does not advocate violence in a Christian's life. But for Luke Jesus teaches and acts assertively and aggressively.[19]

The governing authorities most commonly found in Luke-Acts are Jewish and Roman, and Luke treats them in radically different ways. Luke generally treats Jewish officials negatively. However, he makes a sharp and significant distinction between the high priest and the Sadducees on the one side and the Pharisees on the other. According to Luke, the Christians are the true Pharisees (cf. Acts 26:4-8); so during Jesus' passion and throughout Acts, the Pharisees, at least by name, cease to be opponents of the Christians. In fact, the Pharisee Gamaliel defends the apostles; and Paul, too, finds defenders among the Pharisees (Acts 23:6-10). This reveals Luke's literary astuteness because the high priests belonged to the Sadducee party which was no longer influential in Judaism after A.D. 70. Christianity's opponents have practically vanished.

Before these Jewish officials Luke allows for civil disobedience. To the accusation of the Jewish officials who had governing authority in Jerusalem, Peter and John (Acts 4:19-20) and Peter and the apostles (Acts 5:29) retort that they have to obey God rather than man. Certainly, Luke thinks that the apostles are doing the right thing (cf. Acts 5:38-39); but, by any standards, the apostles are committing civil disobedience. For the Jewish officials had police authority in Jerusalem.

Luke furnishes a varied portrait of the Herodian treatment of Christ and the Christians. Herod Antipas is glad to see Jesus; however, when Jesus refuses to answer him, Herod and his soldiers treat Jesus with contempt and mock him. Yet Herod Antipas does not think that Jesus is guilty (Luke 23:8, 11, 14-15). Herod Agrippa kills James the brother of John; and, since this pleases the Jews, he arrests Peter (Acts 12:2-3). Luke terminates this Herod-story with the sardonic comment: ". . . the angel of the Lord smote him, because he did not give God the glory; and he was eaten by worms and died" (Acts 12:23). In contrast, Luke's treatment of Agrippa II (Acts 25:13-26:32) is gentle and favorable. Agrippa II wants to hear Paul's defense, pleasantly interacts with him, and twice affirms his innocence. In summary, Luke evaluates the Herodian princes in terms of their treatment of Christ and the Christians.

In the narrative of paying taxes to Caesar (Luke 20:20-26), Jesus' opponents are trying to entrap him; they have no real interest in establishing a norm for paying taxes to the Romans. Jesus recognizes their intention, and his answer avoids their trap. Jesus accepts Roman taxes as a reality—nothing more.

Roman authorities deal favorably with Jesus and the Christians.[20] Frequently, to protect themselves from opponents, Jewish or other, the Christians appeal to the Romans. Jesus' passion marks the first major encounter with the Romans.

A. Vanhoye described Luke's passion narrative as "personal and hortatory."[21] Luke calls the reader to follow Jesus in his moral nobility. As a historian, Luke more than Mark or Matthew unfolds the events in well-ordered fashion; he attends to everything which touches on personal relationship with and attachment to Christ. This attachment finds expression in the repeated affirmation of Jesus' innocence and the omission of offensive or cruel details.

Pilate does not behave during Jesus' passion as a courageous official who defends the disadvantaged, but he does try to free him (Luke 23:16, 20, 22; Acts 3:13). The high priests and scribes force Pilate's hand; according to Luke the main blame for Jesus' death falls on them (cf. Luke 24:20). In several places (Luke 22:52; 23:4-5, 10, 13-16) during Jesus' passion, only Luke introduces the chief priests and rulers as Jesus' opponents and distinguishes them from the people (esp. Luke 23:35; cf. 23:13). Jesus' innocence (Luke 23:4, 14-15, 22; cf. 23:41, 47-48; Acts 3:13-14; 13:28) constitutes Luke's main theological message during Jesus' passion. The last words at Jesus' passion are those of the Roman centurion: "Certainly this man was innocent" (Luke 23:47). Jesus' silence during his passion witnesses to his acceptance of his Father's will (cf. Luke 22:42) and to his feelings about the horrid miscarriage of justice (cf. Luke 22:68-71; 23:3). Nowhere does Luke ever say that Jesus has been condemned.

With modifications Luke (23:2, 3, 37, 38) takes over Mark's presentation of Jesus as King (Mark 15:2, 9, 12, 18, 26, 32). This title, surely not a political one for Mark or Luke, recalls Jesus' transcendence over any political force of this world:

> And he [the good thief] said, "Jesus, remember me when you come *into your kingdom.*" And he said to him, "Truly, I say to you, today you will be with me in *Paradise*" [Luke 23:42-43].

According to Luke, the Christians have quite amicable relations with the Romans. Roman laws and customs benefited them. The first Gentile convert is the Roman centurion, Cornelius (Acts 10:1-11:18). At Paphos, Sergius Paulus, the Roman proconsul, believes when he sees the result of Paul's curse on Elymas (Acts 13:6-12). Romans become Christians.

In Philippi, Roman customs and practices are at first used against Paul and Silas (Acts 16:21). But notice of their Roman citizenship causes the magistrates to fear because they beat and imprisoned them; the magistrates apologize, let them out of prison, and ask them to leave the city (Acts 16:35-40). The Jews create a riot at Thessalonica but cannot find Paul. The city authorities require bail of Jason and others and free them (Acts 17:1-9). In Corinth, Roman law again protects Paul. When the Jews bring Paul before the tribunal, Gallio, the proconsul of Achaia, reacts as follows:

> . . . Gallio said to the Jews, "If it were a matter of wrong doing or vicious crime I should have reason to bear with you, O Jews; but since it is a matter of questions about words and names and your own law, see to it yourselves; I refuse to be a judge of these things" [Acts 18:14-15].

In Ephesus, the town clerk fears that Paul's opponents will be charged with rioting, for they cannot justify the commotion (Acts 19:40).

Claudius Lysias, a Roman tribune, rescues Paul from the Jewish mob in Jerusalem (Acts 21:27-36; 23:27). He allows Paul to speak to the people (Acts 21:39-40). Although Lysias had ordered Paul to be examined by scourging, Paul's appeal to his Roman citizenship spares him this humiliation and frightens Lysias because he had bound a Roman citizen (Acts 22:22-29). The high priest, contrary to the law, orders Paul to be struck (Acts 23:2-3); Lysias rescues Paul from the clamorous dissension of the Sanhedrin (Acts 23:9-10) and the ambush of the Jews (esp. Acts 23:12-22, 30). Two centurions and Roman soldiers provide Paul safe conduct to Caesarea (Acts 23:23-25, 31-32). Lysias writes his opinion about the whole affair to Felix, "I found that he was accused about questions of their law, but charged with nothing deserving death or imprisonment" (Acts 23:29).

The Roman procurator, Felix, has a rather accurate knowledge of the Way. Paul defends himself before him; according to Luke, Felix's greed for money (Acts 24:26) keeps him from freeing Paul. His conduct toward Paul confirms his realization that Paul was innocent. Paul remains in custody but enjoys some freedom; his friends are not to be prevented from attending to his needs.

Paul appears before Festus and then before Festus and Agrippa II. When Festus wants to do the Jewish leaders a favor and send Paul to Jerusalem for trial, Paul appeals to Caesar (Acts 25:11-12; cf. 25:21, 25; 26:32; 28:19). Again, Roman law protects a Christian. Paul's appearance before Festus and Agrippa II represents the climax of his defense,[22] and this section (Acts 25-26) strongly parallels that of Jesus before Pilate.[23] Festus' answer to the Jews exhibits how Roman customs protected the Christians:

> I answered them that it was not the custom of the Romans to give up any one before the accused met the accusers face to face, and had opportunity to make his defense concerning the charge laid against him [Acts 24:16].

In Agrippa II we find a man who knows Roman law and customs and the disputes of the Jews, yet this defense ends with a twofold declaration of Paul's innocence. Everyone says, "This man does nothing to deserve death or imprisonment"; then Agrippa II tells Festus, "This man could have been set free if he had not appealed to Caesar" (Acts 26:31-32).

The Lord had instructed Paul that he would have to witness about him also in Rome (Acts 23:11; cf. 19:21). The Roman centurion, Julius, conducts Paul to Rome (Acts 27:2); on the way, at Sidon, Julius treats Paul kindly and allows him to visit friends who care for him (Acts 27:3). When the soldiers plan to kill the prisoners lest any escape, the centurion, wishing to save Paul, prevents them from carrying out their purpose (Acts 27:42-43). Once again, a Roman provides a Christian with kind and fair treatment.

When they arrive in Rome, Paul is allowed to stay by himself with only a soldier to guard him. Paul reports to the local Jewish leaders that although he did nothing against the Jewish people or the customs of the fathers, he was delivered as a prisoner to the Romans. The Romans wanted to free him because they thought he did nothing worthy of death. However, since some Jews objected to this, Paul had to appeal to Caesar (Acts 28:17-19). Actually, Paul endures imprisonment for the hope of Israel which is a resurrection of the dead (Acts 28:20; cf. 23:6; 24:14-15; 26:6-8, 22-23). Amazingly, the Jews in Rome had received no letters about Paul; and no Jew coming to Rome had reported any evil about him (Acts 28:21). An ideal situation for Paul (and Christians) ends Acts; for two whole years Paul lives at his own expense in Rome; he welcomes everyone who comes to him; he preaches the kingdom of God and teaches about the Lord Jesus Christ quite openly and unhindered (Acts 28:30-31). Once in Rome, Paul remains a prisoner but, thanks to the Romans, freely and without hindrance preaches and teaches.

Perhaps Acts 4:27 constitutes the only negative statement about the relationship of a Roman official to Christianity: "For truly in this city there were gathered together against your holy servant Jesus whom you anointed, both Herod and Pontius Pilate, with the Gentiles and peoples of Israel." But here Luke relates a historical reality: Jesus had been crucified, and Pilate was among the perpetrators. In the context, Luke points out that even this crime was part of God's plan (Acts 4:28).

In summary, Luke advocates taking full advantage of the Roman polity. His principle would be: Christians should use every available legal means to protect themselves. Obviously, Luke is not facing a situation of the outright opposition of Roman officials to Christianity as does the author of the Revelation of John. For Luke not all the Jews are opponents of the Christians; and, at least, one of the Herodians, Agrippa II, seems friendly. The Christians are the true Pharisees. Romans become Christians; Cornelius is the first Gentile convert. Roman officials treat the Christians kindly and fairly; they protect them from Jewish and other political abuse and intrigue. Roman laws and customs favor the Christians as they preach about Christ. To the Romans, Jewish religious questions and disputes are of no import. Jesus, unless one wants to make a case for the cleansing of the temple, and the Christians commit no crime; Paul's only "crime" is his belief in the resurrection of the dead. In the overall Lukan theology no political force, Roman included, overcomes God's plan. Most importantly, Paul (Christianity) at the end of Acts resides in the capital city of the world and preaches and teaches freely and without hindrance.

A corollary of the above would be something never explicitly stated by Luke. The activity of the Christians and the tenets of their religion create no difficulty for a sensible, reasonable system of government. Only an irrational government or people, led by religious prejudice and/or hatred, could find fault with Christianity. In any nation ruled by reason, Christians make good citizens.

LUKE'S CALL TO IMITATE THE APPROACH OF JESUS

Earlier this article briefly discussed the imitation of Christ. Under this imitation comes Luke's theme of Jesus as the savior of the weak, oppressed, despised, and sinners. This theme of Jesus as the savior of the disadvantaged unifies the remaining considerations of Jesus in politics and society in Luke-Acts. Luke claims these attitudes for Jesus and all Christians. The headings discussed will be: humility and service, mission to the Gentiles, rich and poor, women, and the sick.

In Terms of Humility and Service

When the apostles fight over which of them is the greatest, Jesus instructs them not to be like the kings of the Gentiles who lord it over their subjects. But among Christians, the greatest should become as the youngest, "a child" (cf. Luke 9:48); the leader as one who serves (cf. Luke 17:10). For Jesus is among them as one who serves (Luke 22:24–27). This attitude of service explains Jesus' responses at his temptation (Luke 4:1–12). Also only Luke reports Jesus' refusal to allow James and John to call down fire from heaven to destroy the Samaritan town (Luke 9:54–55) as Elijah did to the soldiers of Ahaziah (2 Kings 1:10, 12). Jesus merits the title, servant (*pais*; Acts 3:13, 26; 4:27, 30). The apostles appoint the Seven to serve tables (Acts 6:2–3, 6); they will devote themselves to the service of the word (Acts 6:4). Paul, a model for Christians, in his farewell to the Ephesian elders recalls that his ministry in Asia was spent serving the Lord with humility (Acts 20:18–19). The resurrected Christ appoints Paul a servant (*hypēretēn*). This directive of humble service governs every Christian.

Jesus criticizes those who demand social privilege. "Woe to you Pharisees! for you love the best seat in the synagogues and salutations in the market places" (Luke 11:43). He warns his disciples, "Beware of the scribes, who like to go about in long robes, and love salutations in the synagogues and the place of honor at feasts, who devour widows' houses and for a pretense make long prayers" (Luke 20:46–47; cf. 11:43). Jesus himself shared table fellowship even with tax collectors and sinners (Luke 5:27–30; 7:36–50; 10:38–42; 11:37–52; 14:1–6; 15:2; 19:1–10; 22:7–13; 24:28–35). In fact, Luke (Acts 9:19, 43; 10:6, 48; 14:28; 15:33; 16:15, 34; 17:7; 18:3, 27; 21:16; 27:3; 28:2, 14, 17–31) relates numerous examples of hospitality, especially among Christians.

Some examples of humility are proper to Luke. Jesus addresses the parable of the Pharisee and the tax collector to those who trusted in themselves that they were righteous and despised others (Luke 18:9). "For everyone who exalts himself will be humbled, and he who humbles himself will be exalted" explains why the publican went down to his house justified and the Pharisee did not (Luke 18:14). Jesus makes the same observation about the guests who choose the places of honor in his parable about the sitting arrangements at the marriage feast (Luke 14:7–11). He further directs the host:

> When you give a dinner or banquet, do not invite your friends . . . invite the poor, the maimed, the lame, the blind, and you will be blessed because they cannot repay you. You will be repaid at the resurrection of the just [Luke 14:12–14].

More directly addressed to Christians would be the discussion between Jesus and Peter about the parable of watchfulness:

> But if that servant says to himself, "My master is delayed in coming," and begins to beat the manservants and the maidservants, and to eat and drink and get drunk, the master of that servant will come on a day when he does not expect him and at an hour he does not know, and will punish him, and put him with the unfaithful [Luke 12:45–46].

Christians are to be faithful servants who demand no social privilege, not even because of their position or authority. They should not abuse one another or play favorites, unless it be the poor.

Yet power and authority characterize Jesus and his followers. Jesus teaches with authority (Luke 4:32). With power and authority he commands the unclean spirits (Luke 4:36). The power of the Lord is with Jesus to heal (Luke 5:17; cf. 6:19; Acts 10:38); he forgives sins (Luke 7:47–48). Jesus gives the Twelve power and authority over all demons and to cure diseases (Luke 9:1); he gives the Seventy authority to tread upon serpents and scorpions, and over all the power of the enemy; and nothing shall hurt them (Acts 10:19). In Acts, Luke predicates signs and wonders of Jesus (Acts 2:22; 4:30) and the Christians (Acts 2:19, 43; 4:16, 22; 5:12; 6:8; 8:6, 13; 14:3; 15:12). Jesus promises the apostles that they will receive the power of the Holy Spirit (Acts 1:8). Members of the high-priestly family, the rulers, elders, and scribes ask Peter and John, in what power or in whose name they healed the cripple (Acts 4:7; cf. 3:12). Finally, God does extraordinary miracles through the hands of Paul (Acts 19:11). Hence, Jesus and his followers do perform humble service, but divine power characterizes this service done in Jesus' name.

In Reference to the Gentiles

Luke's theme of the mission to the Gentiles represents social advance. No longer does one have to belong to a given people or observe all the details of the Torah (cf. Acts 15:28–29) to be saved. Luke summarizes his position in Peter's statement. "Truly, I perceive that God shows no partiality, but in every nation anyone who fears him and does what is right is acceptable to him" (Acts 10:34–35). God gives the Gentiles the same gift he gave to those at Pentecost (Acts 11:17).

Regarding the Rich and Poor

Luke has a theme of riches and poverty. He appears to favor the poor. Jesus' parents can obtain no place in the inn (Luke 2:17). Shepherds, not Magi, visit him at his birth (Luke 2:16–17); at his presentation in the temple, his parents make the offering of the poor (Lev. 12:8), a pair of turtledoves or two young pigeons (Luke 2:22–24). Only in Luke stand the passages that the Spirit of the Lord is upon Jesus because he has anointed him to preach the good news to the poor (Luke 4:18) and "Blessed are you poor" (Luke 6:20). Material restraint characterizes the Christian missionaries (Luke 9:3–4; 10:4–8; 18:28–30).

On the other hand, Luke can speak harshly to the rich. With the other Synoptics, Luke holds that the rich need God's special help to enter heaven (Luke 18:24–27). Only he reports Jesus as saying, "But woe to you that are rich, for you have received your consolation" (Luke 6:24). The parable of the rich fool (Luke 12:13–21), again properly Lukan, answers the man who wants Jesus to bid his brother to divide the inheritance with him. Jesus' introduction to this parable sets the tone: "Take heed, and beware of all covetousness; for a man's life does not consist in the abundance of his possessions."

Luke furnishes a number of examples of what might be called social action. When Agabus predicts the famine, the Christians in Antioch send relief to those in Judea (Acts 11:27–30). Related to almsgiving would be the scene in Acts 6:1–7; a concern for widows in the daily distribution leads to the first disagreement in the church. Not proper to Luke but relevant here is Jesus' instruction to the rich ruler to give his wealth to the poor and then follow him (Luke 18:22–23). Jesus speaks the parable of the rich man and Lazarus (Luke 16:19–31) to the Pharisees who were lovers of money. The parable mentions no mistreatment of Lazarus by the rich man; Luke condemns the indifference of the rich man. Jesus becomes a guest of Zacchaeus, a rich chief tax collector. Zacchaeus' only words in the narrative are, "Behold, Lord, the half of my goods I give to the poor; and if I have defrauded anyone of anything, I restore it fourfold." This "sinner" surpasses everyone in Luke-Acts in almsgiving except for the poor widow (Luke 21:2–4) and demonstrates tremendous generosity in the kind of restitution he will make. The very amount of restitution hints that he was conscious of being honest. In the early chapters of Acts, Luke portrays an ideal community in which the Christians share their goods; their scope was to care for anyone in need (Acts 2:45; 4:34–35). This ideal community summons us to do whatever will bring about a Christian (and world) community where no needy persons are found. Paul embodies the Lukan spirit when he sums up his ministry before the Ephesian elders:

I coveted no one's silver or gold or apparel. You yourselves know that these hands ministered to my necessities, and to those who were with

12   *Robert F. O'Toole, S.J.*

me. In all things I have shown you that by so toiling one must help the weak, remembering the words of the Lord Jesus, how he said, "It is more blessed to give than to receive" [Acts 20:33–35].

Luke's proclamation about riches and poverty challenges a world dominated by materialism and one of whose chief ideologies is materialistic communism. For Luke, the poor deserve to be "favorites" of us all. The rich must be challenged and informed that "a man's life does not consist in the abundance of possessions." Indifference toward the poor merits only condemnation. If people have been cheated, restitution must be made; and the giving of alms (philanthropy) should surpass even that of Judaism since it is motivated by a hope in eternal life. The ideal community of the early chapters of Acts challenges us to overcome the world's poverty by sharing. For Luke, Paul embodies this spirit and achieves it by hard work.

On questions of justice, Luke displays practicality. John the Baptist answers the tax collectors, "Collect no more than is appointed you" and the soldiers, "Rob no one by violence or by false accusation, and be content with your wages" (Luke 3:12–14). Jesus condemns lawyers because they place heavy burdens on men and do not help them to carry them. The lawyers have taken away the key of knowledge; they do not enter; and they hinder those who do enter (Luke 11:46, 52). Ideally, Christians are not to judge nor condemn but to forgive and give generously (Luke 6:37–38).

With Respect to Women

Women play a significant part in Luke-Acts. Doubtless, Luke's theme of Christ as the savior of the oppressed led to this interest. Luke speaks of widows more than any other New Testament writer. Like the other Synoptics, he narrates the story of Jairus' daughter and the woman with the flow of blood (Luke 8:40–56) and Jesus' rejection of divorce (Luke 16:18). Mark and he (Luke 21:1–4) report the story of the poor widow's generous offering.

Luke has a number of stories about women which are proper to him. Although in a sense all of these stories bear on the topic of women's place in society, some do so more directly. Luke affords more attention to Jesus' mother, Mary (Luke 1–2; 8:19–21; Acts 1:14); he contrasts her faith with Zachariah's unbelief. For R. E. Brown, Mary, the handmaid (Luke 1:38), was an ideal disciple who during Jesus' lifetime (Luke 8:19–21) and after the resurrection (Acts 1:14) obeyed the word of God.[24] Luke mentions John the Baptist's mother, Elizabeth, and the prophetess, Anna. Women recognize Jesus' greatness and associate with him and the apostles (Acts 1:14); they provide for them out of their means (Luke 8:2–3). Luke admires women's determination (Luke 15:8–10; 18:1–8). Priscilla appears to be the equal of her husband in the ministry; in Ephesus Priscilla and Aquila expound to Apollos the way of the Lord more accurately (Acts 18:26). Perhaps, by modern standards, Luke would not be judged a progressive in the area of women's rights;

but by comparison with the other New Testament authors (with the exception of Paul?), he appears progressive. B. Witherington summarizes Luke's treatment of women as follows:

> Women are a continuing theme and example used by Luke as he tries to teach the qualities of a true disciple—one who is loyal and faithful to Christ through trials and joy; and who witnesses to the person and work of Christ; one who serves the Lord and the brethren freely from their own means, etc.[25]

Regarding the Sick

Undeniably, Jesus and his followers heal the sick. Above mention was made of the theme of signs and wonders which Luke predicates of Jesus and his followers in Acts. In addition to the theme of signs and wonders, Luke relates general healing activity on the part of Jesus (Luke 4:40; 5:15; 6:17-19; 7:21-22; 9:11), the apostles (Acts 5:12), the Seventy (Luke 10:17), Peter (Acts 5:15), Philip (Acts 8:6-7), and Paul (Acts 19:11-12; 28:9). Moreover, Luke narrates similar miracle stories of Jesus and his followers. Paul's healing of Publius' father's fever and dysentery (Acts 28:8) reflects Jesus' healing of Simon's mother-in-law's fever (Luke 4:38-39). Peter's healing of the lame man at the Beautiful Gate of the temple (Acts 3:1-10) and of the paralytic Aeneas in Lydda (Acts 9:32-35) and Paul's cure of the man at Lystra who was crippled from birth and had never walked (Acts 14:8-10) resemble Jesus' healing of the paralytic (Luke 5:17-26). Jesus restores life to Jairus' daughter (Luke 8:54-55), Peter to Dorcas (Acts 9:40-41), Paul to Eutychus (Acts 20:10-12). Finally, the identification of Paul and Silas by the spirit of divination in the slave girl, "These men are servants of the Most High God who proclaim to you the way of salvation" mirrors the identification of Jesus by demons when he works cures, "I know who you are, the Holy One of God" (Luke 4:34) and "You are the Son of God!" (Luke 4:41). So, Luke intends that the healing of mental and physical afflictions remain a permanent ministry of the church; needless to say, the disadvantaged are the primary recipients of this healing activity.

CONCLUSION

This article has used redaction (composition) criticism; in Luke-Acts both source criticism and historical criticism would have been less productive. Since the double work, Luke-Acts, comes from the pen of one man, the books were studied together. Although Luke may not have felt obliged to match our sense of consistency, a consideration of his *Sitz im Leben* revealed that he had deeper concerns. First, Christians believe in Christ who became man and died and rose for them. Thus, human nature itself has a radical dignity. As a historian, Luke was convinced that God is the God of history;

for Luke the Christians should model themselves after Christ. One does not oppress the neighbor whom he loves.

The practical application of Luke's opinions on politics and society should avoid two pitfalls; our problems should not be read back into Luke's time, yet Luke's opinions should not be stripped of their true force. The cleansing of the temple was an act of civil disobedience and violence; modern disregard of God could require the use of civil disobedience. But Luke's redaction of Mark's account of the cleansing of the temple hardly advocates the Christian use of violence. He has kept the historical fact but plays it down. Jesus could be assertive and aggressive. Luke shows little regard for Jewish officials; before them, the apostles opt for civil disobedience. On the other hand, the Christians take full advantage of Roman polity; they use every available means to defend themselves. (Luke knows that Christian living leads to persecution, but he sees little advantage in encouraging Christians to seek persecution). This challenges modern Christians to take full advantage of what can be legally done to continue to carry out the task of Christ. If lobbies rule this county, Christians must lobby. Apparently, Luke would have accepted everything which was politically feasible and not sinful.

Christians should imitate Christ, the savior of the disadvantaged. Our humble service permits no demand for social privilege nor abuse of one another. As God offers his salvation to all, we should serve all. This task calls for radical social reform. Structures which do not assist the disadvantaged must be removed. In this sense, commitment to Christ does call for new social patterns. Our respect for one another should dissolve any claims for special treatment. Assertions of humble service, not accompanied by effective measures for the disadvantaged, merit the tag of "mouthings," not service.

When Luke speaks of the rich and poor, he strikes at the truth that "a man's life does not consist in the abundance of his possessions" and that the worth of a human being requires the sharing of our goods with him. Luke condemns indifference to the poor whom we are to favor. In our age of materialism, Luke's proclamation falls on deaf and lethargic ears. We do not want to part with our goods, or our past failures and the enormous dimensions of the problems leave us without spirit. But Luke's theme of rich and poor will din in our ears until we remember his poor.

The same holds for those who are disadvantaged in any way. Whatever rights women are entitled to must be theirs. As Jesus cared for those who did not have good health, so should we. The presence of his life must touch them here and in eternity.

NOTES

1. E.g., Martin Hengel, *Acts and the History of Earliest Christianity* (Philadelphia: Fortress Press, 1979), pp. 50–58. One can hardly find fault with "The historical method which is appropriate here requires extreme care, guarded intensity, responsibility, and reverence toward the truth" (p. 57).

2. One might agree with J.B. Tyson ("The Lukan Version of the Trial of Jesus," *NovT* [1959]:255): "But in Luke the charge of treason and treasonous teaching is clear from the beginning. The best argument for the authenticity of this charge is the fact that the Church and Luke, in particular, attempted to portray the ministry of Jesus and the Christian movement as non-political." In this investigation the author of Luke-Acts is referred to as "Luke" without determining whether or not he was a companion of Paul.

3. The leading representative of this contention has been S. G. F. Brandon, *Jesus and the Zealots: A Study of the Political Factor in Early Christianity* (Manchester: Manchester University Press, 1967) and *The Trial of Jesus of Nazareth* (London: Batsford, 1968). For an attempt to summarize the evidence on both sides of the argument see Oscar Cullmann, *Jesus and the Revolutionaries*, trans. G. Putnam (New York: Harper & Row, 1970), pp. 7–11.

4. J. B. Tyson ("Source Criticism of the Gospel of Luke," *Perspectives on Luke-Acts*, ed. C. H. Talbert [Danville: Association of Baptist Professors of Religion, 1978]) contends that we should treat Luke as the author of the intentional unity of Luke-Acts and approach his Gospel as if we knew nothing about his sources. See also J. Dupont, *Les Sources du Livre des Actes: Etat de la question* (Bruges: Desclée de Brouwer, 1960), esp. pp. 159–160); E. Trocmé, *Le "Livre des Actes" et l'histoire* (Paris: Presses Universitaires de France, 1957), pp. 215–217. For examples of authors who feel they have uncovered sources, cf.: C. C. Torrey, *The Composition and Date of Acts*, Harvard Theological Studies 1 (Cambridge: Harvard University Press, 1916, repr. Kraus); M. Wilcox, *The Semitisms of Acts* (Oxford: The Clarendon Press, 1965); J. A. T. Robinson, "The Most Primitive Christology of All?" *JTS*, new series, 7 (1956): 177–189; C. F. D. Moule, "The Christology of Acts," *Studies in Luke-Acts*, ed. L. E. Keck and J. L. Martyn (Nashville: Abingdon, 1966), pp. 169–171; G. Lohfink, "Christologie und Geschichtsbild in Apg 3:19–21," *BZ* 13 (1969): 223–241; M. Wilcox, "Luke and the Bezan Text of Acts," *Les Actes des Apôtres* (Gembloux: Duculot, 1979), pp. 447–455.

5. Martin Dibelius, *Aufsätze zur Apostelgeschichte* (Göttingen: Vandenhoeck & Ruprecht, 1968), p. 11.

6. After all, redaction criticism implies that the author was the final editor of his sources and not that he composed the piece of literature.

7. For the common authorship of Luke-Acts see: E. Trocmé, *Le "Livre des Actes" et l'histoire*, pp. 38–41; but his contention that Luke 24:50–53 and Acts 1:1–5 are later additions failed to gain the day; H. J. Cadbury, *The Making of Luke-Acts* (London: SPCK and Naperville: Allenson, 1958), pp. 8–11; P. S. Minear, *To Heal and to Reveal: The Prophetic Vocation According to Luke* (New York: Crossroad, 1976), p. 84.

8. As R. J. Karris ("Missionary Communities: A New Paradigm for the Study of Luke-Acts," *CBQ* 41 [1979]: 83–94) indicates, Luke does not always present his narrative in a totally consistent way. An example of this is Luke's application of the title, Christ, to Jesus. At birth Jesus is called Christ (Luke 2:11); and he is called "the Christ" by Peter at Caesarea Philippi (Luke 9:20). In Acts 2:36, Peter states "God has made him both Lord and Christ, this Jesus whom you crucified"; Jesus becomes Christ at his exaltation. Finally, J. A. T. Robinson ("The Most Primitive Christology of All?" pp. 184–185, 188) contends that in Acts 3:20–21 Jesus has not yet become Christ. Thus, this article will not presuppose that Luke must be totally consistent in the expression of his convictions on politics and society.

9. Elsewhere, I have attempted to enumerate and evaluate the efforts made on this

topic to date: R. F. O'Toole, S.J., "Why Did Luke Write Acts (Lk-Acts)," *BTB* 7 (1977): 66–76. Others who hold that more than one exclusive purpose lay behind the writing of Luke-Acts include: W. Ward Gasque, *A History of the Criticism of Acts of the Apostles* (Grand Rapids: Eerdmans, 1975), p. 303; W. G. Kümmel, *Introduction to the New Testament* (London: S.C.M. Press, 1965), p. 115; H. J. Cadbury, *The Making of Luke-Acts*, p. 302.

10. P. Schubert, "The Structure and Significance of Luke 24," *Neutestamentliche Studien für R. Bultmann* (Berlin: A. Töpelmann, 1954), pp. 170–171. E. Plümacher, *Lukas als hellenistischer Schriftsteller* (Göttingen: Vandenhoeck & Ruprecht, 1972), pp. 32–38. W. C. Van Unnik, "Luke's Second Book and the Rules of Hellenistic Historiography," *Les Actes des Apôtres*, pp. 37–60.

11. Hengel (*Acts and the History of Earliest Christianity*, pp. 51–52) expresses it very well: "His imitation of the style of the Septuagint shows that he wants quite deliberately to be in this tradition." See also N. A. Dahl, "The Story of Abraham in Luke-Acts," *Studies in Luke-Acts*, pp. 152–153.

12. This appears to be the position of Robert J. Karris, O.F.M., *What Are They Saying About Luke and Acts?: A Theology of the Faithful God* (New York: Paulist Press, 1979), pp. 48–83. P. Schubert ("The Structure and Significance of Luke 24," pp. 165–186) with more precision speaks of Luke's theology of proof from prophecy. Minear (*To Heal and to Reveal*, p. 85) prefers to speak of "*the prophets* and fulfillment." N. A. Dahl ("The Story of Abraham in Luke-Acts," *Studies in Luke-Acts*, p. 153) phrases it more to my liking, "But Luke alone sets this forth in the form of a historical account which also includes recapitulations of the OT history which is continued in the things now fulfilled."

13. But confer my article, "Christ's Resurrection in Acts, 13, 13–52," *Bib* 60 (1979): 361–372.

14. R.B. Rackham, *The Acts of the Apostles* (London: Methuen, 1912), pp. xlvii, 401–402, 477–478. M.D. Goulder, *Type and History in Acts* (London: SPCK, W. Clowes and Sons, 1964). P. S. Minear, *To Heal and to Reveal*, pp. 122–147. L. T. Johnson, *The Literary Function of Possessions in Luke-Acts* (Missoula: Scholars Press, 1977), pp. 60–78. R. Pesch, "Der Christ als Nachahmer Christi," *BK* 24 (1969): 10–11. V. Hasler, "Jesu Selbstzeugnis und das Bekenntnis des Stephanus vor dem hohen Rat," *Schweizerische Theologische Umschau* 36 (1966): 36–47. Luke has extensive parallels between Jesus and Paul. Adrian Hastings, *Prophet and Witness in Jerusalem* (Baltimore: Helicon Press, 1958), pp. 135–140. W. Radl, " 'Paulus Traditus' Jesus und sein Missionar im lukanischen Doppelwerk," *Erbe und Auftrag* (1974): 163–167, and *Paulus und Jesus in lukanischen Doppelwerk: Untersuchungen zu Parallelmotiven in Lukasevangelium und in der Apostelgeschichte* (Bern/Frankfurt: Herbert Lang, 1975). A. J. Mattill, Jr., "The Jesus-Paul Parallels and the Purpose of Luke-Acts: H. H. Evans Reconsidered," *NovT* 17 (1975): 15–46. R. F. O'Toole, S.J., *Acts 26: The Christological Climax of Paul's Defense* (Rome: Biblical Institute Press, 1978), pp. 22–25, and "Luke's Notion of 'Be Imitators of Me as I Am of Christ' Acts 25–26," *BTB* 8 (1978): 155–161.

15. W. C. Van Unnik, "The 'Book of Acts' the Confirmation of the Gospel," *NovT* 11 (1969): 26–59.

16. In his excellent article, A. J. Mattill, Jr. ("The Jesus-Paul Parallels and the Purpose of Luke-Acts: H. H. Evans Reconsidered," pp. 36–37, 46) apparently feels that the parallels between Jesus and Paul prove Paul's innocence. But A. Feuillet ("L'apparition du Christ a Marie-Madeleine Jean 20, 11–18: Comparison avec

l'apparition aux disciples d'Emmaus Luc 24, 13-35," *Esprit et Vie* 88 [1978]: 222) calls attention to a parallel between "Philip and the Ethiopian Eunuch (Acts 8:25-40)" and "The Disciples on the Road to Emmaus (Luke 24:13-35)." Can this comparison between Jesus and Philip possibly be designed to prove Philip's innocence? To limit the explanation only to Jesus' and the Christians' innocence does not explain those comparisons where the notion of innocence does not occur at all.

17. L. T. Johnson, *The Literary Function of Possessions in Luke-Acts*; R. J. Karris, "Poor and Rich: The Lukan *Sitz im Leben*," *Perspectives on Luke-Acts*, ed. C. H. Talbert (Danville: Association of Baptist Professors of Religion, 1978), pp. 112-125 and *What Are They Saying about Luke and Acts?* pp. 84-104.

18. See Minear, *To Heal and to Reveal*, pp. 81-147; Johnson, *The Literary Function of Possessions in Luke-Acts*, pp. 60-78.

19. See Richard J. Cassidy, *Jesus, Politics, and Society* (Maryknoll, N.Y.: Orbis Books, 1978), p. 41.

20. For a similar opinion, confer Hans Conzelmann, *The Theology of St. Luke* (New York: Harper & Row, 1960), pp. 137-149. However, Conzelmann fails to understand that for Luke the relationship between Christianity and Judaism helps determine Christianity's innocence before the Romans. R. J. Cassidy (*Jesus, Politics, and Society*, pp. 128-130) fails to consider Acts and thus to appreciate Conzelmann's position.

21. A. Vanhoye, S.J., *Structure and Theology of the Accounts of the Passion in the Synoptic Gospels*, trans. C. H. Giblin, S.J. (Collegeville, Minn.: Liturgical Press, 1967), pp. 1-37, esp. p. 9. Vanhoye's genius lies in concise precision; my presentation here depends upon him in no small measure.

22. R. F. O'Toole, S.J., *Acts 26: The Christological Climax of Paul's Defense.*

23. Ibid., pp. 20-28; I have developed the same idea in "Luke's Notion of 'Be Imitators of Me as I Am of Christ' in Acts 25-26" *BTB* 8 (1978): 155-161.

24. R. E. Brown, S.S., *The Birth of the Messiah* (Garden City: Doubleday, 1977), pp. 316-319; see also E. H. Maly, "Women and the Gospel of Luke," *BTB* 10 (1980): 102-104.

25. B. Witherington III, "On the Road with Mary Magdalene, Joanna, Susanna, and Other Disciples—Luke 8:1-3," *ZNW* 70 (1979): 244.

2

Politics or Peace (Eirēnē)
in Luke's Gospel

WILLARD M. SWARTLEY

Contemporary redactional studies of Luke's Gospel owe much to Hans Conzelmann's seminal work *Die Mitte der Zeit* (Eng., *The Theology of St. Luke*). While Conzelmann's theses regarding Luke's periodization of redemptive history and the delay of the parousia have been widely discussed, his corollary thesis that Luke-Acts presents a deep political apologetic has received almost no attention, at least not before Richard Cassidy's *Jesus, Politics, and Society* appeared in 1978. Already in 1972 John Howard Yoder blew the *jobel* horn for Luke's Gospel, calling for a jubilean understanding of Jesus' ministry, accented especially by Luke (*The Politics of Jesus*, chs. 2–3). But the task of examining the contradicting portraits of Conzelmann and Yoder was either swept under the carpet or conveniently swooshed away by the vacuum of our left cerebral hemispheres, at least until Cassidy began his Lukan housecleaning. At about that same time three doctoral dissertations appeared, taking up jubilean aspects of Luke's Gospel (Jacob Elias, Donald Blosser, and Robert B. Sloan).[1] But none of these took up the problem of contradiction between Conzelmann and Yoder.

In this essay, therefore, I will summarize the differing interpretations of Conzelmann, Cassidy, and Yoder; then examine Luke's crucially relevant redactional emphasis on *eirēnē;* and finally propose a method for evaluating these rival interpretations.

THE RIVAL INTERPRETATIONS

Conzelmann's View of Luke

Conzelmann sets forth his view of Luke's political apologetic as an essential part of the situation of the church in the world, occasioned by the delay of the parousia. This understanding expresses itself in distinctive views of the church's relationship to Judaism and to the Empire. The church's relationship to Judaism shows two aspects: continuity with Judaism in order to show Christianity's legitimate place in redemptive history *and* distancing of Christianity from Judaism *in political import* in order to put Christianity in a favorable relation to the Empire. Christianity shows no critical stance toward Rome's political presence; when, however, disturbance of any sort arises, it is incited by Jewish troublemakers.[2]

Conzelmann cites numerous incidents from Luke's Gospel to support his thesis:

1. John the Baptist instructs the military and the government in good morals, making loyalty to government an implicit assumption (3:19).

2. Jesus presents his messianic mission in nonpolitical categories (4:16–18).

3. Herod's interest in Jesus is nonpolitical (9:7ff; 23:8).

4. Jesus' death happens because of divine necessity (*dei*); events of a political nature, such as cleansing the temple, are treated briefly or recast in favorable light (13:31–34; 19:45–46).

5. Jesus' Davidic rule is depoliticized (19:38).

6. Jesus' appearance before Roman authorities is instigated by the Jewish leaders (20:20; 23:1ff.). Even the predicted appearance of believers before kings and governors will vindicate the Christian cause through the wise words given by the Spirit.

7. The accusations of the Jews are lies (23:1f.; 20:20ff.). By choosing Barabbas, Jewish disposition to insurrection is patently demonstrated (23:18ff.).

8. Pilate pronounces Jesus guiltless *three* times, declaring Rome's assessment that Christianity is nonpolitical (23:22).

Within the passion narrative Conzelmann discerns two themes set side by side: "the dogmatic theme of the necessity of the suffering and the 'historical' theme of the guilt of the Jews and of the innocence of the Empire, which appreciates the non-political character of the Gospel and of Jesus' Kingship."[3] Conzelmann thus asserts:

> So ergibt sich eine dreifache Demonstration des Tatbestandes: vor den Juden—die nun lügen müssen; vor den Imperium, das den rechtlichen Befund objektiv fixiert; vor dem römischen Klientelfürsten, welcher dem Befund des römischen Vertreters zustimmt.[4]

These redactional themes continue in Acts; Conzelmann cites the following:

1. A Roman centurion is the first Gentile convert to Christianity (Acts 10).

2. The conduct of a Roman official appears exemplary (13:6).

3. As Christianity spreads into Europe (16:11ff.), Roman law often appears as a friend and a "savior" for Paul (22:1ff., 25; 18:12–17). Hence, Paul appeals to Caesar for his justification before the Roman law (25:23ff.; 26:32).

4. The representation of the Christian gospel as subversive is put so that the reader will see through it and perceive it as framed by the Jews (17:1-7).

5. Luke's apologetic pattern is clearly stated by Paul himself as part of his defense (25:15-16; 23:6ff.; 24:10ff.): accusations against him are falsely instigated by the Jews, but even to the Jews he did no wrong (24:17; 25:10); the Roman law will surely acquit him. As Conzelmann puts it, summing up his view of Luke's apologetic, the church's relation to Israel is adversarial so that the Jews are the troublemakers and Christianity is put into a favorable light. In this way Luke has Christianity enter into conversation with the state "in order to achieve a permanent settlement" between Christianity and the Empire.[5]

Cassidy's View of Luke

Cassidy's description of Luke's view of the political character of Christianity stands sharply at odds with Conzelmann's. Cassidy identifies two major Lukan emphases which show the Gospel to be a potential political threat to the Empire: first, Jesus' teachings and deeds were of revolutionary consequence—socially, economically, and politically; and second, Jesus regularly refused to defer to the existing political authorities; he criticized them severely and maintained a defiant stance, especially against the chief priests.[6]

Cassidy maintains that Luke's social stance shows that Jesus not only responded to the needs of marginal people in society but that his actions and teachings were also responses "to the policies and practices of the political leaders of his time." Cassidy describes five major expressions of Jesus' social stance:[7]

1. Jesus shows concern for the poor, the infirm, the women, and the pagans. Mary's Magnificat introduces Jesus as one who will vindicate the poor, send the rich empty away, and dethrone the mighty (1:52-53); John's preaching also calls the people to share their extra coats with those who have none (3:11). Jesus himself associates his mission with the social themes of Isaiah (4:18-19) which emerge later as the distinctive features of his ministry (7:22-23). This emphasis marks Jesus' preaching also: he announces blessing to the poor (6:20-21) and woe to the rich (6:24-25). Luke's Gospel regards Gentiles favorably (4:38-39), showing a universalist outlook but not endorsing the status quo. It also gives special place to women, showing again its socially revolutionary character (7:11-17, 36-50; 8:2, 43-48; 13:10-13).

2. Jesus takes a clear stand against riches and criticizes the rich. He speaks against accumulating possessions (12:15-21) and counsels to live simply (10:4; 12:22-24). He instructs the rich to give to the poor (12:32-34; 16:9; 18:18-23) and repeatedly warns the rich against the destructiveness and perils of riches (8:14; 16:15, 19-31; 18:24-25; 21:1-4). He praises those who gave up possessions (7:25, 36-50; 19:8-10).

3. Jesus speaks and acts against practices of oppression and injustice

(18:1-5; 20:9-19, 45-47). By affirming new personal and social identity for women, he takes a stand against structural oppression (8:1-3; 10:38-42; 16:18).

4. Jesus calls for social relations to be based upon service and humility (9:47-48; 14:7-11; 17:7-10; 20:46-47). Further, Jesus specifically identifies service and humility as characteristics which mark off his followers from the kings of the Gentiles "who lord it over them" (22:24-27). The model of kingdom behavior stands opposed to the Empire model.

5. Jesus takes a stand against violence; his teaching encourages nonresistance (6:27-31). While speaking negatively of violence (13:1, 31; 19:45-46), he calls his followers to the way of repentance and forgiveness (17:3-4). Sayings that contain imagery of violence are best explained otherwise and do not alter this prevailing ethic (12:49-53; 22:35-38). Jesus calls for the things that make for peace (19:42-44) and regards those who come with swords as inappropriately responding to his ministry (22:47-51).

In addition to these five aspects of Luke's social stance, a potentially serious threat to the Roman Empire, Jesus refused to defer to the political authorities. Numerous incidents show elements of collision between Jesus and the political authorities:[8]

1. Jesus accepts the Pharisees' report that Herod Antipas wants to kill him. He derogatively calls Herod a fox and declares that Herod will not alter the course of his ministry (12:31-33).

2. The antagonism between the chief priests and Jesus is accented by Luke (19:37; 20:19); at his trial Jesus first responds sarcastically (22:67-68) and then noncommittally (22:70).

3. Jesus speaks of Pilate's massacre of the Galileans (13:1-3).

4. The tax dispute puts God's claims in tension with Caesar's, leading to the (false?) accusation that Jesus taught refusal of tax payment (20:21-25; 23:2).

5. Jesus explicitly identifies the kings of the Gentiles with a model of behavior he strongly repudiates (22:24-27).

6. Jesus predicts persecution for his followers at the hands of kings and governors (21:12-15).

7. Even though Pilate (and Herod) declare Jesus innocent, four texts show Rome responsible for Jesus' death: Pilate "gave his verdict" (23:24); Pilate put up the inscription, "This is the king of the Jews" (23:38); a Roman soldier stood beneath the cross (23:47); and Pilate had jurisdiction over the body (23:52).

On the basis of this portrait of the social stance of Jesus and Jesus' refusal to defer to the authorities, Cassidy concludes that Luke shows Jesus to be a potential threat to Rome, certainly if large numbers of people followed his way (and indeed, Luke-Acts accents the growth of the movement). Pilate and Herod were wrong in pronouncing Jesus innocent, in Cassidy's judgment. Cassidy sums up his view of Jesus as Luke presents him:

Although Jesus did not constitute the same type of threat to Roman rule as the Zealots and the Parthians, the threat that he posed was, ultimately, not less dangerous. Unlike the Zealots, the Jesus of Luke's gospel does not make the overthrow of Roman rule the central focus of his activity, nor does he support any of the other forms of government (including that probably advocated by the Zealots) that might have been considered as replacements for Roman rule. Nevertheless, by espousing radically new social patterns and by refusing to defer to the existing political authorities, Jesus pointed the way to a social order in which neither the Romans nor any other oppressing group would be able to hold sway.[9]

How then does Cassidy assess Conzelmann? He challenges Conzelmann's view that Luke does not place Jesus "in conflict with the existing social and political conditions and that Jesus was primarily concerned with a heavenly kingship."[10] Conzelmann fails to treat the texts where "Luke shows Jesus refusing to cooperate with, or actually criticizing, his political rulers." Nor does he note the way Jesus contravened existing social patterns and criticized the kings of the Gentiles.[11]

Yoder's View of Luke

Yoder's interpretation of Jesus in Luke's Gospel, quite compatible with Cassidy's, selects some of the same but also many different Lukan texts to show that Jesus' ministry was, from beginning to end, socially, economically, and politically revolutionary. While Jesus' proclamation of jubilee lies at the center of Yoder's description, a variety of emphases contribute to his thesis as follows.[12]

1. The annunciation texts and John's preaching (Luke 1:46ff., 68ff., cf. 3:7ff.) interpret the messianic advent in starkly socio-political images and hopes; e.g.

> he has put down the mighty from their thrones
> and exalted those of low degree;
> he has filled the hungry with good things
> and the rich he has sent empty away (1:52–53).

The birth narrative of chapter 2 also accents the political features of Jesus' coming: Bethlehem, David's city; "peace on earth"; and the liberation hopes of Simeon and Anna (cf. Matthew's report of Herod's fear and his massacre of babies).

2. Jesus' commissioning and testing (Luke 3:21–4:14) merge the themes of kingly enthronement (Ps. 2) and suffering servanthood (Isa. 42), on the one hand, and then show, on the other, that this unique commission is tested in

the three temptations by Empire models of economics, politics, and religion.

3. Luke introduces Jesus' ministry in the Nazareth synagogue with Jesus' jubilean sermon of Isaiah 61. Jesus' messianic mission is described in expressly social terms:

> to preach good news to the poor,
>   to proclaim release to the captives,
>   to give sight to the blind,
>   to liberate the oppressed,
>   to proclaim Yahweh's year of favor
>   [own trans. of 4:18-19].

Holding that "the year of favor" refers to "the year of jubilee," Yoder argues that Jesus' mission is clearly presented as "a visible socio-political, economic restructuring of relations among the people of God."[13]

4. Jesus' sermon on the plain (Luke 6:12ff.) spells out in detail the socioeconomic consequences of his Nazareth address. Having already established a new social reality in the Twelve, Jesus' teaching supported by his action enunciates an ethic of a new order. Rooted in God's boundless love even for rebellious sinners (6:35f.), Jesus' ethic is strikingly different from natural-law behavior (6:32-34).

5. When Jesus fed the multitude bread in the desert (9:1-22), the crowd wanted to make Jesus their Welfare King. But Jesus withdraws and begins to teach that suffering and cross-bearing are essential components of God's kingdom. His withdrawal is not retreat but a renewed messianic commitment: "The cross is beginning to loom not as a ritually prescribed instrument of propitiation but as the political alternative to both insurrection and quietism."[14]

6. Jesus' teaching on the cost of discipleship (12:49-13:9; 14:25-36), framed by awareness of violent political events (13:1-9; 31f.), instructs followers on the difficult experiences that arise from joining the new community of *voluntary* commitment: division within families and forsaking aspirations to greatness (22:25ff.). To form a new community with such distinctive lifestyles "constitutes an unavoidable challenge to the powers that be and . . . [introduces] a new set of social alternatives."[15]

7. Jesus' epiphany in the temple (19:36-46) depicts Jesus' kingly authority and incites the hostility of the chief priests to his messianic act and claim in cleansing the temple. This leads to a sequence of confrontations between "two social systems and Jesus' rejection of the status quo" (19:47-22:2).

8. The final episodes in Jesus' public ministry (22:24-53) show Jesus' last renunciation of messianic violence. He rejects a Zealot-like kingship by refusing to allow his disciples to defend him with the sword; though able to do so, he does not call twelve legions of angels to deliver him (Matt. 26:53).

9. Jesus' execution and exaltation (Luke 23-24) contain numerous political

accents: traded for Barabbas an insurrectionist, Jesus is crucified as a Zealot leader and "King of the Jews"; the irregularities of the trials accent the threat that the Jewish and Roman authorities felt Jesus to be; and in the post-resurrection narrative, Jesus' disciples still express their long-cherished hope that he would redeem Israel (24:21).

Yoder concludes this sketch of the social, economic, and political significance of Jesus' mission in Luke by declaring that "Jesus was in his divinely mandated prophethood, priesthood, and kingship, the bearer of a new possibility of human, social, and therefore, political relationships."[16]

Yoder follows up this sketch with an even more detailed analysis of the jubilean features of Jesus' mission *à la* Luke. He relates various teachings of Jesus in Luke to the four prescriptions for the year of jubilee (Lev. 25): (1) leaving the soil fallow, (2) the remission of debts, (3) the liberation of slaves, and (4) the return to each individual of his family's property.[17]

Since the command to leave the soil fallow generated anxiety over adequate food (Lev. 25:20–21), Jesus' proclamation of jubilee in A.D. 26 occasions his teaching against anxiety about food and drink (Luke 12:29–31). Similarly, Jesus' model prayer (Luke 12:2–4), when it asks, "forgive us our sins, for we ourselves forgive each one who is in debt to us," is a jubilean expression. Yoder argues that *aphiēmi* means remission of monetary debts and that "forgive us our offenses" is a wrong translation. Two parables, that of the unmerciful servant (Matt. 18:23–25) and that of the unjust steward (Luke 16:1–13) are both illumined when viewed against the jubilean rules for cancelling debts. The merciless servant is condemned for not cancelling a debt, especially because his own larger debt had been cancelled. The dishonest steward is commended because he forgave debts; his prudent jubilean act of repentance brought him friendship from his master's debtors. Yoder also describes the ingenious *prosboul* method of evading debt cancellation (begun by Rabbi Hillel) to prove that such jubilean expectations were taken as serious obligations in the first century. Yoder concludes,

> The two parables of the merciless servant and the unfaithful steward thus confirm what the Nazareth discourse, the Lord's Prayer, and the Sermon on the Mount had already given us to understand. It is really a jubilee, conformed to the sabbatical instructions of Moses, that Jesus proclaimed in A.D. 26: a jubilee able to resolve the social problem in Israel, by abolishing debts and liberating debtors whose insolvency had reduced them to slavery. The practice of such a jubilee was not optional. It belonged to the precursor signs of the kingdom. Those who would refuse to enter this path could not enter into the kingdom of God.[18]

Finally, Yoder relates Jesus' command to "sell your possessions and give alms" (Luke 12:33–34) and the inadequacy of the tithe (Luke 11:42) to Jubilee's prescription to redistribute capital. Jesus' teaching "was a jubilee ordinance . . . to be put into practice here and now, once, in A.D. 26, as a 'refreshment,' prefiguring the 'establishment of all things.' "

This summary of Cassidy's and Yoder's portraits of Jesus in Luke's Gospel presents a major challenge to Conzelmann's argument that Luke-Acts wants to show that the Christian movement is politically nonsubversive and is seeking to establish a permanent settlement with Rome. Before we evaluate these alternative interpretations, another crucially relevant Lukan redactional emphasis merits our attention. Might Luke's efforts to interpret the gospel of Jesus as a gospel of peace illumine the problem posed by the rival observations of Conzelmann, on the one hand, and Cassidy and Yoder on the other?

PEACE: A LUKAN REDACTIONAL EMPHASIS

Eirēnē (peace) occurs fourteen times, in twelve different passages, in Luke's Gospel. This contrasts to only one occurrence in Mark and four occurrences in Matthew (these occur in two verses in ch. 10, vv. 13 and 34). Mark's use occurs in triple tradition and Matthew's in Q material. Mark's and Matthew's uses of *eirēnē* are clearly traditional and insignificant to their theological emphases.[19] But not so for Luke. The majority of Luke's uses occur in pericopes found only in Luke's Gospel. Two uses (11:21; 19:38) are distinctive to Luke, but occur within triple tradition. Two more uses (8:48; 12:51) have parallel uses in Mark and Matthew respectively. One text with three uses of *eirēnē* (10:5–6) is especially difficult to classify: it has one parallel use in Matthew 10:13, it occurs in Matthean material common to Luke (Q) but is majorly altered by Luke, and two of the three uses of *eirēnē* do not have parallels in Matthew's text. This *eirēnē* text therefore is most appropriately considered among Luke's unique uses of *eirēnē*. Luke's *eirēnē* texts, classified into these three categories of use vis-à-vis Matthew and Mark, are as follows:

Group A: Uses of Eirēnē *in Contextual Pericopes Unique to Luke:*
—Luke 1:79: ". . . to give light to those who live in darkness and in the shadow of death, to guide our feet into the way of peace."
—Luke 2:14: " 'Glory to God in the highest, and on earth peace among men with whom he is pleased!' "
—Luke 2:29: "Lord, now lettest thou thy servant depart in peace, according to thy word; . . ."
—Luke 7:50: "And he said to the woman, 'Your faith has saved you; go in peace.' "
—Luke 10:5–6 (see Matt. 10:13): "Whatever house you enter, first say, 'Peace be to this house!' And if a son of peace is there, your peace shall rest opon him; but if not, it shall return to you."
—Luke 14:32: "And if not, while the other is yet a great way off, he sends an embassy and asks terms of peace."

—Luke 19:42: " 'Would that even today you knew the things that make for peace! But now they are hid from your eyes!' "

—Luke 24:36: "As they were saying this, Jesus himself stood among them, and said to them 'Peace to you.' "

Group B: Uses of Eirēnē *Distinctive to Luke, but in Triple Tradition*

—Luke 11:21 (par. Matt. 12:29; Mark 3:27): "When a strong man, fully armed guards his own palace, his goods are in peace; . . ."

—Luke 19:38 (par. Matt. 21:9; Mark 11:10): " 'Blessed be the king who comes in the name of the Lord! Peace in heaven and glory in the highest!' "

Group C: Uses of Eirēnē *with Parallels in Mark or Matthew*

—Luke 8:48 (par. Mk 5:34): "And he said to her, 'Daughter, your faith has made you well; go in peace.' "

—Luke 12:51 (par. Matt. 10:34): "Do you think that I have come to give peace on earth? No, I tell you, but rather division; . . ."

While all Luke's uses of *eirēnē* may carry some redactional intention, any attempt to assess Luke's redactional purpose must assign to those in Group A the greatest significance, to those in Group B a secondary importance, and to those in Group C a still lesser importance. The following commentary discusses Luke's *eirēnē* texts in this methodological order of importance.

Commentary on *Eirēnē* Texts: Group A

Luke 1:79. The *eirēnē* phrase carries a threefold significance: (1) it functions as the conceptual and literary climax to Zechariah's hymn, exalting the Lord God for Israel's now appearing *salvation*, redemption from "our enemies"; (2) it stands, however, in poetic parallel to a phrase which unites Israel's redemption to the giving of light to "those who sit in darkness," plus several previous phrases of distinctively universalist outlook; and (3) it (the *eirēnē* phrase) concludes and climaxes the entire series of Lukan annunciation hymns, setting at the same time the mood for the birth of the Savior child. Luke's use of *eirēnē* is clearly strategic, presaging fulfillment of Israel's messianic peace hopes, e.g., Isaiah 2:1–4, where swords are beaten into plowshares.

Luke 2:14. Heralding peace on earth because of God's limitless benevolence, this use sums up the divine commentary regarding the significance of Jesus' birth. Just as *eirēnē* was the last word of the human annunciation of Jesus' coming (1:79), so *eirēnē* is a key word in the divine commentary on the event of Jesus' birth. The preceding pericope of angelic announcement (vv. 10–12) clearly places the *eirēnē* text within Israel's tradition-hope of a Messiah-Savior, a king par excellence who, like Yahweh of old, will bring salvation to God's people. The text, however, does not limit the Messiah's peace to Israel, but envisions peace on earth among people everywhere.

Luke 2:29. While this use of *eirēnē* may be considered somewhat formular (cf. Gen. 15:15), its strategic function in Luke's birth narratives gives it crucial significance: the word itself is part of a unique prophetic oracle inspired by the Holy Spirit (vv. 25, 26, 27). Simeon, a man whose only credentials are his piety (v. 25) and his waiting for Israel's consolation (*paraklēsis*), can die in peace because Israel's hopes are now going to be fulfilled through the birth of this child Jesus, the Lord's Christ. The parallel themes to peace in the oracle are the appearance of God's salvation which shall be "a light to enlighten the pagans" and a glory to Israel. The death of God's servant *in peace* rests upon the certainty that God's now appearing consolation will have salvific significance both for the Gentiles (mentioned first!) and for Israel, thus fulfilling the universalist messianic hopes of Isaiah 40ff. Thus, through God's servant Simeon's death *in peace*, peace is associated with the fulfillment of Israel's messianic hopes and, specifically, salvific blessing to the Gentiles, thus excluding any notion of vindicating Israel's hopes in nationalistic and exclusivistic categories.

Luke 7:50. This occurrence of *eirēnē* comes at the end of Luke's distinctive story of Jesus and the sinful woman, a story told in the context of a controversy over Jesus' authority and the negative response of the religious leaders. The story itself illustrates positive response, the love of the sinner forgiven much. The phrase "go in peace," climaxing discussion on Jesus' authority, occurs in conjunction with the woman's forgiveness and salvation. However, because this phrase, like 2:29, is somewhat formular (cf. 8:48), it has limited significance when assessing Luke's redactional purposes.

Luke 10:5-6. Occurring in Luke's distinctive account of Jesus sending out the seventy, these three uses of *eirēnē* indicate that (1) the gospel in its essence and distinguishing feature is peace; (2) the missionary imperative to all nations (the seventy symbolizes the worldwide mission) extends the gospel as a gospel of peace; and (3) the purpose of Jesus' mission is to gather together children of peace.[20] This text, together with those in Luke's infancy chapters, is highly significant for assessing Luke's redactional purpose. It is placed close to the beginning of Luke's special section.

Luke 14:32. This use of *eirēnē* is not a direct part of the Gospel's emphasis; it occurs in a story told to illustrate the Gospel's emphasis on the call to discipleship. In the illustrative story, peace functions as the alternative to war, but the story itself commends neither war nor peace. It rather illustrates the necessity of counting the cost when taking up the cross of Jesus. This use of *eirēnē*, then, contributes almost nothing at all to the attempt to assess Luke's redactional interests in *eirēnē*, clearly evident elsewhere.

Luke 19:38, 42. (Though v. 38 belongs to group B below, it is best discussed here because of its thematic continuity with v. 42). These Lukan uses of *eirēnē* occur close to the end of Luke's special section. Jesus' entry into Jerusalem (vv. 28-38) resumes the triple tradition, but Luke adds two *eirēnē* declarations. The first concludes the triumphal entry chorus, sung by a great crowd of Jesus' disciples, according to Luke. The phrase, "Peace in heaven and glory in the highest heavens," climaxing the chant, may be intended as earth's antiphonal response to heaven's declaration in 2:14, "Peace on earth among those of good will.'' It is clearly a Lukan addition and only Luke puts the praise, including "Blessed is the king who comes in the name of the Lord!'' on the lips of disciples, people who have responded positively to Jesus.

Note that the narrative then moves to discussion of who will recognize Jesus for what he truly is. Some Pharisees wanted the disciples rebuked. But Jesus answered, "If these were silent the very stones would cry out.'' Luke is saying that earth must cry out and acclaim Jesus, the king of peace. Earth's people of good will must respond, else the stones will cry out.

Then follows Jesus' lament over Jerusalem; Jesus weeps over the city because it does not know on this day, the day of Jesus' entry, what brings peace. The city does not recognize its king of peace and hence faces judgment and destruction. Failure to recognize and understand peace is the criterion against which Jesus judges Jerusalem, the cornerstone (*Jeru*) of peace (*shalom*). Specifically, judgment comes because the people failed to "recognize their opportunity when God offered it'' (v. 44). This then provides the context for Jesus' cleansing the temple, a prophetic act calling for the justice of God's peace. The passion narrative, framed with this emphasis, then depicts the rejection of the king of peace. The structural function of these two *eirēnē* texts, closing off Luke's special section, underscores the redactional prominence which Luke assigns to *eirēnē*.

Luke 24:36. This occurrence of *eirēnē* is textually problematic. While most manuscripts include the *eirēnē* blessing upon the disciples, a few manuscripts (D and some Itala mss.) lack the phrase. Since the addition can be explained by influence from John, the RSV has decided to omit it. However, the manuscript evidence for including the phrase is overwhelming. In view of Luke's interest in *eirēnē* elsewhere, the phrase should be retained in the text, in my judgment.

God's mission of peace, and not the people's rejection of it, triumphs. The resurrected Lord, upon appearing to the eleven gathered disciples, says, first of all, "Peace be with you!'' In view of Luke's preceding peace emphasis, the phrase must be considered as more than a customary greeting in this context. The words signal the triumph of the incarnation's purpose *à la* Luke. Peace comes to earth in the Messiah, born as Bearer of peace (2:14), proclaimed as Lord of peace (10:5-6), and rejected as King of peace (19:38-42). The worldwide mission of peace (signaled in 10:5-6) triumphs through the risen Jesus, who reassures his disciples that *eirēnē* remains.

Commentary on *Eirēnē* Texts: Group B

Luke 11:21. This use of *eirēnē* is similar to that of 14:32, discussed above. The word peace is not used here directly as part of Luke's gospel emphasis. It occurs within a story-image that illustrates Luke's main point, i.e., that Beelzebul's house (palace) is not "in peace'' because God's kingdom, coming in Jesus, is stronger than Beelzebul. In this illustrative metaphor, *eirēnē* denotes security or safety. While the range of meaning for *eirēnē* is illustrated both here and in 14:32, these uses do not contribute directly to Luke's purposes elsewhere to show that the good news of Jesus is an *eirēnē*-event.

Luke 19:38. This distinctive Lukan use of *eirēnē* does contribute to Luke's purpose to connect the mission of Jesus to peace. See the discussion above on 19:38, 42 in the Group A texts.

Commentary on *Eirēnē* Texts: Group C

Luke 8:48. Jesus' word, "go in peace," to the daughter healed of a hemorrhage functions as a word of blessing. Here the word is associated with physical health; in Luke 7:50 it occurred parallel to the granting of forgiveness of sins. Because the phrase appears formular and is parallel to Mark 5:34, little redactional significance can be attached to it.

Luke 12:51. This use of *eirēnē* appears to directly contradict Luke's efforts elsewhere to describe the significance of the gospel with *eirēnē*. But several factors preclude any contradicting significance. The verse is clearly of Q origin, occurring in a larger section which advances Luke's teaching on Jesus' call to costly discipleship. Further, *eirēnē* is used in a metaphorical saying that illustrates the effect of costly discipleship upon family relationships. It may be, however, that Luke felt the possible contradiction between this saying and his redactional emphases, since Luke's version of the Q saying is toned down from its Matthean sharpness by at least three significant changes: *dokēite* for *nomisēte, dounai* for *baleín*, and, most significant, *diamerismon* for *machairan*. With these changes, Luke protects the word from any notion that the gospel allows the use of the sword against enemies; he clearly assigns to it the meaning of division among household members that the gospel may bring.

Summary of Commentary

Of the four Lukan *eirēnē* texts in Groups B and C, only 19:38 advances directly Luke's redactional purposes evident in the Group A texts, although Luke's modification in 12:51 may witness indirectly to his *eirēnē* redaction. Of the eight Group A texts, 14:32 is of little significance. All the remaining seven texts, plus 19:38 in Group B, serve the purpose of showing that Jesus and the gospel bring *eirēnē*. The themes connected to *eirēnē* in Luke's redactional purpose are many: redemption from oppression, light to the pagans, forgiveness of sins, blessings to the outsiders (Gentiles, a sinner, women), a "yes" to those of good will, peace affirming peace as the hallmark of the missionary growth of the kingdom and the distinguishing character of the Jesus community, acceptance of God's purposes in the Messiah Jesus (and conversely, judgment upon those who reject the peace of the Messiah), and receiving the peace of Christ's presence.

It is important to note that Luke's distinctive occurrences of *eirēnē* occur at structurally strategic places in the Gospel's narrative. Three uses occur in Luke's infancy narratives (1:79; 2:14, 29) and thus set the mood of peace expectancy: the announced coming one will bring *eirēnē* as a new and unprecedented historical reality. A second structurally strategic cluster introduces and ends Luke's special section (10:5-6; 19:38,42). Jesus' teachings on discipleship which leads to the kingdom of God are framed by peace emphases. And conversely, when *eirēnē* is unwelcomed or refused, judgment follows (10:10-12; 19:43-46). Jesus' *eirēnē* thus brings crisis, a point clearly expressed in 12:51. The third structurally crucial occurrence is 24:36 where peace is the resurrected Lord's self-identifying greeting to his disciples.

These uses together make it clear that for Luke peace (*eirēnē)* expresses the very heart of the gospel. Further, his continuing uses of *eirēnē* in Acts corroborate this point (esp. 7:26; 9:31; 10:36; 15:33). In these instances, *eirēnē* describes reconciliation, the advancement of the gospel, breaking down barriers, and celebrating the unity of the church.[21] Quite clearly *eirēnē* essentially describes the mission of Jesus in Luke's double volume on Jesus and his Spirit. How then should this emphasis be understood in relation to the competing theses of Conzelmann, Cassidy and Yoder regarding Luke's political stance? Does peace make a difference?

ASSESSING LUKE'S *EIRĒNĒ* REDACTION VIS-À-VIS THE "POLITICAL INTERPRETATION"

The task of evaluating the significance of Luke's *eirēnē* redaction in the context of the opposing interpretations of Luke's political emphasis requires a two-way analysis. From the one direction Luke's *eirēnē* redaction must be assessed for its bearing upon whether Luke presents a political apologetic for Christianity (Conzelmann) or shows Jesus to be a political threat to Rome (Cassidy) or stresses the revolutionary jubilean significance of the gospel (Yoder). Conversely, from the other direction, whatever correlation *eirēnē* has with these rival interpretations will determine in turn the meaning that must be assigned to *eirēnē* in Luke's Gospel. Does Luke adorn Christianity with *eirēnē* to show Rome that Christianity is a good ally of the Empire's *Pax Romana*? In this case the *eirēnē* redaction supports Conzelmann's thesis, making Christianity a valuable resource for pacification and Luke's political apologetic. Or is Luke's *eirēnē* a confrontive rival force to the *Pax Romana*, thus supporting Cassidy's interpretation? Or is Luke's *eirēnē* an expression of the jubilean gospel, creating an alternative model for human life and relegating the *Pax Romana* to an order of the passing world?

Taking up the first task, how does one assess Luke's *eirēnē* redaction vis-à-vis these rival interpretations? I propose two lines of inquiry to assist this evaluative task: (1) Do these distinctive Lukan peace texts have any textual affinity to the key texts used by Conzelmann, Cassidy, or Yoder respectively; and (2) to what extent do the three interpretations vis-à-vis the *eirēnē* redaction logically cohere with a dozen other Lukan emphases, a test in redactional coherency?

The Test of Textual Affinity

Significantly, none of the *eirēnē* texts occur in structural conceptual affinity to the key texts cited by Conzelmann, except 19:38. Conzelmann cites this text to assert that Luke depoliticized the Davidic kingship, since Luke used the simple term king instead of Mark's "kingdom of our father David," or Matthew's "Son of David." Conzelmann failed to cite Luke's next phrase, "Peace in *heaven* and glory in the highest" (italics mine), which might have been used to serve his argument that Jesus' "Kingship does not stand opposed to the Empire on the political plane." This connection between *eirēnē* and Luke's view of the kingdom, however, supports more firmly the point that Luke protects his use of *eirēnē* from any nationalistic expression of Jesus' kingship. This is in keeping with Luke's use of *eirēnē* elsewhere (1:79; 2:14, 29; 10:5-6). Note also the above suggestion that this is earth's antiphonal response to heaven's good news in 2:14 (it *must* be said by the disciples, else the stones will cry it out! 19:40). Were other Lukan *eirēnē* texts connected to those texts cited by Conzelmann to support his thesis, the view that 19:38 witnesses to a political apologetic would need to be considered more seriously. But such evidence is not to be found.

When one assesses Cassidy's thesis in the same way, the two parts of his thesis fare differently. The second part, that Jesus refused to defer to the authorities, shows only one connection between *eirēnē* and texts cited in its support. That text is 19:42 where peace *is not* because Jerusalem does not know the things that make for peace. Cassidy uses 19:47 as part of his textual evidence to document the chief priests' hostility toward Jesus. Jesus' cleansing of the temple (vv. 45-46) also shows that Jesus initiated confrontive judgment against the temple's aristocracy, primarily the chief priests (see also the prophetic judgment of vv. 43-44). This is important evidence in support of Cassidy's thesis that Luke focuses upon the role of the chief priests in the passion narrative (see note 11). *Eirēnē*, however it is to be defined, stands in sharp opposition to that particular historical situation (vv. 45-47): for it there is no peace!

But all the other Lukan verses cited by Cassidy to show that Jesus did not defer to the authorities have no structural textual connection to Luke's use of *eirēnē*. On the basis of this testing then, Luke's redactional use of *eirēnē* provides us no evidence for judging between a pro-Roman or anti-Roman redactional emphasis. Might these opposing emphases, both appearing in the text, *à la* Conzelmann's and Cassidy's citations, simply concur with the entire New Testament's portrait in which some texts view government positively (Rom. 13:1-7; 1 Pet. 2:13-17; 1 Tim. 2:1-4; Titus 3:1) and some view it negatively (1 Cor. 6:1-6; 2:6-8; Mark 10:42-45; Matt. 4:8-10; Luke 4:5-8; Eph. 6:12; Rev. 13)? Both the Jewish view of the powers and the historical realities produced this bifurcated emphasis. In this case Conzelmann and Cassidy are correct in identifying these opposing emphases. Both portraits of

Jesus' and Christianity's relation to the authorities are to be found in Luke-Acts and must be considered as part of Christianity's experience with the state. They reflect the history of Jesus and the views of the church and Luke. This means also that neither view can be ascribed to Luke's redactional purpose in such a way as to exclude the opposite emphasis. While the Empire and its representatives may be viewed as either friend or foe, Jesus and the early church did not set forth a theological rationale or political apologetic that locked the Empire or state into either category.

The first part of Cassidy's thesis regarding Jesus' social stance, however, as well as Yoder's similar emphasis on the revolutionary impact of Jesus' teachings and mission has some significant correlations with Luke's *eirēnē* redaction. Both writers use 1:51ff. and 19:36ff. to present the revolutionary socio-political character of this Gospel. The *eirēnē* theme emerges as the climax to the annunciation hymns and the *eirēnē* redaction in 19:38, 42 is especially prominent. Further, Cassidy cites several times the story of Jesus and the sinful woman (7:36–50) to show Jesus' acceptance of marginal persons (both sinners and women); the story concludes with an *eirēnē* word. Cassidy also uses Luke 10:4 to depict the simple life-style of Jesus' followers; this verse precedes the very significant *eirēnē* texts of 10:5–6.

This degree of structural correlation between Luke's *eirēnē* redaction and his emphasis upon the revolutionary impact of the gospel—socially, economically, and politically—on the one hand, and the absence of any such structural correlation with pro-Roman or anti-Roman emphases provides the basis for two conclusions. First, it is clear that the *eirēnē* of the gospel of the kingdom is not a puppet, nor even an ally of the *Pax Romana*. If Luke really wanted to dish up a political apologetic for Christianity, he missed a good chance! Nor does the *eirēnē* of his Gospel emerge with a primary agenda to confront the Empire, seeking either to condemn it or convert it. Rather (and second), the *eirēnē* of the Gospel stands in the service of making all things new—socially, economically, and politically. The variety of Lukan themes associated with his *eirēnē* texts embraces almost every aspect of life, showing clearly the inadequacy of existing political and religious alternatives, be they Zealot, Pharisee, Sadducee, Essene, or Roman.

The Test of Coherency with Other Lukan Redactional Themes

Evidence from this testing will be only briefly sketched in order to serve a collaborative function to that above. Of the dozen or so recognized redactional themes of Luke's Gospel, three fail to logically cohere with Conzelmann's thesis that Luke develops a political apologetic for Christianity. Luke's presentation of Jesus blessing the poor and warning the rich (see Walter Pilgrim's recent study)[22] does not comport well with the economic model of the Empire. Nor is the teaching compatible with long-term settling in, a point which in itself casts suspicion upon Conzelmann's thesis that the delay of the parousia plays an important role in Luke, thus producing the development of a political apologetic. Further, Luke's emphasis on persecution and martyrdom stands in principle against his thesis, especially Luke's mention of "kings and governors" as the persecutors (Luke 21:12) and Pilate's leading position in an account of those responsible for Jesus' death (Acts 4:27). Nor can Luke's pro-temple redaction[23] be easily reconciled with a political apologetic since the temple structurally focused political threats to Rome. Any notion, therefore, of a Lukan redactional purpose to create a political apologetic in which Christianity seeks a permanent settlement with Rome is mistaken.

The Lukan emphases of Cassidy and Yoder fare better on the coherency test. Their portrait of Jesus' mission as revolutionary—socially, economically, and politically—fits well with the Lukan teaching on the rich and the poor, with Luke's universal outlook which puts the despised Samaritans and the enemy Gentiles in positive light, with Luke's positive emphasis on women, with Luke's accent on God's and Jesus' love for sinners, with Luke's emphasis on salvation (*sōtēria*) and with Luke's highlighting of the Holy Spirit as God's agent to create a new order. Luke's well-known missionary vision and imperative also fit well with this emphasis. Further, Luke's concern to accent Jesus' and the church's place in redemptive history is readily correlated with these themes: they show how God establishes the new order for humanity. The persecution and temple themes which contradicted Conzelmann's thesis are also congruent with Cassidy's and Yoder's interpretations. Finally, Luke's *eirēnē* redaction, examined above, coheres well also with their proposals.

The Meaning of *Eirēnē* in Luke

Having ascertained which "political" interpretations Luke does and does not associate with *eirēnē*, we are now able also to formulate some notion of the meaning of *eirēnē* in Luke's Gospel. The *eirēnē* of the Gospel does not serve the cause of "making peace" with the Empire, nor with the Jewish political leaders for that matter. While it occurs as a climax to hymns with Maccabean overtones (1:47–55, 67–79), its use is strategically connected with blessing to the Gentiles, the oppressor-enemies (1:79; 2:32). Though Jesus is born with the credentials of Davidic kingship (2:11),[24] the peace he brings upon earth is not restricted nationally, politically, socially, or economically. It is for all those willing to accept it. Likewise, the missionary peace of 10:5–6 is set within the context of Luke's distinctive mission of *the seventy*, symbolizing the gospel's going to all the nations of the world. But if one is not a child of peace, he is shut out of the kingdom of God which has come near in *eirēnē*. This explains Jesus' hard words concerning Jerusalem in 19:43–44, spoken because the city refused "the things that make for peace." Nonetheless, 24:36 assures the reader that the peace of the kingdom triumphs. *Eirēnē* then, while it is essentially universalistic, a gospel-blessing for all people, also brings judgment. It sets forth criteria which some affirm and some reject.

The variety of uses in Luke also clearly disassociates *eirēnē* from any restrictive personalistic meaning in which peace is a matter of the heart or only an individual and merely personal experience. *Eirēnē* is associated with relational and structural realities (Israel's freedom and Gentile-enemy blessing, the forgiveness and acceptance of despised sinners [7:36-50; cf. 15:1ff.], all nations hearing the gospel, and the *things* that make for peace). This point gains importance when *eirēnē* is equated with salvation, as occurs in Marshall's commentary on Luke.[25] In his earlier volume Marshall identified Luke's recurring use of the term savior in the birth narratives.[26] In fact every use of *eirēnē* in these chapters occurs in a context where *sōtēria* also occurs (see 1:47, 68-79; 2:10-14, 29f.). Building upon its broad meaning in the Old Testament, Marshall says that *salvation* in Luke also has a wide range of meaning, denoting the sum of God's blessings, rescuing people "from every human distress and from divine judgment." It refers especially to the bliss which God confers "on his people at the end of the age." Marshall cites numerous Lukan uses of the verb *sōzō* where *save* is connected to healings of various kinds.[27]

Marshall is correct in seeing the close relationship between peace (*eirēnē*) and salvation (*sōtēria*) in Luke's Gospel. Marshall's comment on 2:14 is helpful:

If the glory of God in heaven is revealed in the coming of his Son, the effect for men on earth is summed up in *eirēnē* (1:79). Here, however, more than the cessation of strife is meant, and the word is used to indicate the full sum of the blessings associated with the coming of the Messiah (Is. 9:5f.; Mi. 5:4). He brings a new situation of peace between God and men in which his blessings can be communicated to them; *eirēnē* is thus tantamount to *sōtēria*.[28]

In subsequent verses where *eirēnē* occurs, Marshall regularly equates it with *sōtēria* and refers back to this discussion of 2:14.[29] While *eirēnē* and *sōtēria* are indeed related in meaning, the weakness of this approach is that it misses Luke's special interest in *eirēnē* and precludes the discovery of nuances in meaning for *eirēnē* that *sōtēria* may not connote.

Just as Luke inherited Old Testament meanings for *sōtēria* so he also inherited meanings for *eirēnē* in Israel's multifaceted use of *shalom*. These meanings include well-being, health, salvation, trusting relationships, and, perhaps most significant, social justice. Shalom's semantic field includes righteousness (*tzedeqah*), justice (*mishpat*), steadfast love (*hesed*), and faithfulness (*emunah*).[30] Granted, Luke may contribute new meanings and nuances to the word, such as correlating it with the universal welcome of the gospel. But these meanings of *shalom* match exactly those themes developed by Cassidy and Yoder in describing Jesus' social stance in Luke. The larger pervasive emphases of Luke's Gospel support a justice-shalom interpretation of Luke's *eirēnē*. For this reason the ready equation of *eirēnē* with *sōtēria* must be cautioned against, for it leads too quickly in the direction of collapsing the distinctive meaning of *eirēnē* (and *sōtēria* for that matter) into "peace between God and men" or "the bliss that God confers at the end of the age" (see above). To be sure, these points are not wrong, but they are abortive when viewed against Luke's major attention to social themes which show the *eirēnē*-gospel to be of revolutionary consequence, socially, economically, and politically—here and now.

At the same time it is important to remember that Luke's *eirēnē* does not serve an ideology or apologetic that either *consistently* courts or condemns the state and political leaders, though both critical and favorable comments may appear, as Conzelmann and Cassidy have shown. The *eirēnē* of the Gospel has its own mind and mission. It will not be seduced into either the Pietist or Sadducee-Zealot perversions. It creates its own agenda, seeking to find more "children of peace" and to testify to all people about "the things that make for peace."[31]

NOTES

1. Jacob Elias limits his study to Luke 4:16–30 and argues that jubilee is not a redactional emphasis in this pericope. The themes rather express the messianic hope of eschatological reversal ("The Beginning of Jesus' Ministry in the Gospel of Luke" [Th. D. diss.: Toronto School of Theology, 1978]). Robert B. Sloan, Jr., argues for jubilean emphasis in Luke but holds that it is eschatological in character. He then criticizes Conzelmann's view that Luke de-eschatologized the Gospel (*The Favorable Year of the Lord: A Study of Jubilary Theology in the Gospel of Luke* [Austin, Tex.: Schola Press, 1977]). Donald Blosser surveys the meaning of jubilee in Israel's long tradition history and argues that numerous texts in Luke reflect jubilean emphasis. He criticizes Sloan for assigning to jubilee in Luke a metaphorical eschatological function. Luke's narrative shows that Jesus called for Jubilee practices here and now ("Jesus and Jubilee, Luke 4:16–30: The Year of Jubilee and Its Significance in Luke" [Ph.D. diss.: St. Andrews University, 1979]).

2. Hans Conzelmann, *The Theology of St. Luke*, trans. Geoffrey Buswell (New York: Harper & Row, 1961), pp. 138–148.

3. Ibid., p. 140.

4. "Thus the threefold demonstration of the facts is given to the Jews—who now must tell lies: to the Empire, which objectively defines the legal position; and to the ruler owing allegiance to Rome, who agrees with the findings of the Roman representative" (ibid., p. 141). I quote this from the German original because the English translation does not adequately reflect the threefold circumstance. *Die Mitte der Zeit: Studien zur Theologie des Lukas* (Tübingen: J. C. B. Mohr [Paul Siebeck], 1954; 2nd ed. 1967), p. 120.

5. Ibid., pp. 141–144 and 138 in the English translation.

6. Richard J. Cassidy, *Jesus, Politics, and Society: A Study of Luke's Gospel* (Maryknoll, N.Y.: Orbis Books, 1978), pp. 78–79.

7. The following five-point summary is of chapters 2 and 3 of Cassidy's book, pp. 20–49.

8. This summary is of chapters 4 and 5 of Cassidy, pp. 50–76.

9. Ibid., p. 79.

10. Ibid., p. 129.

11. Ibid., pp. 129, 130. Cassidy also notes that while the innocence of Pilate is one theme in the passion narrative, it is only one theme. Another more pervasive theme is Luke's effort to be "precise about the major responsibility that the chief priests and their allies had in securing Jesus' death" (ibid., p. 130). In his dissertation, Cassidy expands this point by noting how this theme permeates the larger passion narrative (19:47; 20:19, 26 and cf. vv. 27, 40). He notes that Luke wants to document the "unrelenting efforts of the chief priests to destroy Jesus." But the chief priests and their allies do not represent all Jews or Judaism en toto. See Cassidy, "The Social and Political Stance of Jesus in Luke's Gospel" (Ph.D. diss.: Graduate Theological Union, 1976), pp. 337–338, 366, n. 41.

12. John Howard Yoder. *The Politics of Jesus* (Grand Rapids, Mich.: Eerdmans, 1972). The following summary is of chapter 2, pp. 26–63.

13. Ibid., p. 39.

14. Ibid., p. 43.

15. Ibid., p. 47.

16. Ibid, pp. 62–63.

17. This section summarizes chapter 3 of Yoder's *Politics of Jesus*, pp. 64–77.

18. Ibid., p. 74. In this quotation and elsewhere Yoder does not limit his citations to Luke. Arguing that this portrait represents Jesus, he follows mostly but not exclusively Luke's Gospel. This approach has its strengths for Yoder's purposes. But it also has liabilities when one seeks to assess the Lukan portrait on the basis of Yoder's work. I have addressed this issue more extensively in an unpublished paper, "An Exegetical Analysis of Yoder's *Politics of Jesus* with Further Probings of the Jubilean Interpretation of Jesus," 1978.

19. I do not mean that Matthew and Mark have no interest in the subject. Both develop similar emphases with related vocabulary (e.g., Matthew's *dikaiosune* and Mark's *hodos* theology). Certainly Matthew's distinctive *makarioi* hoi *eirēnoporoi* (5:9) and Mark's distinctive *eirēneuete* en *allēlois* (9:50) need to be considered here as well.

20. William Klassen regards this phrase "son of peace" to be a unique and most significant expression, close in meaning perhaps to a "son of Torah." The phrase thus denotes dedication to the way of peace, the giving of one's life in service to its cause (cf. "peace-maker" in Matt. 5:9). See Klassen " 'A Child of Peace' (Luke 10:6) in First Century Context," *NTS* 27 (1981), 496–497.

21. John R. Donahue has called attention to this emphasis in Luke-Acts as well; see his article, "The Good News of Peace," *The Way* (London) 22 (April, 1982), 88–89. See also note 31 below.

22. Walter Pilgrim, *Rich and Poor in Luke's Gospel: Wealth and Poverty in Luke-Acts* (Minneapolis: Augsburg, 1981).

23. Francis D. Weinert surveys the literature on this topic and correctly argues against those, including Conzelmann, who contend that Luke has a negative view of the temple. Instead, Luke shows a markedly positive view of the temple, evident especially in the early chapters of both Luke and Acts and elsewhere. See Weinert, "Luke, the Temple and Jesus' Saying about Jerusalem's Abandoned House" (Luke 13:34–35), *CBQ* 44 (Jan., 1982), 68–76; "The Meaning of the Temple in Luke-Acts," *BTB* 11 (Mar., 1981), 85–89.

24. This bold depiction by Luke sharply contradicts Conzelmann's commentary on 19:38, that Luke depoliticizes Jesus' kingship by deleting titles that reflect Jesus' Davidic heirship.

25. I. Howard Marshall, *The Gospel of Luke: A Commentary on the Greek Text* (Grand Rapids, Mich.: Eerdmans, 1978), pp. 95, 112, 419, 715, 716.

26. I. Howard Marshall, *Luke: Historian and Theologian* (Grand Rapids, Mich.: Zondervan, 1970), pp. 97–102.

27. Ibid., p. 95.

28. Marshall, *Gospel of Luke*, p. 112.

29. See above, note 25.

30. See, for example, Ps. 72:1–7; 85:8–13; Isa. 32:1, 16–18; 48:18; 54:10, 14; 60:17; Amos 5:22b, 24. See also G. von Rad, *TDNT*, II, pp. 404–406.

31. Joseph Comblin's studies of *eirēnē* in Luke-Acts, focusing mostly on the uses in Acts (7:26; 9:31; 10:36; 15:33), complement this interpretation. Comblin argues that in Acts, Luke uses *eirēnē* to describe the reconciliation of Jews and outsiders in Christ: an Israelite and an Egyptian (7:26); Samaritans also have come into the kingdom (9:31); Gentiles also receive salvation (10:36); and the jeopardized unity of Jews and Gentiles in Christ is restored (15:33). This is the mystery of the church (Paul, Eph. 3:6) which stands as testimony to the Empire, a *Pax Christi* which has achieved what the *Pax Romana* could never do.

Uncritically following Conzelmann's view that Luke wants to show harmony between the church and the Empire, Comblin fails to adequately assess the evidence in Luke-Acts where Jesus and the church are put into critical tension with the Empire, even though he notes that the church's experience was persecution from the Empire and that the *Pax Christi* was inherently a challenge to the *Pax Romana*. See Joseph Comblin, *Theologie des Friedens: Biblische Grundlagen* (Graz, Vienna, Cologne: Verlag Styria, 1963), pp. 359–383, and his earlier essay, "La Paix dans la Théologie de saint Luc," *ETL* 32 (1956): 439–460.

3

Luke's Perspective on Tribute to Caesar

J. DUNCAN M. DERRETT

A millenarian and charismatic movement is likely to be in trouble with the state, since the essence of such a movement, at its very origins, is protest. The state is alerted, and will attempt to infiltrate it, and, if its momentum persists, direct it. Buddhism when it penetrated into China and the Christianity of the Counter-Reformation when it began to consolidate itself in Japan both found that the movement, to justify itself, must make out that it does not deny the sovereignty of the emperor. The difficulties which both faiths encountered were prolonged. Buddhism found a formula in the advantage which the state might draw from the cult and from the association of rulers with endowments. The Tokugawa government in Japan was shrewd enough to realize that the famous formula, "Render unto Caesar . . . ," enjoined only a most qualified submission to the ruler, without specifying either the conditions subject to which the Christian might, with a good conscience, obey his ruler, or the persons whose exclusive right to "bind and loose" could decide in any emergency where the line was to be drawn.[1] The government designated the religion of the "Batiren" (Padres) an "evil religion," a position which persisted well into our century.

Nowadays it is obvious that several different interpretations of the formula can exist.[2] One is the notion that there are two distinct spheres—this is the traditional Catholic exegesis—Caesar's and God's; neither should trespass on the ground demarcated for the other. This outlook was emphatically that of Publius Petronius, legate of the Emperior Claudius, as far back as A.D. 43–44 (Josephus, *Ant.* 19.305)! In a sense this is the outlook to which the United States notably subscribes: there is the field of religion, which the Constitution guarantees, and there are secular matters into which religion (whichever religion) may not enter except so far as the state permits or requires.

A well-approved interpretation is more true to historical probability. Christ enjoins us to render to Caesar what is really Caesar's, subject to the overriding requirements of God.[3] Fr. Cassidy's own view of the formula is a forthright one:

> Far from having any independent existence of its own, Caesar's realm, the social order of the Roman empire, was in Jesus' view a part of the larger order of creation, whose only author was God. Therefore the Romans' social patterns were to be evaluated against the standard of the social patterns desired by God, and supported or not on that basis.[4]

But the modern teachers who confidently preach this message, not least in their commentaries on Luke's Gospel, would be astounded to have to answer for the blood of Bishop Lewumb, and the many other modern martyrs who have preferred obedience to God to the commands or the requirements of tyrants. In his ivory tower, the academic can confidently write of the superiority of God, the creator, over the authority of the created, namely the administration. He can conveniently ignore the question, "Who decides what belongs to Caesar?" and pass on to the next pericope calling for exegesis (in our case the question of the Sadducees).

LUKE'S CONCERN TO PROVIDE GUIDANCE

Since Luke was writing for a church which had had at least forty years' experience of living with hostile Jewish and sceptical Gentile onlookers, which had, according to Paul's evidence, experienced actual persecution from the side of the Jewish authorities, and which was welcoming the catastrophe of the fall of the city and the temple with mixed feelings, it is of interest to see how his rewriting of the Marcan passage of the tribute-money (Mark 12:13–17) in 20:20–26 contributes to our guidance. Without departing from Mark, without adding anything not inherent in his text, without intruding or excluding anything according to any whim or fashion, Luke contrives to present the passage, which to him is more vivid than it was, evidently, to Matthew, as actual *guidance*, and therefore capable of being trusted even in an emergency. That this is so is shown by his use of the word *apocrisis* in v. 26. They "wondered at his *answer*." The word *apocrisis* was later to become a technical term for a *rescript*: it is what we lawyers call a *responsum*, a technical answer to a technical question, particularly in the field of behavior (so Luke 2:47!). The question is put to the authority (rabbi, Roman jurisconsult, mufti, or pandit) according to the culture, and he gives a *responsum*. Those who believe in his wisdom and authenticity as exponent of the culture are bound to respect and follow the formula he gives them. And "Render unto Caesar" is a formula if ever there was one.

Moreover, we know that Luke believed it to be a piece of (quasi-) legislation, if one can use that rather unsuitable word. No doubt it was a precept, and no more; but the same could be said of the entire Law of Moses.

"And they were not able to catch hold of him by his word[5] *in the presence of the people* . . ." (v. 26). God's chosen emissary does his great works, and utters his message, in front of the people (of God): that is the biblical formula.[6] Judged by the people, who are the audience (and, we are to understand, the beneficiaries of the *responsum*), Jesus' answer was faultless. Therefore, the cryptic formula was *not* merely a piece of evasion, a clever ambiguity, a trap into which the questioners were pushed. It was something that the people of God could welcome, especially since the previous sources of norms, the Law and the Prophets, did not say anything about Tiberius. Even Daniel threw no light on payment of tribute.

That the information was for use either to prevent, dispel, or dissipate persecution is shown at v. 20. All the verse, like all the portions diverging from Mark, is made up, with few exceptions, with Lukan words or words which appear here only in the Gospels.[7] Here we have Luke's own composition, his commentary, his evaluation. "And setting a watch upon him,[8] they [i.e., the scribes and chief priests, 20:19], despatched agents [not necessarily *secret* agents][9] in the guise of righteous men, in the hopes of catching hold of him by his word,[10] with the intention that he should be *handed over* to the government and the power of the governor." The question eventually put to Jesus is about *rule*. He himself will be *handed over*,[11] as he predicted his followers would be handed over, precisely to rulers and governors.[12] The expression "handing over" is a technical one. Jews would later, and it is clear they could also earlier, claim the absolute right to hand over for punishment, if need be for destruction, to the secular power, any fellow Jew who jeopardized the race, who put his fellow Jews in peril.[13] We know from Paul that Jews who refused the message of Christ attempted to delate Christians to the Romans as troublemakers and seditious persons.[14] Their own rather delicate relations with the secular power were threatened by the movement springing up in their midst, and it was their responsibility to put their house in order and cast these sectarians out. But that was not enough. They must bring them before rulers. And the pattern for all this was Christ himself.

Since the attempt, which Luke himself actually depicts (23:2), to delate Christ before the ruler (unsuccessfully, as Luke shows), was based on his allegedly teaching his followers to refuse tribute to Caesar, the truth of Christ's attitude and his actual teaching on the subject would be vital for the church. A wise man would advise his people at least to pay taxes or risk charges of insurrection (so Agrippa as reported in A.D. 66 at Josephus, *War* 2.403–440). Was the church a separate government? It was, like all Asian normative systems, incapable of separating secular from religious, and its teachers would be unconscious of that distinction of which the Romans and their pupils (including ourselves) were and are so proud, namely which kept *ius* (law) and *fas* (religious precept) clearly apart. But did the church regard itself as entitled to delimit the rights of the state to command actual obedience? So thorny a subject had evidently to be settled in some measure with the aid of a short formula, apparently cryptic and ambiguous, and, as Luke himself shows at 23:2, capable of authorizing the hearers (those who sent the agents) to assert, with witnesses to hand, that Jesus prevented the payment of tribute to Rome which would otherwise have been paid!

THE MEANING OF LUKE'S ACCOUNT

To see what value Luke obtained from "Render unto Caesar" we must unwind the story as he unwound it. First the questioners, as has always been noticed, pretended that they were certain that whatever Jesus answered would be *true*,[15] and *impartial*. They chose, as it were by accident, to attribute to Jesus the divine quality of objective judgment.[16] No doubt this suggests that he will reply unfavorably to Caesar's claims, seeing that these were regarded almost universally as merely *de facto* and not *de iure* valid. They insinuate that whatever answer he gives is to be the "Way of God." This Marcan phrase correctly prepares us to understand that Jesus' *responsum* is indeed the Way. Our expectations from that formula are increased dramatically. "Is it permitted [in the sense of permitted by the Jewish law] for us [being subject to the Torah of Moses] to give tribute [Luke generalizes somewhat from the Marcan *census* to all taxation likely to be imposed, not merely on Rome's provincials but even on others] to Caesar [as representative of the Roman state]?" Jesus catches sight[17] of their wickedness (in posing a trap question in the form of a religious question), and says, "Show me a denarius." Without mentioning that he looked at it—Mark is interested in the actual inspection of the coin[18]—Luke continues with his question, "Whose image and inscription does it bear?" They are now placed in the position of answering a question, a question, however, the answer to which is already known: "Caesar's."

The words that follow have been a source of anxiety to the church, and ingenuity for exegetes, since they appear to be without logic. Asian, and not less Jewish than other Asian, minds have never pretended to be logical, nor to proceed in what Westerners have understood, since the time of Aristotle at the latest, as allowable sequences of demonstration. No one doubts the historicity of this *logion* of Christ, but what exactly was meant is, as we have seen, open to debate. Luke himself by the slightest of touches puts us into a position to guess what we should understand *him* to suppose it meant. "And he said to them, *Therefore* render the things of Caesar to Caesar and[19] the things of God to God." Matthew also (Matt. 22:21) introduces a *therefore* (*oun*), but the effect is quite different. Placed as it is in the Matthean sentence it by no means implies that the conclusion follows logically, nor necessarily follows, from what had preceded. Luke's *toinun*, at the commencement of the sentence, however, most certainly means that the formula, cryptic or not, arises directly out of the answer "Caesar's."[20] Caesar is the lord of all, whose coinage may not be refused, and whose very name strikes the hearer with terror.[21]

Mark's mind is on a Wisdom passage[22] about obedience to kings which perhaps he, rather than the historical Jesus, called into play. He places the formula directly after the answer, as if it were an original saying, the fruit of meditation on the question and the presentation of the coin. This bore an anomalous, idolatrous portrait, with the implication of being used in currency in a territory ruled by its originator. Luke takes the sequence of ideas more strictly. *Because* they admitted that the coin which they had handy was a coin of the current ruler of the locality, that fact (not the admission of the fact) provided the answer to the question.

"The things of Caesar" means the rights of Caesar, just as the "things of God" means the rights of God. This form of words, which covers the concept of "right," which, as a modern and Western concept, had not yet surfaced as such in that Asian environment, is plainly traceable as a biblical expression. *Kol d⁴var-hamelech* (literally "all the things of the king") means the king's rights (in fact, his "matters"), and *kol d⁴var-YHWH* means the rights of God: the contrast, and possible opposition as between them, can be observed where this phraseology occurs, namely at 1 Chron. 26:32 and 2 Chron. 19:11. The questioners' question implies that Jesus and they share a system of norms, and the answer is therefore couched in biblical terms. The questioners knew what was Caesar, and they knew what was Caesar's coin. They could comprehend duties toward Caesar. Caesar is a man, as his portrait shows, and, as scholars noticed long ago, the *image* is, though Caesar does not know it, the image and likeness of God himself.[23] That is why there are duties toward man, as well as duties toward God, and God has (quasi-)legislated in respect of both.[24]

Duties toward man include duties to pay debts, and among those are the duties to pay taxes to human rulers.[25] Rulers did not claim that they taxed their subjects just for their own amusements. On the contrary they claimed to do this to provide for defence, the buildings of public works, etc. To the extent that they ruled they were entitled to taxes, even under the extremely disagreeable and inefficient systems of tax-collection in vogue in those days. Jesus starts off from the undeniable position that if the coins of Caesar are current in a region, and his writ runs, as it were, the inhabitants owe a duty of paying taxes which nothing in the religion disputes. It is not the case that Jesus was indifferent to the topic. The fact of rule is something which, if once accepted by the questioner, fixes him with the obligation to pay taxes. It would be a fair question to ask Zealots or the like, who are said to have disputed (see Josephus, *War* 7.417ff) the validity of Roman rule, whether they abstained from using the Roman silver coinage. It is likely that the question never occurred to them.

Having thus disposed of the Jew's duty, under the law of God, to pay taxes, he finds no incongruity in requiring that they render the "things of God" to God. Once again "things of" means, virtually, rights. Duties toward God are set out in tedious and copious detail in the Hebrew scriptures. These also include duties toward the fellow man. Righteousness and peace are among the requirements; also love not only of the neighbor, but even of the enemy, as illustrated by the precepts about helping the enemy's baggage animals, etc.

We come straight to the point. What if the ruler not merely demands payment of taxes, but also demands, as Frederick the Great did of the Quakers, that they serve in his armies against whatsoever enemies of his under whatsoever conditions? How can one reconcile obedience to the ruler with the commands of God, which are admittedly superior? In refusing to obey the ruler one in fact serves under superior orders, against which he rages in vain! The state, utilizing secrecy, deception, and hypocrisy, urges the citizen to take up arms, and show, either deliberately or in consequence, all possible beastliness against fellow human beings, whose guilt is not established to the satisfaction of his conscience. And if one refuses, one's blood is upon one's head. Or is it?

CONSIDERATIONS REGARDING CIVIL DISOBEDIENCE

As I read Luke I find no difficulty. He has unwound the problem for us, though he leaves it to the individual conscience (as his Master did) what the implications are. Provided one pays taxes to the ruler in all cases where this is consistent with the duty toward God, one has performed one's obligation. The question is therefore not about *obedience* as such. The Gospel does not directly pose or answer the question of a duty of general obedience, about which the Tudor and Stuart monarchs and their clerical servants were so much concerned. On the contrary, the question is about *tribute*. When it comes to *obedience* we have quite a different story. The dreadful truth is stated so plainly that nothing serves but to quote the passage verbatim:

> But before all this happens they will set upon you and persecute you. You will be brought before synagogues and put in prison; you will be haled before kings and *governors*[26] for your allegiance to me. This will be your opportunity to testify; so make up your minds not to prepare your defence beforehand, because I myself will give you power of utterance and a wisdom which no opponent will be able to resist or refuse [cf. 20:26!]. Even your parents and brothers, your relations and friends, will betray [literally, "hand over"] you. *Some of you will be put to death*; and you will be hated by all for your allegiance to me. But not a hair of your head shall be lost. By standing firm you will win true life for yourselves [Luke 21:12–19 NEB].

In other words, as elsewhere in the gospel, one saves one's life (in the world to come) by losing it in this world at the hands of those who rise up, as the state will, against a charismatic movement which simply defies it.

The crisis arises in this way: because taxes, once levied, are at the disposal of a pagan power, pagan, if for no other reason, because it *is* power (*exousia*) which is in Satan's gift (Luke 4:6), they will be used in part in ways contrary to God's precepts. Jesus himself has no hesitation in speaking of the "kingdom" of Beelzebub (Mark 3:22–24): "kingdom," unless it be that of God, almost implies devilish activities. By *knowingly* conniving at such uses, one is disobeying God's commands. One cannot give to God the "things of God" if one voluntarily pays taxes knowing that they, or some of them, will be used for repugnant purposes! Thus the obligation to pay taxes is not absolute. The distinction between taxes and obedience, and between absolute obedience and due obedience is not brought out literally by the Gospel passage. The further New Testament material in this area needs to be looked at afresh.

Let us ask first whether Christ's *responsum* would have been the same had the Romans been content, as other governments might well have been, to receive taxes in Jewish aniconic copper coinage or in the form of comestibles, e.g., sacks of corn? Does Jesus' answer really depend on the image and inscription? Obviously not. That was a rhetorical device, as elsewhere (Matt. 21:42, Luke 10:26, etc.), to provide an answer from the interlocutors' own knowledge. The question was about taxation (*phoros*), not about obedience; and the right to taxes, even if not stated in the Law and the Prophets, arises from political subjection. The king's right to impose taxes and to impress labor is clearly defined and delimited in the passage at 1 Sam. 8:10–17 (see especially the LXX version), which professedly charts an innovation. It does not follow from political subjection that one must comply with the ruler's requirements in every particular: the story of the Three Saints in the Furnace was a vibrant piece of Jewish mythology and we have no trace anywhere of scepticism on Jesus' part as to its utility. On the contrary, the predictions quoted immediately above go the other way.

The need to present the church's teaching on civil obedience arose prior to Luke, but it is noticeable that Luke does not enlarge the tribute story in order to provide a bogus *responsum* on the subject. Jesus spoke about the tribute, and to tribute the *responsum*, even in Luke, still relates. Even in Acts there is no suggestion that need was felt to project a comprehensive teaching of submission to power or the powers. On the contrary the ethic projected is to negotiate with rulers (Acts 16:35–39) or to suffer patiently. Actual disobedience to rulers is found from no less persons than Peter and John (Acts 4:19, 21, 29). Centuries later the saintly ascetic Leontius, so we are told in the *Life of St. Theodore of Sykeon*, was overtaken in his cell when the Persians conquered Byzantine territory. They considerately bade him depart. He refused and was put to death.

OTHER NEW TESTAMENT PASSAGES REGARDING OBEDIENCE AND TRIBUTE

It may be argued that we have three passages in New Testament literature which do not differentiate between tribute and obedience. It may be argued that we are entitled to read back their teaching into the tribute story, and to cite "Render unto Caesar" as the Batiren will have done to the Tokugawa inquisition, as proof that Christ himself was of that mind. But if we look at those passages (it is convenient to do so in reverse historical order) we shall find nothing to disturb our present dichotomy. Obedience to rulers is not absolute but conditional.

By the time of Titus 3:1 the proposition of Christian obedience is well established, and can be stated shortly: "Remind them to be subordinate to governmental authorities [or, to rulers and powers],[27] to be docile [or, docilely obedient], *ready for every good work.*" The passage states that the members of the church are to slander no one, not to pick quarrels, to show forbearance and a consistently gentle disposition toward all people. The author, whoever he was, did not say "ready for any kind of work ordered by government, good and bad alike!" In fact, he is concerned that Christians should not give the church (and therefore the Savior himself) a bad name by refusing what are called *liturgies*, i.e., public service obligations, which had to be shared out and were shared out by cities and territories according to local custom, which might have arbitrary elements in it.

When 1 Peter was written the basic proposition needed to be spelled out, needless to say for the enlightenment of friend and foe alike. Does that author require absolute obedience? No. Before we look at the relevant passage it is essential to bear in mind the contemporary opinion, not confined to Christianity, that if one is unjustly punished one gains merit (see the quotation from Luke 21 above) and therefore one should be submissive even to tyrannical or unjust rulers *in respect of suffering uncomplainingly the punishment they mete out to those who do not conform to their arbitrary requirements.*[28] The *disciplinary* power of the state is from above, even if it is unjustly or incompetently employed: so we may infer from John 19:11. 1 Peter 2:13–17 is extremely frank and clear. Though written in such a tone as to conciliate sceptics, its meaning is beyond doubt.

> Subordinate yourselves to every human institution for the sake of the Lord, whether to the king as the superior or to governors as deputed by him for the exacting of justice from criminals or for the commendation of those who do good. For such is the will of God that men of good conduct shall put the ignorance of thoughtless persons[29] to silence. So do, as *free men*, not as if your freedom were a screen for evil-doing, but as bondsmen of God. Honour everyone, love the brotherhood,[30] fear God, honour the king.

Notice how honor is distinguished from love here, evidently as a lower relationship, and how the king, though appearing in the emphatic final position, is "last but not least." The final verse of the passage quoted is a recipe for juggling: all the obligations have to be complied with simultaneously. It is not a question of the king's being honored by God's "bondsmen" to the detriment of the rights of God.

The position is clarified if we go still further backwards toward Luke's time and their Master's. In the famous thirteenth chapter of the Epistle to the Romans, Paul is speaking at length about civil subjection. The conditional subjection to authority is stated in an uncompromising way, though with extraordinary tact for a pugnacious man such as Paul was, a man prepared to place Christ above all "rule and power" (Col. 2:10). Here we need only reproduce some portions of the passage, namely Romans 13:1-2, 6-8:

> Let every soul [meaning "person," including the flesh] be subordinate to the superior powers. There *is* no power except from God, and the existing powers are ordained by God. Therefore one who places himself in opposition to [any such] power has resisted an institution [or, provision] of God. . . . [Paul goes on to explain that the ruler exists for the punishment of vice and the reward of virtue.] That is also why you pay *taxes*. The authorities [i.e., the "powers"] are in God's service and to these duties they devote their energies.[31] Discharge your obligations to all men; pay tax and toll, reverence and respect to *those to whom they are due*. Leave no claim outstanding against you, except that of mutual love. He who loves his neighbor has satisfied every claim of the law. . . .

It is a religious obligation for the church to obey even a pagan "power." Social organization is likely to be pagan in almost every conceivable case, such being its characteristic. But there is the higher requirement of sanctifying the Divine Name, and the highest requirement of all, that of love. "Love cannot wrong a neighbor; therefore the whole law is fulfilled [or, "summed up"] in love" (Rom. 13:10). There can be absolutely no question but that, fixing the *responsum* "render unto Caesar" to the admission about the circulation of that coinage, Luke expected his hearers to understand that in paying their taxes the members of the church were obligated to consider whether a breach of obligations toward God might arise after that payment, and out of payment, and therefore to do their best to see that the taxes were applied not merely for the repression of crime and the forwarding of works of virtue, for, e.g., national defense properly so understood, but for such purposes as "bondsmen of God" would naturally foster and promote.

NOTES

1. Had the identity (and limits) of this been clear the state could have seen to it that, as in the then contemporary Western Europe and as in the Orthodox Church in Eastern Europe now, only those would be "elected" who conformed to the government's requirements.

2. Derrett, *Law in the New Testament* (London: Darton, Longman, and Todd, 1970), Ch. 14. The most striking earlier treatment, more exhaustive than any purely theological study, is Ch. 9 of E. Stauffer (numismatist, ancient historian, professor of theology), *Christus und die Caesaren*, 7th ed. (Munich and Hamburg: Siebenstern

Taschenbuch, 1966), pp. 102–124. He does not observe the distinction insisted upon in this paper.

3. This view is clearly propounded by N. Geldenhuys, *Commentary on the Gospel of Luke* (London and Edinburgh: Marshall, Morgan, and Scott, 1956) and I. Howard Marshall, *The Gospel of Luke, A Commentary on the Greek Text* (Grand Rapids, Mich.: Eerdmans, 1978), both on this text.

The most recent survey of all relevant literature is K. Aland, "Das Verhältnis von Kirche und Staat in der Frühzeit," *Aufstieg und Niedergang der römischen Welt* 23, part 1 (1979), pp. 66ff., at pp. 172–174. Aland's own view is that the saying is a rebuff (*Abweisung*), a refusal to admit something. The demands of the state are genuine, but they are secondary, subordinate. As with the temple-tax, Christians must regard demands for revenue as *indifferent*. Incidentally, an attempt is made by Fr. Cassidy to relate Matt. 17:24–27 to civil taxes, "Matthew 17:24–27—A Word on Civil Taxes," *CBQ* 41 (1979): 571–580.

4. Richard J. Cassidy, *Jesus, Politics, and Society: A Study of Luke's Gospel* (Maryknoll, N.Y.: Orbis Books, 1978), p. 58.

5. The word *rhēma* alludes to the conventional way of referring to the Word of God: Gen. 15:1, 18:14, etc.; Matt. 4:4; cf. Luke 3:2; 5:2; John 3:34, 8:47; etc.

6. See, e.g., Exod. 4:30, 11:3, 13:22, 19:11; Deut 3:28, 31:7.

7. Luke used no source independent of Mark: T. Schramm, *Der Markus-Stoff bei Lukas* (Cambridge: Cambridge University Press, 1971), p. 170. The following words are Lukan: *orthōs, phoros, katanoēsas, apokrisei, esigēsan. Exousia* ("power") is a favorite of Luke's. The following are *hapax legomena* in the New Testament: *enkathetous, hypokrinomenous. Epilabōntai* is not only peculiar to New Testament Greek in this sense, but is found only in this passage. *Lambanein, prosōpon,* and *panourgia* are found in no other Gospel, and so too the most important particle *toinun*.

8. Luke 6:7 (taken from Mark 3:2), 14:1. The ungenerous and even cowardly implications of the word *paratērein* are brought out very clearly in Polybius, *Hist.* 18.3, 2. However, there is another implication in Luke. The teacher teaches by his actions and reactions, and his pupils watch him, for he is their pattern. The "people" are the background to this, as to other incidents, and Jesus is a model.

9. *Enkathetoi* are people sent as agents; *enkathiēmi* implies surreptitious infiltration (Plutarch, *Pyrrh.* 11.4). At Josephus, *War* 6.286 *enkathetoi* are (false) prophets employed as secret agents by the "tyrants." *Enkathetos* at Polybius, *Hist.* 13.5, 1 means agent in the sense of "fifth column."

10. See n. 7 above.

11. On the technical term (=1 Heb. *mesîrâ*) and its history see Derrett, "Haggadah and the Account of the Passion," *Downside Review* 97 (1979): 308–315; "Handing Over to Satan: An Explanation of 1 Cor 5:1–7," *Revue internationale des Droits de l'Antiquité*, 3rd ser., 26 (1979):11–30; "The Iscariot, mesîrâ, and the Redemption," *Journal for the Study of the New Testament*, 8 (1980): 2–23.

12. Mark 13:9 par.

13. Otherwise they are guilty of misprision of treason. An interesting example occurs at Josephus, *War* 6.301–305.

14. Acts 17:1–9 (Paul the source of information).

15. *Orthōs legeis* normally means "say what is no less than the truth." Wetstenius, commenting on the passage, says that they admitted that the persons against whom the Parable of the Wicked Vinedressers had just been aimed were correctly identified.

However that may be, the gospel irony intends that the crafty questioners should be fixed with what indeed turns out to be a truthful answer.

16. See Acts 10:34, Gal. 2:6, alluding to Deut. 10:17. Cf. 1 Sam. 16:7, 2 Chron. 19:7.

17. Cf. Prov. 8:5 LXX.

18. Because of Eccles. 8:2.

19. Semitic usage does not distinguish rigidly between "and" and "but."

20. Citing Plato, *Symp.* 178d, Xenophon, *Anab.* 3.1, 36, etc., Liddell-Scott-Jones, *Greek-English Lexicon* confirms that *toinun* implies, "Well, then . . .", s.v. p. 1801, meaning 3, but the instance cited from Plato, *Men.* 76a, under meaning 2 ("especially an answer which has been led up to by the same speaker") is relevant.

21. Epictetus, born circa 55, was a contemporary of the Synoptic evangelists. He often speaks of "Caesar" (sic). His name strikes terror (Disc. 4.1, 41–50, 60); he is the lord of all (ibid., 4.1, 12); and no subject may refuse to accept his coinage (ibid., 3.3, 3–4).

22. Above, Note 18.

23. Gen. 1:27, 5:1, 9:6; Ps. 8:5ff. G. F. Moore, *Judaism* (Cambridge: Harvard University Press, 1958), I, pp. 397ff., 446f., II, p. 85.

24. On the customary division of the Decalogue see remarks in W. P. Paterson, "Decalogue," in J. Hastings, ed., *Dictionary of the Bible* (Edinburgh: T. and T. Clark, and New York, Scribner's, 1898), I, p. 581; S. R. Driver, "Law (in Old Testament)," ibid., III (1900), p. 67; and E. Kautzsch, "Religion of Israel," ibid., Extra Vol. (1904), p. 634. Moore, *Judaism*, II, pp. 86–87. The Great Commandment insists on the dichotomy without suggesting a difference in obligation: Mark 12:28–34 par. On the contrary, it makes "all the Law and the Prophets" hang from both together. The emphasis on duties to man expressed at Mark 10:17–31 par. is remarkable. The distinction between "transgressions between man and his fellow" and "transgressions between man and the Omnipresent" is noticed in connection with repentance and the Day of Atonement: Mishnah, Yoma 8:9 (Babylonian Talmud, Yoma 85b). Maimonides, *Guide of the Perplexed* III.35 (= 77a), trans. and ed. S. Pines (Chicago and London: University of Chicago Press, 1974), II, p. 538.

25. Matt. 17:25. Tanhuma on Gen. 8:16 (Moore, *Judaism*, II, pp. 116–117); Palestinian Talmud, Sheq. 3, 47c, 33 at Hermann L. Strack and Paul Billerbeck, *Kommentar zum Neuen Testament aus Talmud und Midrasch* I, *Das Evangelium nach Matthäus*, 3rd ed. (Munich: C. H. Beck, 1961), p. 885. Judas of Gaulanitis or Galilee opposed such payment: Josephus, *Ant.* 18.4, *War* 2.118.

26. Here, as elsewhere, the emphasis is of course mine.

27. The variant readings are *archais exousiais*, the *lectio difficilior* which is usually printed, and *archais kai exousiais*, which is at once intelligible. The author cannot possibly have been unaware of Luke 20:20 (our passage) or Luke 12:11; cf. 1 Cor. 15:24, Eph. 1:21, 3:10, Col. 1:16, 2:10, 15—in fact, it was a cliché.

28. 1 Peter 2:18ff., *Did. Apost.* 11.

29. Evidently those who alleged that the church did not recognize civil power, pagan political scientists!

30. I.e., members of the church, with whom each member must identify: honor and fear being something short of identification.

31. We hope! The passage is written on the supposition that the pagan governments to which the church looked for protection against Jewish rioters, etc., would exercise their prerogatives properly.

4

Reciprocity in the Ancient World and in Acts 15:23-29

FREDERICK W. DANKER

Problems relating to the question of the historical value of St. Luke's account of the meeting at Jerusalem, as recorded in Acts 15, continue to invite inquiry. As a contribution to the discussion I propose to focus on selected Hellenistic features that are found especially in verses 23–29, with principal reference to their formal and thematic aspects.[1]

LUKE'S CONSCIOUSNESS OF ROMAN PATTERNS

A prerequisite for serious exposition of this text is awareness of the Graeco-Roman bureaucratic context in which St. Luke appears to have lived and had his being. Two examples drawn from other parts of Acts will serve to illustrate how deeply conscious he was of that aspect of his environment.

The first is a letter formulated by Luke as an appropriate communication by a tribune named Claudius Lysias. The form of the greeting, "Claudius Lysias to his Excellency the Governor Felix, greetings" is constant over the centuries. In 288/7 B.C.E. Seleukos I begins a letter to the people of Miletos with the words, "King Seleukos to the Council and the People of Miletos, greeting."[2] About four hundred years later, Caelius Florus, procurator of Lycia under Hadrian, addresses the millionaire philanthropist Opramoas in similar terms: "Caelius Florus to the Honorable Opramoas, son of Apollonios, greeting."[3]
Luke also knows what to put into a letter of this type. As Ernst Haenchen observes, the content of Luke's version of Lysias' letter reflects a Roman

subordinate's interest in appearing as efficient as possible under trying circumstances. In the process Luke also succeeds in magnifying the prestige of Rome's star criminal.[4]

The second example is the speech of Tertyllos, Acts 24:2–8. Hans Conzelmann calls attention to a number of Graeco-Roman rhetorical patterns found in the speech.[5] Of special interest is the close resemblance of Tertyllos' preamble (verses 2–3) to the preambles in Graeco-Roman dedicatory inscriptions.

In the celebrated calendaric inscription found at Priene, Caesar Augustus is praised for his contributions to the peace and the stability of the world.[6] The lengthy sentence in which this accolade is expressed begins with *epe[ide]* (whereas). The corresponding structure in Tertyllos' speech is a genitive absolute, which incorporates the themes of peace (*eirene*) and stabilization achieved through the providential concern of Felix (*diorthomaton ginomenon . . . dia tes ses pronoias*). Besides contrasting Felix's political contributions and Paul's activism, Tertyllos treats Felix like an emperor and ranks him with the many benefactors whose virtues are celebrated in inscriptions that are to be found in nearly every corner of the Mediterranean world.

A common motif in such accolades is the universal outreach of the benefactor's generosity,[7] and very little risk is incurred in concluding that Tertyllos' comprehensive phrase, *pantei te kai pantachou* is to be construed with what precedes.[8] The verb *apodechometha* is then used absolutely, being the standard term for grateful receipt of benefits conferred.[9] The reference to *epieikeia* is in keeping with the bureaucratic tone, for "leniency" is frequently recognized as a valued attribute in public officials.[10]

LUKE'S CHALLENGE IN ACTS 15

It is quite apparent that the public functions of Lysias and Tertyllos invited the type of syntax and diction used in the communications assigned them by Luke. And the historian was equal to the task. The rhetorical challenge confronting Luke in the writing of Acts 15 was, however, more complex. He had to find a medium that would bridge the bureaucratese to which Graeco-Roman Antioch would be accustomed, in the minds of Luke's public, and the protocol practiced in Jewish Jerusalem. He found his answer in the Hellenistic decretal form that was used to promulgate decisions relating to matters of state or to honor local citizens or foreigners who had rendered services worthy of special honor.[11]

In the calendaric inscription cited earlier, the Asian League records two resolutions. Both include a preamble, followed by declarations of decision. The first of these proclaims that the New Year is to begin for all cities on September 23, which is the birthday of Augustus, and it further declares that Paullus Fabius Maximus, who proposed the unique mode of honoring Augustus, is to be recognized with an appropriate inscription on a marble stele. The second decree orders that elections are to be scheduled in such a way that all officials may enter office on the same day.

The following inscription from Eretria (about 302 B.C.E.) illustrates the principal formal lines of the honorary decree:

Damadias, son of Phanokleios, of the Deme Aphareuthen, moved as follows: *Whereas* [*Epeidē*] Glaukippos and his brothers Hippodamas and Apollonios render exceptional service to King Demetrios and to the people of Eretria, and extend themselves in behalf of the citizens who are rendering naval service, the People *resolved* [*edoxen*] that Glaukippos and Hippodamas and Apollonios the son of Dionysios, all from the tribe of Antigonis, be *proxenoi* and *euergetai* of the people of Eretria, both they and their descendants, and that they be entitled to own property and dwelling, and that they, like the other people of Eretria, be free from imposts for incoming and outgoing goods, and that their persons be inviolate, assured of security in time of peace or of war, on land or on the sea, and that they have first access to the Council and the People, immediately after the sacred rites. It was further resolved to inscribe this resolution on a stone stele and to place it in the temple of Olive-bearing Apollo.[12]

Luke's threefold use of the verb *edoxe* (Acts 15:22, 25, 28), meaning "resolved," clearly signals the decretal contours of verses 23–29, which consist of a preamble that is introduced by the standard term *epeidē* (verse 24) and of the formal resolution (verses 25–26), introduced by the verb *edoxe*.

Imbedded in the resolution is the motif of the endangered benefactor, which finds repeated expression in honorific expressions.[13] This motif takes various forms in the Graeco-Roman world. In an inscription dated in the first part of the second century B.C.E., a gentleman named Agathokles served zealously as envoy during various periods of crisis that befell his city: *prothymon heauton parechomeno[s e]m (=en) pasi tois tēs poleōs kai[r]ois.*[14] Similarly, declares Luke's decree, Barnabas and Paul have offered their lives in the service of Jesus Christ, *paradedōkosi tas psychas autōn hyper tou onomatos tou kyriou hēmōn Iēsou Christou.* The inclusion of this motif is integral to Luke's depiction of the manner in which harmonious relationships between the community in Jerusalem and Gentile areas of the church are achieved. Because of their faithful service, Paul and Barnabas are recognized also by Jerusalem as benefactors of all Christians under the one Lord Jesus Christ.[15]

LUKE'S RESOLUTION IN PERSPECTIVE

Quite obviously the major resolution of the leaders and assembly in Jerusalem would have been meaningless had its contents not been shared with the public whom it was designed to benefit. Therefore, in accordance with Hellenistic custom, St. Luke imbeds the resolution concerning envoys (verses

24–26) in an official letter, which invites comparison with a letter from Aitolia, in which an envoy named Sosikles is commended for his faithful services:

> From the Strategos of Aitolia:
> Dikaiarchos to the Council and People of Magnesia, greeting. *Whereas* [*epei*] the sacred envoy whom you sent has comported himself with honor during his stay among us and has completed in an appropriate manner his duties relative to the sacrifices in service of the gods, and has well discharged his responsibilities in connection with the Pythian Contest, and has shown laudable concern for the directors of the Contest and for colleagues who served as sacred envoys, therefore we, in deliberative assembly, together with the Amphictyonic Council, have honored him, and we have *resolved* [(*kri*)*nomes*] to write you concerning him. You will do well therefore to receive with favor our commendation of Sosikles and the honors that have been bestowed on him. Farewell.[16]

This Aitolian letter consists of an initial greeting, followed by a resolution which authorizes the communication of an earlier resolution and concludes with an admonition to the addressees. Similarly, the letter in Acts 15 begins with a correspondingly simple form of address: "The apostles and elders, (your) brothers, to (our) Gentile brothers and sisters in Antioch, Syria, and Cilicia. Greeting" (v. 23). Then follows the resolution concerning the envoys (verses 24–26). However, the manner in which the contents of the principal and earlier resolution are presented differs somewhat from the rhetorical procedure in the Aitolian letter.

At verse 24 Luke offers a clue as to how part of the preamble or "whereas" of the principal motion read. Verse 28 summarizes that resolution. Luke has in effect intercalated the resolution concerning the sending of the envoys between two parts of the main resolution and then imbedded this mixture between initial and terminal epistolary features. Since it was customary in the Graeco-Roman world for bearers of letters to share further details orally with the addressees,[17] Luke has the authors of the letter state that the envoys, Jude and Silas, are to announce verbally "the same things" (*ta auta*, verse 27), that is, the contents of the main motion and presumably the gist of the discussion that accompanied it. Luke reveals the seam in his rhetorical construction, for the proleptic statement sounds harsh to ears that are tuned to Western rhetoric. But his tactic is clearly discernible. He aims to bring into close juxtaposition the principal contents of the main decree and the concluding admonition: *ex hōn diatērountes heautous eu praxete* (verse 29).

The phrase *eu praxete* in this concluding admonition has not received adequate treatment. There is no substantial progress from Jackson-Lake, *The Beginnings of Christianity*[18] to Haenchen, *The Acts of the Apostles*:[19] both refer to the epistolary formula: "If you do this, you will do rightly," but no real clue is given to the meaning. The formulation is indeed firmly entrenched in the Graeco-Roman world, but it is important to note the specific semantic flavor generated by the inclusion of this expression in an official or semi-official decree in which the deep structure of Mediterranean social expectation and diplomatic protocol is uncovered.

THE ELEMENT OF RECIPROCITY

A basic element in that structure is the process of reciprocity. Even the most powerfully entrenched must be able to count on the good will of their subjects. To reinforce their image, Graeco-Roman rulers and magistrates therefore emphasize the quality and quantity of benefactions that have been or will be conferred on the populace. At the same time they remind their subjects that the endorsement of official policy will ensure an undiminished flow of beneficence. Typical in this connection is the letter of Eumenes II to the Karians:

> [It is our wish] that you should share in the sacrifices and [in the contests. We have therefore sent as envoys] Megon of Ephesus, whom we consider one of our friends and one who is held in [high] honor, and Kalas of Pergamon, adjudged by us [to be a person of merit], and who as a citizen has attained everything that befits his age, [and who has been chosen] by his city because it joins us in this proclamation. You will do [well], then, first out of consideration for the Goddess and then for our person, to give [these men] a courteous hearing and to recognize the [Nikephorion festival and the inviolability of the sanctuary]. In so doing you will quite evidently [be sharing] in the advancement of her honors and you will find us very eager [in the future] to do everything in [our power] that is advantageous to your people. You will hear [from the envoys] at greater length about these matters. Farewell. Megon delivered it on the sixth of Anthesterion.[20]

Like the letter of the Aitolians, the similarity of this communication to the epistle recorded in Acts 15:23–29 commends it as a heuristic medium for determining Luke's meaning in verse 29. (1) Both texts contain a preamble and an official decision imbedded in an epistolary structure that terminates with the word *errōsthe*. (2) Both documents refer to matters that are to receive further elucidation upon delivery of the letter by envoys. (3) The grammatical structure of participle followed by finite verb is identical in the concluding admonition of both letters. In the letter of Eumenes, the words [*kalōs oun po*]*iēsete* (you will do well) are explicitly interpreted by the clause: "In so doing you will find us very eager to do everything in our power that is advantageous to your people." Such amplification is typical of the grandiloquent Asiatic style.[21] The letter from Aitolia has, like Acts 15:29, a more condensed version of the formulation, beginning with *eu oun poiesēte*. For the phrase *eu poiesēte* Luke has *eu praxete*, which is an even more precise formulation in a context suggestive of public policy.[22]

Quite evidently Luke's brief phrase *eu praxete* is generated by the depth structure of the socio-cultural context common to the public envisaged for the audition of Acts 15, as well as for the recipients of the letters sent by Eumenes and by the Aitolians. The portions of text that deal with the good fortunes of the recipients are in all three texts generated by the common expectation of reciprocity in the types of relationships outlined in the documents. In short, the recipients of Jerusalem's letter can be assured of the abiding goodwill of the community in Jerusalem if they will abide by the few provisions spelled out in the correspondence, and as relayed by the envoys.

The followers of Jesus who are located in Jerusalem thus come off in Luke's recital as benefactors who are bestowing their bounty on the Antiochenes by lifting all sanctions, except those specifically mentioned in Acts 15:29.[23] The restrictions are from Luke's standpoint understandable. At 15:21 he has Simeon say in explanation of the restrictive requirements that the Mosaic legislation is well known throughout the world, a statement that scarcely registers the difficulty alleged by Martin Dibelius, whose viewpoint is shared by Haenchen.[24] The point is that the regulations of Moses respecting dietary practices and recognition of close consanguinity are so entrenched in the minds of people, both Jews and Gentile sympathizers, that departure from the norms would be terribly offensive. Well versed in Greek culture, Luke knows the meaning of *nomos* as inherited custom.[25] Repeated reading of the legislation of Moses in the synagogues of the Graeco-Roman world has over the centuries grown a deeply rooted plant of tradition.

The few restrictions, suggests Luke, are far outweighed by the general lifting of legal sanctions, some of which, as Luke endeavored to display in his Gospel, were unbearable.[26] Besides such manifestation of generosity, Jerusalem's leadership knows the virtue of collegiality, and Luke signals the fact through his references to the principals responsible for the actions taken in Jerusalem. These references (Acts 15:22, 23) would be especially meaningful to many of Luke's public who lived in cities where local affairs would be decided by the traditional system of popular ratification of resolutions that had been proposed by a city council.

Although Rome held a tight rein on the provinces, various degrees of rights were granted to cities. Most of these had to do with trivial policy-making and the dispensing of honors.[27] Under Roman domination deliberative assemblies were but a shadow of their former selves, but the established Greek pattern of ultimate decision by the popular assembly, or *demos,* retained its hold on the Graeco-Roman world. In practice the council or *boulē* made proposals *(probeulēmata)* but the *demos* voted on them and made additions or amendments. The collegial action of the two bodies is therefore ordinarily expressed in the phrase: "It was resolved by the Council and the People."[28] This collegial tradition underlies Luke's phrasing in Acts 15:22: *Tote edoxe tois apostolois kai tois presbyterois syn holei tei ekklēsiai,* "Then the apostles and the elders, together with the entire assembly, resolved. . . ." The apostles and presbyters form the *boulē,* and the *ekklesia,* or assembly, is to be understood as the *demos* of the Christian community. Luke emphasizes the democratic atmosphere that prevails in the Christian community at Jerusalem, at least with respect to the decision to send envoys with a letter of encouragement to the Christians in Antioch.

Since provincial assemblies could write as entities to other assemblies,[29] Luke's concentration on the apostles and elders as authorities for the letter is not to be ascribed to epistolographic convention. Rather, Luke aims to emphasize that the highest authorities in the Christian community at Jerusalem have taken the lead in expressing concern for their Christian brothers and sisters at Antioch. At verse 28 Luke returns to the more familiar Hellenistic pattern: "The Holy Spirit and we resolved." Here the Holy Spirit assumes the place of the traditional *boulē*, and the pronoun *hēmin* includes all the human participants in the formulation of the decree. Through emphasis on the Holy Spirit Luke provides an antidote to misconceptions that might develop from a reading of his concluding account in Acts 28 concerning the refusal on the part of some representatives of Israel to participate in the mission to the Gentiles. The Jewish Christians in Jerusalem are collegially aligned with the Holy Spirit.

THE CHARACTER OF LUKE'S ACHIEVEMENT

Despite some inelegance that results from his attempt to blend two resolutions within a formal communication, Luke has achieved a remarkable degree of unity in Acts 15:23–29 by giving expression to various facets of the reciprocity system that was in vogue in the Graeco-Roman world. His sketch of what he thinks happened in the earliest days in Jerusalem is to serve as a guide for resolving related problems in the period after the destruction of Jerusalem. He shows how the culturally ingrained reciprocity system, which features the ubiquitous figure of the civic benefactor, can serve as a model for stabilization of the Christian congregations as they go about their task of witness to the one Name that spells the ultimate benefaction of salvation offered to the entire world (Acts 4:12).

Our study demonstrates that Hellenistic rhetorical patterns have penetrated Luke's description of alleged proceedings at Jerusalem to a greater extent than hitherto recognized. The evidence appears to confirm the view that the evangelist-historian is not so much interested in recapturing the past as in offering assistance to Christian communities in meeting their current responsibilities.

NOTES

1. I am grateful to the publishers for permission to use material from Frederick W. Danker, *Benefactor: Epigraphic Study of a Graeco-Roman and New Testament Semantic Field* (St. Louis: Clayton, 1982).

2. W. Dittenberger, ed., *Orientis Graeci Inscriptiones Selectae*, 2 vols. (Leipzig, 1903–1905), 227.1.

3. R. Cagnat et al., eds., *Inscriptiones Graecae ad res Romanes pertinenentes* (Paris: Ernst Leroux, vols. 1 and 2, 1911, vol. 3, 1906, vol. 4, 1927), III, 739. 4. 13. 1-2.

4. Ernst Haenchen, *The Acts of the Apostles: A Commentary*, trans. B. Noble (Philadelphia: Westminster, 1971), see pp. 647-650.

5. Hans Conzelmann, *Die Apostelgeschichte*, Handbuch zum Neuen Testament (Tübingen: J. B. C. Mohr, 1963), pp. 130-131; Eng., *The Acts of the Apostles*, trans. B. Noble (Minneapolis: Augsburg, 1972).

6. F. Hiller von Gärtringen, *Inschriften von Priene* (Berlin: Georg Reimer, 1906), hereafter *Priene*, no. 105, 31-41 (= Robert K. Sherk, *Roman Documents from the Greek East: "Senatus Consulta" and "Epistulae" to the Age of Augustus* [Baltimore: Johns Hopkins University Press, 1969]), n. 65.

7. The praise of Menas, son of Memes, is typical. This decree, passed by the city of Sestos in gratitude for his services as an envoy and as sponsor of gymnastic activities, emphasizes that Menas shared sacrificial meat with outsiders as well as with the local participants; Dittenberger, *Orientis Graeci Inscriptiones*, 339. 65-67.

8. Compare Haenchen, *Acts of the Apostles*, pp. 652-653; the *Berkeley Version of the New Testament*; and *The New English Bible. The Revised Standard Version, New American Bible,* and *Today's English Version* are among those that construe with what follows.

9. For example, *Priene* 44. 8-10: "So that the people might show themselves grateful to the people of Alexandria and graciously receive both the crown voted by them and the honor accorded the judges."

10. Compare Cagnat, *Inscriptiones Graecae*, III, 739. 2. 5. 56. See also Phil. 4:5; 1 Tim. 3:3; 1 Peter 2:18.

11. As Eivil Skard pointed out in *Zwei Religiös-Politische Begriffe, Euergetes-Concordia*, Avhandlinger Utgitt as det Norske Videnskaps-Akademi i Oslo, II. Hist.-Filos. Klasse. 1931, no. 2 (Oslo, 1932), pp. 14-15, inscriptional bureaucratese has influenced literary writers more so than literary writers the chancery.

12. Greek text in Charles Michel, *Recueil d'inscriptions grecques* (Paris: Ernst Leroux, 1900), no. 344.

13. See *Benefactor*, chapter entitled "Endangered Benefactor."

14. Luigi Moretti, *Iscrizioni storiche ellenistiche: testo critico, traduzione e commento*, II (Florence: La Nuova Italia, 1975), no. 131. 5-6.

15. The pronoun *hēmōn* stresses the collegiality.

16. Greek text in Otto Kern, *Die Inschriften von Magnesia am Maeander* (Berlin: W. Sherman, repr. de Gruyter, 1967), no. 91 d. On the role of envoys in the Graeco-Roman world see D. Kienast, *RE* (= *PW* or Pauly-Wissowa) Supplement 13 (1973): 587-590. References to two are frequent; compare *Priene* 47. 22; 54. 34; 71. 37-38 and see Luke 10:1; Acts 13:2. D. J. Mosley, "The Size of Embassies in Ancient Greek Diplomacy," *TAPA* 96 (1965): 260, cites literary evidence. For formal appointment of an embassy compare W. Dittenberger, *Sylloge Inscriptionum Graecarum*, 4 vol., 3rd ed. (Leipzig, 1915-1924), 797, concerning a message of congratulation transmitted to Emperor Gaius in A.D. 37.

17. Compare C. Bradford Welles, *Royal Correspondence in the Hellenistic Period: A Study in Greek Epigraphy* (London, 1934; repr. Chicago: Ares, 1974), p. 201, relative to the Letter of Eumenes II cited below, Welles, no. 49a, line 10.

18. F. J. Foakes Jackson and Kirsopp Lake, *The Beginnings of Christianity*, Part One: *The Acts of the Apostles*, 5 vols. (New York: Macmillan, 1933); Vol. 4, *English*

Translation and Commentary, repr. (Grand Rapids, Mich.: Baker Books, 1965), on Acts 15:29.

19. Haenchen, *Acts of the Apostles*, pp. 453–454.

20. Greek text in Welles, *Royal Correspondence*, no. 49a, p. 198.

21. Dittenberger, *Orientis Graeci Inscriptiones*, 383 (translation in *Benefactor*, n. 41) is an excellent example of the Asiatic style. See Ulrich von Wilamowitz-Möllendorf, "Asianismus und Atticismus," *Hermes* 35 (1900): 1–52.

22. Luke's usage has traditional roots; see, for example, Plato *Alkibiades* 116b: *hostis kalōs prattei, ouchi kai eu prattei*? (One who comports oneself well is treated well, is that not so?) For inscriptional use of *prassō* see *Priene*, Index VIII, p. 293, s.v. For Luke's use of *prassō* with civic overtones see Acts 17:7; 19:36; 25:11, 25; 26:26, 31.

23. To relieve others of burdens affords a prime claim to honor. Tiberius Julius Alexander, prefect of Egypt during the reigns of Nero and Galba, assures the Province of Egypt that he does not wish to have it "burdened with new and unfair levies" (*mē barynomenēn kainais kai adikois eispraxesi*), Dittenberger, *Orientis Graeci Inscriptiones*, 669. 5 (translation in *Benefactor*, n. 51). Compare Paul's boast in 1 Corinthians 11:9.

24. Haenchen, *Acts of the Apostles*, p. 450.

25. Compare Werner Jaeger, *Paideia: The Ideals of Greek Culture*, 3 vols., trans. Gilbert Highet (New York: Oxford University Press, 1944), vol. 3, p. 248.

26. By the statement in Acts 15:10 concerning the "yoke . . . which neither our fathers nor we were able to bear," Luke perhaps has reference to the view that Mosaic legislation itself required constant reinterpretation to make it bearable for Jews in the face of fresh exigencies. In view of such flexibility it is historically incorrect to generalize and accuse all Jewish religious leaders of legalism. On the other hand, no religious group, and certainly not Christianity in its various institutionalized forms, is exempt from the charge of imposing burdens that are difficult for the rank and file to observe without some compromise or reinterpretive adjustment. The same is true of Pharisees, some of whom receive a bad press in portions of the Gospels. A goodly number of Pharisees probably did not fit the caricature that is often ascribed to them. It is, however, equally improbable that some would not have felt uncomfortable in the presence of Jesus, who beyond a doubt made waves. Hence Luke includes the charge of scribes and Pharisees that Jesus broke the Mosaic law by pronouncing forgiveness to a paralytic (Luke 5:21). In 8:43–48 he displays the anxiety of a woman who must overcome cultic scruples about even touching the hem of Jesus. And at 11:37–38 Pharisees are dismayed by Jesus' cavalier attitude toward ritual cleansing. At 13:14 the head of a synagogue would have preferred postponement of a healing to some day other than the Sabbath, but with no regard for the woman who had already suffered intolerable anguish. According to 15:2 Pharisees and scribes complain that Jesus entertains people who do not conform to accepted cultic regulations or who are of questionable moral character. On the historical problems associated with Acts 15 see especially G. Zuntz, "An Analysis of the Report about the 'Apostolic Council,' " in *Opuscula Selecta: Classica, Hellenistica, Christiana* (Cambridge: Cambridge University Press, and Santa Clara, Cal.: Rowan, 1972), pp. 216–249.

27. Provincial extravagance in the dispensing of honors was prejudicial to Rome's economic interests. Measures were therefore taken to control the traffic in these incentives to vanity. On imperial restraint of provincial prodigality see Frank Frost Abbott and Allan Chester Johnson, *Municipal Administration in the Roman Empire*

(Princeton: Princeton University Press, 1926), pp. 149-150, 388-389.

28. As in the Letter of the Aitolians cited above. On the history of *probouleumata* or proposals of the Council see Wilhelm Hartel, *Studien über Attisches Staatsrecht und Urkundenwesen* (Vienna: Karl Garold's Sohn, 1878).

29. *Priene* 53 and 54, for example, record exchanges between the city of Iasos and Priene respecting a judge who had served Iasos out of Priene; see also 44:18-20, 125; 54. 42; Dittenberger, *Sylloge Inscriptionum Graecarum*, 426. 9-10; and compare Ernst Nachmanson, "Zu den Motivformeln der griechischen Ehreninschriften," *Eranos* 11 (1911): 100.

5

The Women at Luke's Supper

QUENTIN QUESNELL

It has been commonly assumed that only the Twelve were with Jesus at the Last Supper. So secure does this reading of the Gospel seem that it has for centuries underlain both artistic depictions of the Last Supper and ecclesial polity. Yet in the 1955 edition of *The Eucharistic Words of Jesus*, Joachim Jeremias expressed his surprise at the absence of the women who appear elsewhere in the Gospels, and in his 1966 edition he questioned whether the explicit statements of Matthew, Mark and Luke reflected the full historical fact.[1]

Before exegetes today, however, can hope to find the historical facts behind the Gospels, they have to be sure they understand the special teaching of each Gospel taken singly. There are significant and important differences among the Gospels which reveal the particular purposes of each individual evangelist.

This study will not draw historical conclusions, but limit itself to the preliminary step. Following the method of consistent editorial analysis (redaction criticism)[2] it will try to make clear the written tradition of one evangelist, the author of Luke-Acts.[3] It will lay out all the evidence in the Gospel and in Acts pointing to the fact (1) that Luke thought a larger group than just the Twelve were at the Supper with Jesus; and (2) that within that larger group Luke included the women.

THOSE PRESENT BEFORE AND AFTER THE SUPPER

First of all, let us look at some things Luke tells us about the group that were around Jesus *before* the Supper. Luke says early on that Jesus chose the

This paper was originally presented, in honor of the jubilee of John L. McKenzie, at the 39th general meeting of the Catholic Biblical Association of America. It has been rewritten for inclusion in the present collection.

Twelve *out of* a larger group of disciples: "He called his disciples, and, choosing from them Twelve . . ." (Luke 6:13); "a great crowd of his disciples" (6:17). Luke makes clear early in his narrative that others besides the Twelve traveled constantly with Jesus (8:1–3). When he introduces Jesus' immediate family into his account of the public life (8:19–21), he does it in a way that prepares the reader for the fact they will be counted later among Jesus' faithful followers (Acts 1:14).[4]

Luke adds to the sending of the Twelve (9:1–6) a parallel sending out of the Seventy-two (10:1–16). At the final approach to Jerusalem, Luke describes Jesus as accompanied by an "entire multitude of disciples" (*hapan to plēthos tōn mathetōn*; 19:37). And finally in Acts 1:21, looking back over the whole Gospel story, Luke tells us through the mouth of Peter that, over and above the Twelve, a group of other disciples had been present "in every time in which the Lord Jesus went in and out among us, beginning from the baptism of John until the day he was taken up from us."

Now in each of the points just mentioned, Luke departs from the story as told by Matthew and Mark. Therefore we have reason to think that these points were not just incidental to Luke. If they add up to a pattern, the pattern is not one of which the author was unaware. But they do add up to a pattern. They show that Luke's Gospel gradually builds up a larger and larger group around Jesus. By the time of the arrival at Jerusalem, the group contains at least the Twelve, the Seventy-two, the women (of whom only three are named, but "many others" noted [8:3]), the mother and brothers of Jesus.[5] Luke thinks the group is large enough to deserve being called "the entire multitude of his disciples" (19:37), though it is presumably not much larger than the figure he gives in Acts 1:15—"about 120 persons."

If we turn to examine carefully the persons Luke tells us about *after* the Supper, we see this larger group active at every point. Luke mentions a group of Jesus' followers, larger than the Twelve, present at Jesus' cross: "all those known to him, and the women who had followed him from Galilee" (23:49).[6] Luke 24 repeatedly mentions a larger group gathered together the day of the resurrection. For instance, in 24:9, "returning from the tomb, they announced all these things to the Eleven *and to all the rest*."[7] In 24:13–36, "two of them" (24:13)[7] . . . "one named Cleopas" (24:18) [not among the Twelve] . . . "returning to Jerusalem found gathered together the Eleven and those with them" (24:33).

These two returning disciples "told what happened on the way . . . and while they were telling these things, he himself stood in the midst of them" (24:26). In the midst of whom? Clearly in the midst of the people just named as present; the two returning from Emmaus and "the Eleven and those with them." Therefore Luke thinks that all Christ's words in the remainder of this same scene (24:36–51) are addressed to a group larger than just the Twelve. He opens their eyes to understand the Scriptures, he promises the Spirit and a mission to all the nations, and he blesses them as he ascends into heaven before them.[8]

The same scene is retold in Acts 1:1–12, with so many of the details repeated that the reader must conclude Luke thinks the personnel are the same: the group larger than the Twelve, referred to in Luke 24:33 and 36.[9] But just in case one doubts because of the difference in the time of the two scenes (only Acts 1:1–12 is said to take place after forty days of appearances [Acts 1:3]) Jesus' words in Acts 1:8 make the fact unmistakable: "You will be my witnesses in Jerusalem and in all Judaea and Samaria and even to the ends of the earth." These words imply an audience larger than the Twelve, for in Luke's story later it is "those scattered" by the persecution in Jersualem who "evangelized the word throughout Judaea and Samaria" (Acts 8:4). But, Luke notes, those scattered included "everyone *except* the apostles" (Acts 8:1). Moreover, in the later development of Luke's story, further preaching and witnessing "to the ends of the earth" are performed by Paul, by Barnabas, Silas, Timothy, and others, but not by any of the Twelve.[10]

Moreover, immediately after Christ's ascension, Luke describes a group larger than just the Twelve: "And when they came in, they went up to the upper room, where there were dwelling Peter and John and James and Andrew, Philip and Thomas . . . These were all persevering together in prayer with the women and Máry, the mother of Jesus, and with his brothers" (Acts 1:13f). ". . . the number of persons together was about one hundred and twenty" (Acts 1:15).

Luke also describes a group larger than just the Twelve receiving the Spirit at Pentecost. "They were *all* together . . ." (Acts 2:1).[11] During the Pentecost scene, "Peter, standing up with the Eleven, raised his voice and addressed [the crowds] saying . . . '*These* are not drunk as you suppose . . .' " (Acts 2:14). Peter and the Eleven are doing the speaking.[12] They are no longer acting in a manner supposed drunken. They are defending "these" against that suspicion. Who then are "these"? They are the rest of the community, whom Luke thinks of as continuing their ecstatic prophesying [speaking in tongues] while Peter and the Eleven go on explaining.[13] The same point is clear from verse 16, where the speakers say, "*This* is what was foretold through the prophet Joel." "This" refers to something the crowd sees going on while Peter, with the Eleven, stands giving the explanation. The same is suggested in verse 23: "[Jesus] having received from the Father the promise of the Holy Spirit, has poured out *this which you are seeing and hearing.*"

Thus, after the Supper as before, Luke continues to present the reader with a community which is much larger than just the Twelve. The community of about 120 which he has portrayed gradually gathering around Jesus in the course of the Gospel continues present and active at the end of the Gospel and on through Acts 1 and 2.[14] It will prove itself the core of the expanding church-community of the rest of Acts.[15]

CHARACTERISTICS OF THE SUPPER ROOM

Next, let us take a close look at the *places* Luke refers to in the last chapters of the Gospel and the early chapters of Acts. Luke says that after entering Jerusalem with "the entire multitude of disciples" (19:37), Jesus spends his days teaching in the temple (19:47; 21:37) and his nights on the Mount of Olives (21:37). Where does Luke think the disciples are spending their days? He does not explicitly say, but presumes they are always at Jesus' side, for as soon as Jesus has something to say to them, he simply begins speaking "to the disciples" (20:45); they do not have to be summoned or reenter the scene on their own. Similarly in 22:8, "he sent Peter and John, saying . . ."—Luke thinks they were at his side all along. At any rate, the part of the temple Jesus frequents is large enough not only for all Jesus' disciples (20:45), but also for "all the people" (20:45; 19:48; 21:38). Where do the disciples spend their nights? Luke does not say, but he does think of Jesus' habitual resting place on the Mount of Olives as being out of doors.[16] And when he writes, in 22:39, that Jesus "went to the Mount of Olives according to his custom," he adds specifically "and his disciples followed him."

When it is time for the Supper, Jesus asks for a "*kataluma*, where I may eat the Pasch with my disciples" (Luke 22:11–12 = Mark 14:41–42). *Kataluma* is an inn, a lodging-place, a spot to stay overnight. (Cf. Luke 2:7, "there was no room for them in the *katalumati*.") Of course one can also use a *kataluma*, as they do here, to take a meal in, "though," as F. Büchsel explains in *TDNT* 4 (1967), p. 338 and note 7, "it does not mean dining-room."

Jesus is offered a "large upper-room (*estrōmenon*)." Although this may mean "paved" or "paneled," most English versions take it as "furnished" (BAG). The verb *strōnnuō* (or *strōnnumi* or *stornumi*) means "to spread out." LSJ therefore specifies, "furnished with *strōmata*," where *strōmata* are "anything spread or laid out for lying or sitting upon, mattress, bed . . . bed-clothes, coverings of a dinner-couch." At any rate, Luke describes the room chosen for the Supper as one in which people might spend a longer time.[17]

This is interesting, because the post-resurrection events of Luke 24 all center around an unspecified place in the city (24:49, 52) where "the Eleven and the rest" (24:9), "the Eleven and those with them" (24:33) are all together. (Acts 1:12–14 seems to understand Luke 24:49 as well as Acts 1:4 as directives that they are to *stay* in that place.)[18] In Acts 1:13 Luke says that the group returned to Jerusalem, "entered and went up to *the* upper room (*to huperōon*"). In that room, the Twelve, the women and Jesus' mother and brothers are then said to be "*katamenontes*" (Acts 1:13–14). Now the verb *katamenō* means "to stay, abide, dwell, live." The form here is periphrastic: "*hou ēsan katamenontes*: where they are staying," a form indicating "permanent residence."[19]

Again, Acts 1:15 takes place in a room large enough for Peter to rise in the midst of "about 120 persons." The place seems, by ordinary rules of narration, to be the same place spoken of in the two preceding verses (1:13–14) as the dwelling-place for the Twelve, the women, Mary and the brothers. In fact, Acts 1:21 makes no sense unless Joseph Barsabbas and Matthias, as well as the larger group from among whom Luke says they were selected, have been with the Twelve constantly up to the time of Christ's ascension (1:22 *anelēmphthē* reflects 1:11: *ho analēmphtheis aph' humōn*).[20]

This same picture underlies Acts 2:2. Luke there speaks of the *"oikon hou ēsan kathēmenoi."* All the standard translations confuse Luke's image by rendering this "the house where they were sitting." *Kathēmenoi* does mean sitting when used in conjunction with a chair, but not when used with reference to a house. Linked with mention of a house, the normal sense of *kathēmai* is "to stay, dwell, abide."[21] To speak of the house where people were sitting would make sense only if their posture played some essential role in the story.[22] Here it does not.[23] Luke uses *kathēmai* to mean "stay, abide, dwell" in Luke 1:79 and 21:35 and he uses *kathizō* in the same meaning in Luke 24:49 and Acts 18:11. The construction here is again periphrastic, emphasizing that their residing was ongoing, habitual.

The place references too, therefore, add up to a consistent picture. Luke shows a large community living with Jesus on his travels to Jerusalem and staying with him during the days he preached in the temple and during his nights on the Mount of Olives. Luke shows them at Calvary with him, and then together in one place all during the day of resurrection (Luke 24:9, 33, 36); mentions on the day of ascension that they were living together (Acts 1:13); shows them praying and acting together (Acts 1:15–26); mentions on the day of Pentecost the house in which they were (still) staying.

The simplest, most natural reading of Luke's story would take him to mean they continued living in one large, furnished lodging—the one Jesus had taken special trouble to provide for them the night before he died (Luke 22:11–12).[24] Still, Acts 1:13 does not specifically say that the upper-room (*to huperōon*) is the same identical one as the upper-room (*anagaion*) of Luke 22:12. Moreover Acts 1:15 does not explicitly *affirm* that the assembly Peter addresses is in the same upper-room as the group was living in, in the two preceding verses. Moreover Acts 2:2 does not say that its *oikos* (a common word for house) is the same *oikia* (another common word for house) as that in Luke 22:10.

Therefore we cannot say it is absolutely certain Luke thought all these events happened in one same place, even though that would be the natural way to read the story. What we can be certain of is that, in whatever place or places, Luke pictured these events as happening to a group much larger than just the Twelve, and that the members of that group were living and acting together on a regular basis both before and after the Supper.[25]

ANALYSIS OF JESUS' TEACHING AT THE SUPPER

With that understood, we can turn to a consideration of the Supper itself. First we have to consider the words Luke records as spoken by Jesus himself at the Supper. We will notice that nothing in their content indicates that they are addressed to the Twelve alone. And, more curiously still, some of those words are clearly inconsistent with any suggestion that the group at the Supper was limited to the Twelve alone.

For instance, Luke 22:15–16, 18: "With desire I have desired to eat this Pasch with you before I suffer. For I say to you that no more will I eat it until it be fulfilled in the kingdom of God. . . . I will not drink from now on of the fruit of the vine until the kingdom of God comes." These words indeed mark the Supper in Luke as Jesus' farewell to his faithful companions.[26] But Luke has provided Jesus with many more faithful companions than just the Twelve. Nor does anything in Luke call for a special farewell from the Twelve alone.[27]

Look at Luke 22:26: "Let the greater among you be as the youngest, and the leader as the one who serves." A comparison of the *meizōn* and the *neōteros*, the *hēgoumenos* and the *diakonōn*, seems out of place when addressed to the Twelve alone. If Peter (and John?—cf. Acts 3 and 4) might be *meizōn*, who among the Twelve could reasonably be characterized as "the younger, the neophyte"?[28] And if Peter is the *hegoumenos*, who of the Twelve is "the one who serves"? The verse seems to demand a larger and more structured community than just the Twelve.[29]

In Luke 22:28 Jesus says: "You are those left persevering with me (*diamemnēkotes*) in my trials (temptations, *peirasmois*)." To what temptations he refers is disputed, with perhaps the majority of exegetes tending to take the phrase as anticipation of the passion.[30]

In any case, the Twelve are not in Luke the only ones who persevere with Jesus. There are "all those who have accompanied us in every time in which the Lord Jesus went in and out among us, beginning from the baptism of John even to the day on which he was taken up from us" (Acts 1:21). Before the passion, his "human temptations" are witnessed by more than the Twelve.[31] In the passion, Luke's women, Simon of Cyrene, and Joseph of Arimathaea persevere with Jesus at least as much as do his Twelve.[32] Luke has no equivalent of John 6:66, where the Twelve remain when many other disciples fall away. Luke 22:28, then, is consistent with the presence of a larger group, and somewhat anomalous if taken as directed exclusively to the Twelve.[33]

Jesus' next statement at the Supper is Luke 22:29–30: "I bequeath to you, as my Father has bequeathed to me, a kingdom,[34] [v.30a] that you may eat and drink at my table in my kingdom. [v.30b] And you will sit on thrones judging the twelve tribes of Israel." We had best break this statement down into parts for careful consideration. As to the first part, Luke 22:29, the words do not indicate of themselves that only the Twelve are addressed. There is nothing in the rest of the Gospel of Luke which suggests that the kingdom will be inherited by the Twelve alone, rather than by all the saints.[35]

The same may be said of the second part (22:30a). The promise in Luke is not limited to the Twelve. Many from afar "will sit at table in the kingdom of God" (13:29) while those "who ate and drank in your presence" on earth will be cast out (13:26). "The poor and the crippled and the blind and the lame" (14:21) as well as many "from the highways and byways" (14:23) "will eat bread in the kingdom of God" (14:15).[36]

But most interesting of all is the third part of the statement (22:30b). Jesus in Luke does not specify the number of thrones on which those he addresses will sit. Matthew 19:28 says explicitly, "you will sit on twelve thrones." By not mentioning any number, Luke leaves the saying consistent with the presence of a larger audience than just the Twelve.[37]

The whole saying promises all Christ's disciples a share in his kingdom, rule, and judgment as they had persevered with him. This more common eschatological interpretation sees in vv. 28–29 and 30b imagery familiar since Daniel 7:9–27, especially vv. 9–10, 13–14, 18, 22, 25–27.[38]

Jesus' next saying is Luke 22:31–32: "Simon, Simon, Satan has demanded you [pl.] that he might sift you [pl.] . . .; you [s.] being once converted, strengthen your brothers." S. Brown argues convincingly that "brothers" of v. 32 refers not to the other Eleven, but to all Jesus' followers, just as the same word (*adelphous*) does 36 times in Acts.[39] Strengthen (*stērizō, epistērizō, stereoō*) denotes "apostolic exhortation to the missionary churches." But if that is true, then you (*humas*) must also refer to all Jesus' followers. Otherwise the saying would mean: Satan has requested you (Twelve) to sift you (Twelve); but I have prayed for one of you (Peter) so that he may strengthen other brothers elsewhere.

After foretelling Peter's denial, Jesus' next words are in Luke 22:35: " 'When I sent you out without purse and bag and sandals, did you lack anything?' They answered, 'Nothing.' " These words are inconsistent with the presence of only the Twelve.[40] Jesus sent not the Twelve but the Seventy-two without "purse and bag and sandals." The list is taken from Luke 10:4: "*mē bastazete ballantion, mē pēran, mē hupodēmata.*"

The roughly equivalent instruction given to the Twelve in 9:3 did not contain the words *ballantion* or *hupodēmata*. It did list purse (*pēran*) but accompanied it with "staff . . . bread, money, two chitons." The question and response of 22:35 imply that Jesus is talking not only to the Twelve, sent out in Luke 9, but to at least some of the disciples sent in Luke 10.[41]

THE PRESENCE OF THE TWELVE AT THE SUPPER

All of the above adds up to so consistent a pattern that we now must wonder why the pattern has not been already seen and admitted as compelling evidence of the presence of a larger group. One answer to that is easy: Luke explicitly says, "When it was the hour, he reclined, and the *apostles* with him." Since Luke 6:13 says that "apostles" is the name Jesus gave to those Twelve whom he chose from among his other disciples, this verse is commonly understood to exclude from the Supper anyone but the Twelve.

Nevertheless, Earle Ellis has recently argued that in spite of Luke 6:13 it is by no means certain that Luke limits "apostle" exclusively to the Twelve.[42] His conclusion is that the Twelve are in Luke indeed a special group, but they are a special group within a wider group of apostles.[43]

Ellis's arguments are attractive and quite persuasive. Nevertheless, Acts 1 focuses strongly on completing the Twelve-group by replacing Judas, and Matthias is "numbered with the Eleven Apostles" (Acts 1:26). There follows a period where Luke puts considerable stress on the central role of the apostles in the community: cf. the preaching of 2:14, 37, 42; the supervisory functions implied in 4:35–37; 6:1–6; 8:14; 9:27, in the light of *episkopē* (1:20). Luke 22:14, near the end of the Gospel, stands so close to this section of Acts that I hesitate to explain Luke 22:14 by appealing to the fact that Luke does sometimes clearly give "apostles" a wider sense. While welcoming Ellis's suggestion, therefore, I would rather attempt an explanation of 22:14 which remains valid even if "apostles" there is taken to denote the Twelve.

Before the Supper, Jesus says he is "to eat the Pasch *meta tōn mathētōn*" (22:11). After the Supper, Jesus goes to the Mount "and the *methētai* follow him" (22:39). But as the Supper begins, Jesus "reclined, and the apostles with him" (22:14). If the text is accurate, and if apostles means the Twelve, then the verse still need be no more than a highlighting of one group among the *methētai* (vv. 11 and 39). It would mean that Luke made special mention of the fact that the Twelve were a part of this major event, the introduction to the passion and its normative interpretation (cf. 22:15–16, 17–22, 27–28, 36–37). Their central position in the Christian community in the first chapters of Acts will demand their having shared the events and having understood the events to which they witness (Acts 1:21–22). Luke makes special note of their presence at this critical point.[44]

THE PRESENCE OF A LARGER GROUP

But nothing in the text or context of 22:14 suggests that the Twelve were alone with Jesus at this time. Besides the contrary indications already listed in this study, there is the fact that in Luke the construction "he did X and the apostles with him" never excludes the presence of others. For instance, Luke writes in 8:1: "Jesus went about preaching and evangelizing the kingdom and the Twelve with him." But this does not mean that only the Twelve were with him, for the next verse goes on to add: "And some women. . . ."[45]

Again, Acts 1:13 says: "Where there were dwelling Peter and John and James . . . [= the Eleven]." But this does not mean only the Eleven, for the following verse adds: "These were all persevering together in prayer with the women and Mary the mother of Jesus and his brothers."[46]

All of this argument is on the presupposition that the text of 22:14 is accurately and precisely preserved. But there is question about the text. "The apostles" is the reading of P75. B. the first hand of Sinaiticus and D. But a corrector of Sinaiticus changed that "apostles" to "the Twelve," thus strengthening what he thought must be the sense following Matthew and Mark. Further correctors of Sinaiticus combined those two into "the Twelve Apostles," and this reading was followed by C, by Alexandrinus, by W, and became the Koine reading. Thus the manuscripts show a tendency to render the Supper fellowship more narrow, to make it reflect more explicitly the later ecclesiastical tradition. This tendency, at an earlier stage, could have changed an original Lukan *mathētai* into *apostoloi*. There is manuscript foundation for this suggestion, though it is numerically small: the Sinaitic Syriac at 22:14 does read *mathētai autou*.

Adding all this together, the reader is left with a choice. One can take this single word "apostles" in a single verse as absolutely determinative of all the rest, so that it alone overturns all the indications previously adduced of a Lukan pattern of development in regard to the persons around Jesus—a pattern consistently followed through everything else he writes about places and through all the words he tells us that Jesus spoke at the Supper. Or one can conclude that since this one word stands alone against everything else in the Supper account and the Gospel, there must be something wrong about the way we are reading this one word. Perhaps Luke intended us to read it in the wider sense he himself sometimes uses elsewhere; or perhaps he meant it to affirm a narrower sense without denying the larger number; or perhaps the word is a textual error, the result of some later mistaken "correction."

By standard rules of interpretation, one word, especially one word around which so many questions still hang, cannot outweigh consistently repeated contrary indications. The reasonable conclusion is that Luke did think of the group at the Supper as larger than just the Twelve.

WOMEN AS DISCIPLES OF JESUS

Our next specific concern is to show, if possible, that Luke intends us to include the women among that larger group. The first step is to establish the fact that when Luke says "the disciples," he includes the women under that term.

Everyone grants this point in regard to Luke's use of "disciple" (*mathētēs*) in Acts. There it stands simply for "believer," for "Christian."[47] For instance, in Acts 9:1–2, Saul "breathing threats and slaughters against the *disciples* of the Lord, went to the high priest and asked from him letters to Damascus to the synagogues, so that if he found *any belonging to the Way*, men as well as women, he might lead them out to Jerusalem."[48]

But if Luke uses "disciples" in Acts to include all believers, women as well as men, one should not maintain without clear and compelling evidence that he uses the word differently in his Gospel. There is no such evidence. Scholars have simply presumed until recently that Luke's Gospel normally intended what the other Synoptics intended. Redaction criticism, however, prefers to judge Luke by Luke-Acts.

Moreover an unmistakable demonstration that Luke used "disciple" in the same way in the Gospel can be found in Luke 24:6. There the angel says to the women: "You remember how he spoke to you, being still in Galilee, saying 'The Son of Man must be handed over to the hands of sinful men and crucified and the third day rise.' And they remembered his words."[49] The Lukan passion predictions in Galilee (9:22, 44) were directed to "the disciples," with orders to them in one instance not to mention the predictions to anyone else (9:21).[50] These predictions were made before the appointment of the Seventy-two, but after the introduction of the Twelve and of the women (8:1–3). When Luke here has the angel at the tomb ask the women to remember those predictions, adding explicitly that they did remember them, Luke shows he thinks of the women as among those who heard Jesus' words; namely, among the disciples.

Finally, the word "disciple" occurs in Luke 19:37 for "the great throng of disciples" who arrived with Jesus at the gates of Jerusalem. But in 23:55 Luke speaks of "the women who had been traveling with him out of Galilee." Therefore, the great crowd of "disciples" had included women.

Two further instances must be mentioned in which the word "disciple" does not occur but the description clearly unites in one group the women and the rest of Jesus' followers. In Luke 8:1–3 it is said that Jesus "journeyed from city to city, town to town, preaching and evangelizing the kingdom of God; and the Twelve with him; and certain women . . ."[51] Jesus, the Twelve and the women are three subjects of the verb *diōdeuen* (singular, to agree with the nearest subject). Thus not only the Twelve journeyed, preached, and evangelized, but also the women.[52]

And in Luke 24:13 Luke begins the story of how "two from among them *(duō ex autōn)*" met Jesus on the way to Emmaus. These two (Cleopas and his wife?) tell the Stranger, whom they do not recognize, how "some women from among us" had found the tomb empty. Exegetes universally speak of these two as "two of the disciples." Yet the women are here described as being of the same group.

Finally, if we look systematically at all references to the group of disciples in the course of the Gospel, we find that nothing is ever said to exclude women, and that many things are said which demand that we include women in the group.

Moreover, the women are the first ones after the Twelve who are explicitly shown joining the group around Jesus (Luke 8:1–3). Then Luke shows the women present at all the events which form the core of the Lukan kerygma: the cross (Luke 23:49), the burial (23:55), the resurrection announcement (24:1–8). They are there at the first appearance of the Lord and receive his final message (Luke 24:36–53), receive the understanding of the Scriptures, are named his witnesses, are promised a world-wide mission and the gift of power from on high, as was shown above. They are present during the forty days of appearances, for those appearances (Acts 1:3–4) are summed up in Luke 24:36–53 (cf. Note 9 above), and the women were present for the events and words of 24:36–53.

That this was Luke's understanding is confirmed by Acts 13:31: Jesus appeared "over many days," "*tois sunanabasin autō apo tēs Galilaias eis Ierousalēm*."[53] Now the only persons Luke ever explicitly calls "those who accompanied Jesus from Galilee to Jerusalem" are the women. Cf. Luke 23:49 "*sunakolouthousai autō apo tēs galilaias*"; and Luke 23:55 "*suneleluthuiai ek tēs galilaias autō*."[54] Nor is there any other reference in Acts to the forty days of appearances.

Moreover, the women are present for the Pentecostal outpouring of the Spirit. The speech of Acts 2:14–36 explains the phenomena witnessed by the crowds as the fulfillment of Joel's prophecy. Jesus "receiving from the Father the promise of the Holy Spirit has poured out this which you are seeing and hearing" (Acts 2:33). "This is the thing foretold through the prophet Joel: 'Your sons and daughters will prophesy. . . . On my servants male and female, I will pour out my Spirit' " (Acts 2:17–18). Luke modifies the LXX text by adding "*mou*" twice, and by adding "*kai prophēteusousin*" to Joel 3:2. He also omits the last half of Joel 3:5, which would have limited salvation to Israel.[55] He included, however, Joel 3:1b–2, in spite of its references to "your daughters" and to God's "female servants." This is strange, if Luke envisioned the Spirit being poured forth only on males in the scene which the Joel text is to explain.[56]

Moreover, by adding "*mou*" to both "*doulous*" and "*doulas*" he changes what had been in Joel a description of one class in Israelite society into a reference to God's chosen ones: "*my* servants, male and female," rather than just "the male and female servants."[57] Thus Luke makes the words refer to "these" (Acts 2:15) who are experiencing "this" (Acts 2:16) foretold through Joel. This would be strange, if among "these" there were no women.

Thus it is clear that Luke not only includes women as following Jesus everywhere during his teaching career right up to the Supper (their predominant role in the Lukan infancy narratives is too obvious to mention), but he also includes them in each of the events that follow the Supper.

LOCATING THE WOMEN DISCIPLES WITHIN JERUSALEM

Now we must give detailed study to something that must strike any reader of the Gospel: the many comings and goings of the women after the crucifixion. As long as these movements are left part of a blurred background, one fails to notice that they too add up to a consistent picture. The movements show that Luke considered the women part of the group of disciples living together at the time of Jesus' arrest and during the days which followed.

Luke 23:56: "The women saw the tomb and how his body was placed, and *returning* they prepared perfumes and spices."

Luke 24:1: "Saturday they rested according to the commandment. On the first day of the week very early they went [*ēlthon*] to the tomb, bearing the perfumes they had prepared"; 24:9: "*Returning* from the tomb, they reported all these things to the Eleven and to all the rest."

The action implied in these returns merits our attention. The verb is *hupostrephō*. The women return from the tomb (23:51) in order to rest over the sabbath and to prepare spices. Where they return to is not stated. Then Sunday morning again they return (24:9) from the tomb, and this time the place-where-to is specified: it is the place where the Eleven and the rest were.

The question is, of course, whether "return" is meant strictly this second time. Does 24:9 mean the women returned on Sunday morning to the Eleven and the rest in a strict sense, implying that they had earlier that morning *left* the Eleven and the rest in order to go to the tomb? Or is it just a way of saying that they "withdrew from the tomb to go elsewhere"?

Similarly one must ask whether 23:56 meant strictly that they returned to the same place in which Luke last thought of Jesus' disciples together—whether the mountain or the upper room; or was it just a way of saying that the women left the tomb and went home—whatever home they had found?

Both questions come down to one: Is *hupostrephō* simply another word for motion, with some sense of withdrawal, turning back, turning away? Or is it specifically (in Luke) a verb for going back and into a place from which one earlier departed? There is only one way to decide, and that is by examining all Lukan occurrences.

Luke uses *strephō* as well as eight different compounds of *strephō*.[58] *Hupostrephō* is Lukan, occurring elsewhere in the New Testament only in Mark 14:40, Gal. 1:17; Heb. 7:1; 2 Peter 2:21, but in Luke-Acts 32 times: 21 times in the Gospel, 11 times in Acts.[59] Let us then, setting aside the two verses which concern us here (23:56 and 24:9), examine Luke's 30 other instances of this word.

In 19 of them there is an explicit statement of to where the return was.[60] Of the remaining 11 instances, 9 were preceded a few verses earlier by a clear statement of departure from a definite place.[61] Of the remaining 2 instances, one is unmistakable from context.[62] The last (4:1) might be an instance in Luke of using *hupostrephō* for mere withdrawal. But no commentators ever seem to take it that way.[63]

Thus in all 30 instances Luke uses *hupostrephō* to mean return in the strict sense of going back to a place from which one earlier departed. Applied to our two texts, this evidence indicates that Luke thought the women *returned*, after the burial, to the place they had been the night before the crucifixion. *There* they remained over the sabbath and prepared their ointments (23:56). Sunday morning they went to the tomb (24:1) from that same place. After seeing the angels, they *returned* to that same place and reported to the Eleven and the rest (24:9), who had themselves been there all the time.

JESUS' WORDS ASSUME THE PRESENCE OF WOMEN

Finally we must return to the words Jesus spoke at the Supper in Luke. They give us our last and most important set of arguments. There is no doubt that some of these words are especially appropriate if spoken to the women and are very strange if the women be omitted.

For instance, in Luke 22:15 Jesus says: "With intense longing I have desired to eat this Pasch with you before I suffer." The Last Supper in Luke has the note of farewell from those who had followed him closely.[64] But the women have been with him since 8:1–3, heard the passion-prediction of 9:22, and are described at the cross and tomb as "having accompanied him from Galilee" (23:49, 56). Their exclusion would be all the more puzzling in that "to eat the Pasch" would normally be done in a family, with parts of the ritual assigned to women and children. Thus E. Schweizer, commenting on Mark, considers the absence of women an argument against Mark's Supper being a Passover.[65]

In Luke 22:26–27 Jesus says, "Let the greater among you be as the younger and the leader as the one who serves." The younger ones and those who serve were hard to identify among the Twelve.[66] But the *only* persons in Luke who are said to serve Jesus or the rest of the group (*diakoneō*) are Peter's mother-in-law (4:39), the women from Galilee (8:3),[67] and Martha (10:40). All of these are women.

In Luke 22:28 Jesus says: "You are those having persevered with me in my temptations." If this refers to trials during Jesus' teaching and preaching career, others than the Twelve must be said to have shared those trials,[68] and the women—traveling with him since 8:1—as much as any.

If this in any way looks forward to the trials of the passion (as most understand it), then, to apply it to the Twelve, one first has to explain why Judas' defection and Peter's denials do not contradict it. Then one has to use an argument from silence (Luke's omission of Mark 14:50) and an ambiguous reference on Calvary ("all his acquaintances stood afar off—*pantes hoi gnōstoi autō*").[69]

On the other hand, to apply it to the women is easy. Luke explicitly says that the women were with Jesus at his cross (23:49), at his burial by one not of the Twelve (23:50–55), that they prepared ointments for him over that sabbath (23:56), and returned to his tomb on the third day after his death (24:1). Twice during those accounts Luke recalls that they had been following Jesus ever since Galilee (23:49, 55). The picture of their perseverance could hardly be more clear.

CONCLUSION

The conclusion then is that Luke did think in terms of a larger group at the Supper than just the Twelve. Specifically, he thought of the Christian community he had been at pains to build up around Jesus through the course of the Gospel, and around which he would develop the church of Acts. Further, Luke thought of the women as part of that community, sharing in all its life and actions. When he showed that community gathered for the Last Supper, he never imagined future readers might doubt that the women were present.

NOTES

1. Joachim Jeremias, *The Eucharistic Words of Jesus*, rev. ed. (New York: Scribner's, 1966; repr. Philadelphia: Fortress Press, 1977). Cf. p. 46: "According to Mark 14:17 (par. Matt. 26:20) Jesus celebrated the Last Supper with the Twelve. It is not possible, however, to assume from this that the women mentioned in Mark 15:40;

Luke 23:49, 55 were excluded; in Eastern texts the argument from silence is inadmissible in such cases."

2. For the principles and criteria of "konsequente Redaktionsgeschichte," cf. Quesnell, *The Mind of Mark: Interpretation and Method through the Exegesis of Mk. 6.52*, Analecta Biblica, 38 (Rome: Biblical Institute Press, 1969), pp. 45–56.

3. That Luke has some special concern for women has often been noted. Cf., for instance, H. J. Cadbury, *The Making of Luke-Acts* (New York: Macmillan, 1927), pp. 234 and 263–265; H. Flender, *St. Luke, Theologian of Redemptive History* (Philadelphia: Fortress Press, 1967), p. 9.

4. Raymond E. Brown, "Roles of Women in the Fourth Gospel," *TS* 36 (1967): 697: "For Luke, the hearers of the word of God do not *replace* Jesus' mother and brothers as his true family; for his mother and brothers hear the word of God and do it and so are part of the true family of disciples." This was suggested earlier by W. C. Robinson, "On Preaching the Word of God (Luke 8:14–21)" in *Studies in Luke-Acts*, ed. L. Keck and L. Martyn (Nashville: Abingdon, 1966), p. 133 and note 20, with confirmation from Luke 4:24 (the omission of Mark's charge that the prophet is not accepted "among his relatives and in his own household" [Mark 6:4]).

Further confirmation is possible from Luke 11:27, where the woman's praise of Mary's motherhood is turned to the fact that Mary is one of those who "hear the word of God and keep it": cf. H. A. W. Meyer, *Critical and Exegetical Handbook to the Gospels of Mark and Luke* (New York: Funk and Wagnall, 1884), p. 402; B. S. Easton, translating *menoun* as "truly," in *The Gospel according to St. Luke: A Critical and Exegetical Commentary* (New York: Scribner's, 1926), p. 184; and A. Plummer, explaining *menoun* in *The Gospel according to St. Luke*, ICC (New York: Scribner's, 1896), p. 558.

Further confirmation is possible from Luke's earlier mention of Mary's relation to the word: Luke 1:38, 45; 2:19, 51.

5. At a minimum, this means 91 persons (taking the smaller figure from Luke 10:1, the "many others" as at least 3, and "the brothers" as at least 2). But the Seventy may be 72, the brothers 4 (as in Mark 6:3, Matt. 13:55–56, plus perhaps "sisters"), and "many others" could be any reasonable number. Cf. G. Lohfink, *Die Sammlung Israels: eine Untersuchung zur lukanischen Ekklesiologie* (Munich: Kösel, 1975), p. 72.

6. "*Gnōstoi*" properly indicates a wider circle of "acquaintances." Cf. W. Dietrich, *Das Petrusbild der lukanischen Schriften*, BWANT 94 (Stuttgart: Kohlhammer, 1972), p. 125 and note 220.

7. "*Autōn*" has an antecedent "the Eleven and all the rest" (v. 9). Cf. S. Brown, *Apostasy and Perseverance in the Theology of Luke*, Analecta Biblica, 36 (Rome: Biblical Institute Press, 1969), p. 75 and note 300.

8. Cf. S. Brown: "opens the minds of the apostles and the other disciples" (*Apostasy and Perseverance*, p. 80; cf. p. 54. note 192). Also G. Klein, "Lukas 1, 1–4 als theologisches Programm," in *Das Lukas-evangelium: Die Redaktions- und Kompositionsgeschichtliche Forschung* (Darmstadt: Braumann, 1974), p. 183; G. Lohfink, *Die Himmelfahrt Jesu: Untersuchungen zu den Himmelfahrts-und Erhöhungstexten bei Lukas*, STANT 26 (Munich: Kösel, 1971), pp. 113, 147, 150; A. Plummer, *Gospel according to Luke*, p. 558; S. G. Wilson, *The Gentiles and the Gentile Mission in Luke-Acts*, SNTMS 23 (Cambridge: Cambridge University Press, 1973).

9. Cf. Lohfink: ". . . beide Abschnitte sich gegenseitig interpretieren" (*Himmelfahrt*, p. 158); K. Lake in F. Foakes Jackson and Kirsopp Lake, *The Beginnings of Christianity*, Part 1, *The Acts of the Apostles,* 5 vols. (London: Macmillan, 1933);

Vol. 5, *Additional Notes* (Grand Rapids: Baker Books, 1966), p. 475; E. Jacquier, *Les Actes des Apôtres*, 2nd ed. (Paris: Gabalda, 1926). E.g., the promise of his Father (Luke 24:49; Acts 1:4); receive power from on high (Luke 24:49; cf. Acts 1:8) staying in Jerusalem (Luke 24:49, 47; Acts 1:4); witnesses to all nations, beginning from Jerusalem (Luke 24:47b-48; Acts 1:8); ate before them (Luke 24:43; cf. Acts 1:4); ascended (Luke 24:51; Acts 1:9); return to Jerusalem from opposite Bethany (Luke 24:52, 50; cf. Acts 1:12; [on *heōs pros Bēthanian* = Mount of Olives, cf. Lohfink, *Himmelfahrt*, pp. 164-67]).

10. S. Brown confesses the anomaly: "Since in their own person the apostles are merely witnesses to the people (Acts 13:31), Luke must have thought of their witness as being extended to the ends of the earth in the person of missionaries like Paul and Barnabas . . ." (*Apostasy and Perseverance*, p. 127). S. Wilson calls it "an anomaly of which Luke may well have been unaware. It is best understood as a Lukan creation, which does not accord with some of the more traditional material he relates elsewhere" (*Gentiles and the Gentile Mission*, pp. 93-94). But W. Dietrich shows that "*sunelthontes*" of Acts 1:6 must refer to others present over and above the Twelve (*Petrusbild*, pp. 186-187). Cf. Lohfink (*Himmelfahrt*, p. 269) and G. Schille, "Die Himmelfahrt," *ZNW* 57 (1966): 186.

11. H. A. W. Meyer pointed out that "*pantes homou epi to auto*" would be a peculiar expression for a gathering of twelve people, especially when the immediately preceding scene had been an account of "about 120" (Acts 1:15-26) (*Die Apostelgeschichte* [Göttingen:Vandenhoeck & Ruprecht, 1870], p. 48). Cf. Jackson and Lake, *The Beginnings of Christianity*, vol. 4, *Translations and Commentary*, p. 17: "Wendt, Blass and others, following Chrysostom (Hom. 4) think that it refers to the 120 of 1.15."

12. On "Peter's speech" as the act of the Twelve, cf. also J. Dupont, "Les discours de Pierre dans les Actes et le chapître XXIV de Luc," in *L'évangile de Luc: Problèmes littéraires et théologiques*, ed. F. Neirynck, BETL 32 (Gembloux: Ducolot, 1973), p. 372; also Dietrich, *Petrusbild*, p. 199.

13. Cf. E. Haenchen, *The Acts of the Apostles* (Philadelphia: Westminster, 1971), p. 167: "the one hundred and twenty persons of 1:15"; p. 167, note 4: "It is not only the Apostles who receive the Spirit: while they stand forward (v. 14) the ecstatic event further extends to the others—cf v. 33 [= vollzieht sich . . . an den anderen weiter: Haenchen, Tübingen: J. B. C. Mohr, 1963, *Apostelgeschichte*, p. 131]; p. 183: "the ecstatic speaking with tongues is still going on in the background"; p. 178, note 10: "*touto estin* shows that the Christians—apart from the Twelve—are imagined as still given over to ecstasy, though somewhat in the background of the scene." Cf. also J. Kremer, *Pfingstbericht und Pfingstgeschehen: eine exegetische Untersuchung zu Apg 2:1-13*, Stuttgarter Bibelstudien 63 (Stuttgart: KBW, 1973), pp. 95-97.

14. Cf. Hans Conzelmann, *The Theology of St. Luke* (New York: Harper & Row, 1961), p. 73: "The description of Jesus' itinerant preaching served to present an account of the assembling of witnesses." Also Lohfink, *Sammlung Israels*, pp. 39-40; 70.

15. "About 120" (Acts 1:15); "added about 3000" (Acts 2:41); "added to their number day by day" (Acts 2:47); "about 5000" (Acts 4:4); "increasing in number" (Acts 6:1); "many tens of thousands" (*posai muriades*: Acts 21:20). Cf. Lohfink, *Himmelfahrt*, pp. 178-179: *Sammlung Israels*, pp. 75; 77. Also P. Zingg, *Das Wachsen der Kirche: Beiträge zur Frage der lukanischen Redaktion und Theologie* (Göttingen: Vandenhoeck & Ruprecht, 1974).

16. Cf. 21:37: "*ēulizeto*": W. Manson. *The Gospel of Luke* (New York: R. Smith,

1930), p. 238: "encamped without the city"; A. Plummer, *The Gospel according to Luke*, p. 488: "used to go and bivouac"; A. R. C. Leaney, *A Commentary on the Gospel according to St. Luke*, 2nd ed. (London: Black, 1966), p. 272: "their encampment." Luke says Jesus, having gone there "according to his custom" (22:39), "once arrived at the place" (22:40), withdrew "about a stone's throw"—an apt expression only if Luke thought of the place as outdoors.

Moreover, Luke never says Jesus spent his nights in the village of Bethany (contrast Mark 12:11–12, 19–20; Matthew 21:17; and cf. Cadbury, *The Making of Luke-Acts*, p. 249), although he envisions the village as situated "toward [*pros*]" the Mount of Olives. Nor does he have Jesus dine "in Bethany in the home of Simon the leper" (Mark 14:3). Finally, Luke's Mary and Martha live not in Bethany (contrast John 11:1), but "in a certain town" through which Jesus passed in Luke 10:38–42.

17. The point seems emphasized in D, which reads *anagaion oikon estrōmenon*.

18. The suggestion has often recurred that the room was somewhere in the temple. H. A. W. Meyer (*Apostelgeschichte*, p. 35) names "de Dieu, Lightfoot, Hammond, Schoettgen, Krebs." Haenchen adds Holtzmann and (hesitating) Loisy (*Apostelgeschichte*, p. 120). Most recently, cf. H. Flender, "Die Kirche in den Lukas-Schriften" in *Das Lukasevangelium* Wege der Forschung, 280 (Darmstadt: Wissenschaftliche, 1974), pp. 269–270, 273). Jackson and Lake (*Beginnings of Christianity*, 4:10) say "probably the *anagaion*" of Luke 22:12.

19. Cf. Haenchen, *Acts*, p. 153, note 3, and p. 149, note 7.

20. Cf. S. Brown: "Not only the Twelve have witnessed all the events of the Age of Jesus; otherwise it would have been impossible to find a successor for Judas" (*Apostasy and Perseverance*, p. 54, note 192; also p. 89). J. Jervell points out that "to be eye-witnesses to guarantee the Jesus-tradition" is "a task that can be fulfilled by the wider circle of disciples" (*A New Look at Luke-Acts* [Minneapolis: Augsburg, 1972], p. 78).

21. As in Gen. 38:11 (bis); Exod. 16:29; Judg. 8:29; 4 Kings 14:10: 2 Chron. 25:19; 26:21; Judith 11:23, etc. Similarly often with "in the city, the mountains, the country, etc."

22. As it does, for instance, in Deut. 6:7 and 11:19, where "sitting in your house" is contrasted with "walking on the way, lying down, rising"; or Ezek. 8:1: "as I was sitting in my house, and the elders of Israel sitting before me . . ." (so too 4 Kings 6:32).

23. The occasional suggestion that they were seated as in the typical posture for prayer at once presumes they were praying and overlooks Luke 22:41; Acts 7:60; 9:40; 20:36; 21:5, in all of which Luke explicitly says people are praying but shows them kneeling down to do it: *theis (thentes) ta gonata*.

24. For "Luke's attention to the matter of lodging," cf. Cadbury, *Making of Luke-Acts*, pp. 249–253; also Conzelmann, *Theology of St. Luke*, pp. 73–80; 93–94; and Lohfink, *Himmelfahrt*, p. 269 and note 10.

25. Lohfink, *Sammlung Israels*, p. 94.

26. As in H. Schürmann's title, *Jesu Abschiedsrede*, NTAbh 20, 4 (Münster, 1957).

27. Jesus chose the Twelve (Luke 6:13), but the special closeness implied in Mark's "he appointed Twelve that they might be with him" (Mark 3:14) cannot be found in Luke. Cf. S. Brown: "All of the *mathētai* have been called 'to be with' Jesus, so that the phrase cannot designate a function reserved to the Twelve" (*Apostasy and Perseverance*, p. 88); and also on *sun autō eimi* as a technical expression for disciple (p. 83).

28. H. A. W. Meyer saw the problem, when he wrote that *neōteros* "does not refer to one in the circle of the Twelve, but it means one who is younger than the others, and

denotes a believing youth. It must be supposed that such were present, performing the service" (*Handbook to Mark and Luke*, p. 544).

29. As Conzelmann notes, "Features from the primitive community have naturally been projected back" (*Theology of St. Luke*, p. 47). Cf. R. H. Fuller, *The Mission and Achievement of Jesus: An Examination of the Presuppositions of New Testament Theology*, SBT 12 (Naperville, Ill.: Allenson, 1954), p. 57, with reference to Heb. 13:7, 17, 24 and 1 Tim. 5:1, 2, 11, 14; 1 Peter 5:5.

30. Cf. S. Brown *(Apostasy and Perseverance,* p. 7, expressing his own disagreement with Conzelmann and the rest). In Luke the disciples are never said to abandon Jesus and flee (contrast Matt. 26:31, 56; Mark 14:27, 50). Cf. Conzelmann, *Theology of St. Luke*, pp. 81, 199; Brown, *Apostasy and Perseverance*, pp. 62–74.

31. Cf. S. Brown, *Apostasy and Perseverance*, p. 9, referring to Luke 11:16, 10:25.

32. Luke 23:26, 49, 50–56. Cf. Easton, *Gospel according to St. Luke*, p. 336.

33. S. Brown, while highlighting the perseverance of the Twelve (*Apostasy and Perseverance*, pp. 53–81), also demonstrates Luke's great concern with the perseverance of all Christians (pp. 49–51; 114–120), with explanations of Luke 8:15; 21:19; Acts 11:23; 14:22. Both Judas' defection and Peter's denials offer him serious problems (pp. 68–71; 82–97).

34. Or: "as my Father has bequeathed to me a kingdom, I bequeath to you that you eat and drink at my table in my kingdom." Whether the object of *diatithemai* is *basileia* or the *hina* clause is very disputed. Cf. Note 36.

35. On the contrary, the kingdom of God is evangelized to all (Luke 4:43; 8:1; etc.); is said to belong to "you poor" (Luke 6:20); to the disciples is given to know its secrets (8:10); and "to you [= the disciples; cf. 12:22] the kingdom" is given (12:32). The many references to being in the kingdom, entering the kingdom, receiving the kingdom, etc. also apply to all.

36. S. Brown would avoid the difficulty with 22:29 by understanding *basileia* as "royal rule," reflecting "the impending role in the Church" of the Twelve (*Apostasy and Perseverance*, p. 64). But he does this only by omitting 22:30a "since it appears to be an insertion" (p. 64, note 251). J. M. Creed, in *The Gospel according to St. Luke* (London: Macmillan, 1930), p. 269, pointed out the awkwardness of taking *basileia* as "rule" in v. 29 while taking it as "kingdom" in v. 30. Creed suggests (as does Behm in TDNT 2, 104) that *basileia* (22:29) is the object of *dietheto*, and *diatithemai* governs the clause "*hina esthēte.*"

In fact, the image of eating and drinking at the king's table is not expressive of ruling, "the twelve tribes of Israel" is not really established as a Lukan image for the Christian community, and it is very doubtful that the actions of the Twelve in Acts could reasonably be described as exercising "royal rule" as from "thrones." Most would agree with Schürmann (*Abschiedsrede,* p. 41) and Lohfink (*Sammlung Israels*, pp. 79–83) that the promises of thrones and kingdom are eschatological. Cf. V. Taylor, commenting on Luke 22:30 in his *The Gospel according to St. Mark* (London: Macmillan, 1952), p. 622: "the rule of the saints, which belongs to the end time." Luke's references to receiving or possessing the kingdom, to inheriting it or to God's dispensing or bequeathing (*diatithemai*) the kingdom or willing his *diathēkē*, pertain to all believers. Cf. Acts 20:32; Luke 10:25; 18:18; Acts 3:25.

Even the note of intimacy ("at my table") is common in Christian tradition, though not occurring elsewhere in Luke-Acts. Cf. "share the table of the Lord" (1 Cor. 10:21) and "I will come in to him and eat with him and he with me" (Rev. 3:20; with the following verse on the sharing of thrones!).

37. Cf. H. E. Tödt, *The Son of Man in the Synoptic Tradition* (Philadelphia: West-

—

minster, 1965), p. 64; and Easton, *Gospel according to St. Luke,* p. 326: "the numeral would have been an easy addition for Matthew, and may have specialized for the apostles a promise originally made to a much wider group."

S. Brown (*Apostasy and Perseverance*, p. 84) and Taylor, *The Passion Narrative of St. Luke: A Critical and Historical Investigation* (Cambridge: Cambridge University Press, 1972), p. 64, and Jervell (*New Look*, p. 86) suggest Luke's reason for the omission might be that Judas was present but would never sit on a throne. This leaves unexplained not only Matthew 19:28 (where Judas is also present), but also Luke 22:19b, 28, 29, all of which Luke leaves addressed to Judas even though none of them will find fulfillment in him personally.

38. There, after times of persecution, thrones are placed, the Ancient of Days takes his throne (v. 9), one like a Son of Man is presented to the Ancient of Days (v. 13) and given dominion and glory and kingdom (v. 14), and this last is explained to mean that the saints of the Most High shall receive the kingdom (v. 18) and judgment will be given to them (v. 22: *"kai tēn krisin edōke tois hagiois tou hupsistou"*). Allusion to the same promise is made in Rev. 3:21 and 20:4. Cf. 1 Cor. 6:2.

39. Cf. S. Brown, *Apostasy and Perseverance*, pp. 72–73.

40. Cf. F. Danker, *Jesus and the New Age according to St. Luke: A Commentary on the Third Gospel* (St. Louis: Clayton, 1972), p. 224: "Luke is ordinarily careful about observing correspondence between various parts of his writing. All the more remarkable, therefore, is the wording in v. 35—a clear echo of 10:4, which is part of the account of the sending of the Seventy (two). The Twelve, however, were sent out earlier and with different specifications." Even V. Taylor asked in 1926 "whether in Lk 22:35-8 we have not some indication that more of Christ's followers than the Twelve were present at the Supper, a point which bears on the use of the term 'apostles' in Lk 22:14" (*Behind the Third Gospel: A Study of the Proto-Luke Hypothesis* [Oxford: The Clarendon Press, 1926], p. 43). Cf. Creed, *Gospel according to St. Luke*, pp. 270–271.

41. Reminiscence and recall are, along with prophecy and fulfillment, among Luke's editorial devices for binding his story together with backward- and forward-looking allusions. Cf. Luke 22:61; 24:6, 44; Acts 11:16.

42. In a paper for the Columbia University Seminar for Studies in the New Testament, November 22, 1974: "Observations on the Concept of Apostleship and the Dating of Luke-Acts." Ellis's arguments include: Acts 14:4,14, where the term "apostle" is applied to Paul and Barnabas; Acts 1:2, where "apostles" is used for the group which is clearly identical with the larger group of Luke 24; the paralleling in Luke 24:9 and 10 of "announced these things to the Eleven and to all the rest" with "said these things to the apostles"; the fact that the nearest antecedent for "two of them" in 24:13 is "the apostles"—although the two of them are not of the Twelve; the fact that the meeting of Acts 15 has James as one of its two principal spokesmen, even though the meeting convenes "the apostles and elders" and James is not one of the Twelve; the fact that Acts 1:25 says someone is needed "to take the place of this ministry and this apostolate" from which Judas fell away, since the words "this ministry [of the Twelve] imply theirs is one specific ministry among others, and similarly "this apostolate" [of the Twelve] implies theirs is one apostolate among others.

Cf. S. Wilson, who recently surveyed some of the vast literature aimed at clarifying Luke's notion of "apostle" (*Gentiles and the Gentile Mission*, pp. 109–120) and concluded that "the title 'Apostle' as such was not important to Luke" (p. 117).

43. In confirmation one might point to Acts' use of the expression "the apostles

and elders in Jerusalem" (15:2; 16:4; cf. 15:6, 22, 23), "the apostles and brothers in Jerusalem" (Acts 11:1), and even "the apostles in Jerusalem" (8:14). There were elders in other places (Acts 14:23; 20:17; 21:18); and the implication of the phrases is that Luke knew there were apostles in other places as well. Cf. V. Taylor, commenting on Acts in his *The Gospel of St. Mark,* pp. 625-626.

44. Their presence will be especially underlined again in 24:44, 46 by the reference to the third passion-prediction (Luke 18:31-33), which only the Twelve heard (cf. Jervell, *New Look,* pp. 80-81); in Acts 1:2 by the reference to the *apostolois hous exelexato,* an unmistakable echo of Luke 6:13; at Acts 1:13 by listing their names; and at Pentecost by their risking to speak ("Peter with the Eleven": Acts 2:14). Cf. J. Wanke, *Die Emmauserzählung: Eine redaktionsgeschichtliche Untersuchung zu Lk 24:13-35,* Erfurter Theologische Studien 31 (Leipzig: St. Benno, 1973), pp. 48-49 and 73-75 for an account of this as characteristic of Luke.

45. Cf. S. Brown: "In 22:14 *sun autō* is not to be understood as signifying merely physical presence" (*Apostasy and Perseverance,* p. 83). It expresses "the apostles' solidarity with Jesus and their abiding faith in him" (ibid.). Cf. Easton, *Gospel according to St. Luke,* p. 318: "That others were present is not impossible, but the wording does not say so." Easton notes that "Weiss [B. Weiss, *Das Evangelium des Lukas* (Göttingen: Meyerk, 1901)] thinks that 'the apostles' includes more than the Twelve."

46. Cf. Acts 15:22, where "all the church" is suddenly revealed to have been present (thus occasioning much discussion of sources: cf. W. Dietrich, *Petrusbild,* pp. 307ff and note 259); Luke 7:9, where the previously unmentioned "crowd" is addressed; Luke 23:11, where Herod's "armies" turn out to have been present; 4:14, where "the lame man" is seen standing where only Peter and John had been mentioned; etc. The most famous instance of this is perhaps Luke 9:18, where "Jesus was praying alone" is followed by "and the disciples were with him."

47. Cf. K. H. Rengstorf in *TDNT* 4, pp. 457-459, and BAG: "Even after Jesus' departure from this life, those who followed him were called *mathētai*"; "Acts uses mathētai almost exclusively to denote the members of the new religious community, so that it almost = Christian."

48. Cf. Acts 6:1, 2, 7; 9:36, 38-39; 11:26; 18:26-27; 21:4-5.

49. Cf. Creed, *Gospel according to St. Luke,* p. 294: "We must suppose, therefore, that the women were among the disciples at 9:18, 43."

50. S. Brown explains that the prohibition bears on the *necessity* of the Messiah's suffering (*Apostasy and Perseverance,* p. 61). That is precisely what the women are here said to remember. It also seems to be what Cleopas and his companion are rebuked for not knowing (Luke 24:25-26).

51. Cf. Wm. C. Robinson, Jr., "On Preaching the Word of God (Luke 8:4-21)" in *Studies in Luke-Acts,* ed. L. Keck and L. Martyn (Nashville: Abingdon, 1966), pp. 131-132: Luke 8:1-3 is intended to contrast "with Luke 6:13ff., 17, 20, to note the larger group of followers whom Jesus here instructs about Christian missions, and who form the group of those who in Luke's view were qualified witnesses"; and cf. Robinson's *Der Weg des Herrn: Studien zur Geschichte und Eschatologie im Lukas-Evangelium,* TF 36 (Hamburg-Bergstedt: Reich, 1965), pp. 37ff. Cf. also G. Klein "Lukas 1:1-4," p. 187 and notes 62 and 63.

52. C. Stuhlmueller rightly comments: "Jesus imparts a new dignity and role to woman in granting her a right . . . even to participate in the ministry" (*JBC* 44:77). Cf. Leaney, *Commentary on Luke,* p. 149: "The women from Galilee, later to be

witnesses of the resurrection, are shown playing their part as witnesses from the first alongside the Apostles'' (cf. Acts 1:14–21).''

53. Cf. S. Brown on 23:49, 55: *"sunakolouthousai* and *suneleluthuiai* of discipleship!'' (*Apostasy and Perseverance,* p. 88). The central importance of the idea expressed here is developed in Brown's section on ''The Way of the Lord'' (pp. 131–145).

54. Conzelmann comments on Acts 13:31: '''The witnesses' include more than the Twelve'' (*Die Apostelgeschichte,* HNT 7 [Tübingen: Mohr, 1963]). Cf. Jervell, *New Look,* p. 112, note 88.

55. Cf. M. Rese, *Alttestamentliche Motive in der Christologie des Lukas,* SNT 1 (Gütersloh: Mohn, 1969), pp. 50–51.

56. Cf. Chrysostom: ''The Spirit is poured out upon the 120, for Peter would not have quoted to no purpose the testimony of the prophet: 'Your sons and your daughters . . .' '' (Homilies on Acts, Homily 4).

57. Cf. Haenchen, *Acts,* p. 179.

58. *anastrephō* (2); *apostrephō* (2); *diastrephō* (5); *epistrephō* (1); *metastrephō* (1); *sustrephō* (1); *hupostrephō* (32 = in Luke 21 times, in Acts, 11).

Luke once uses *anastrephō* in the sense of physical return (Acts 5:22) and three times (out of 17) gives *epistrephō* this sense (Luke 2:39; 17:31; Acts 15:36).

59. D would add one more, Acts 19:1. This variant also expresses physical return (''to Asia''), but will not be included in the following statistics.

Acts 13:34 applies the physical meaning to a spiritual reality. Commenting on Psalm 16:10 (LXX): ''You will not give your Holy One to see corruption'' (Acts 13:35), and contrasting Jesus with David, who ''was gathered to his fathers and did see corruption'' (Acts 13:36), it says God raised Jesus ''from among the dead, never more to *return* to corruption.'' (BAG takes *diaphthora* in this verse as = the grave.)

60. Luke 1:56; 2:45; 4:14; 7:10; 8:39; 11:24; 17:15; 24:33, 52. Acts 1:12; 8:25, 28; 13:13, 34; 14:21; 20:3; 21:6; 22:17; 23:32.

61. Luke 2:20 (cf. 2:15); 2:43 (cf. 2:39, 41); 8:37 and 8:40 (cf. 8:22); 9:10 (cf. 9:2, 6); 10:17 (cf. 10:1); 17:18 (cf. 17:15); 19:12 (cf. 19:12 [sic]); Acts 12:25 (cf. 11:30).

62. In 23:48, ''. . . returned, beating their breasts,'' there is no doubt that the people return to a place from which they had set out—either Jerusalem or their own homes. The commencement of their journey was noted in 23:26–27: ''As he was led out . . . a great multitude of the people followed him.''

63. ''Jesus, full of the Holy Spirit, returned from the Jordan and was led by the Spirit in the desert, being tempted forty days by the devil.'' Brown points out that the context makes clear (*peirazomenos,* contemporaneous with *egeto*) that ''in the desert'' is place-where, not place-to-which (*Apostasy and Perseverance,* p. 18). The true goal, then, is not stated until 4:14, ''returned to Galilee.''

So too Conzelmann (*Theology,* p. 20, note 4): ''Chapter 4:1 stresses the final departure from the Jordan, and 4:14 mentions Galilee as the destination.'' If so, *hupestrepsen* in 4:1 follows the standard Lukan usage, being resumed and completed in 4:14. Easton presumes the same when he reasons the desert must be north of the Jordan baptismal scene and on the edge of Galilee (*Gospel according to St. Luke,* pp. 45–46); cf. his note on 4:14 (p. 50): ''completes the journey.''

64. Cf. p. 64 and n. 26 above.

65. Cf. E. Schweizer, *The Good News according to St. Mark* (Richmond: Knox, 1970), p. 295. Cf. Mishnah, Pesah 8:1; 10:4.

66. Cf. p. 64 and n. 28 above.

67. The text tradition is split as to whom the women served in 8:3. BD have *autois*, Sinaiticus and A have *auto*. Conzelmann remarks that the women have been "turned into deaconesses" (*Theology*, p. 47; "zu diakonissen stilisiert"—*Mitte*, 40).

68. Cf. p. 64 and n. 31 above.

69. The phrase embodies elements from cries of desolation in two psalms: "*emakrunas tous gnōstous mou ap'emou*" (Ps. 87:9 LXX) and "*hoi eggista mou apo makrothen estēsan*" (Ps. 37:11 LXX).

6

Reconciliation and Forgiveness in Luke's Gospel

J. MASSYNGBAERDE FORD

St. Luke's Gospel is remarkable for the degree to which it emphasizes the reconciling and forgiving character of Jesus. In the paper which follows, the dramatic Lukan passages opening and closing Jesus' ministry will be analyzed from this perspective. In addition, consideration will be given to the way in which Luke presents Jesus responding to tax collectors and Samaritans.

THE BEGINNING OF JESUS' MINISTRY (LUKE 4:16–30)

At the outset it is important to realize that Luke radically revises the whole beginning of Jesus' ministry if we contrast his Gospel with those of Mark and Matthew. For Luke—from a theological view, even if not from a geographical or historical aspect—Jesus' inauguration of his ministry begins with his homily at his home town of Nazareth (Luke 4:16–30) and this whole event is the keynote to his ministry.[1] In the synagogue at Nazareth Jesus presents himself as the anointed prophet predicted in Isaiah who announces the favorable year of the Lord. There are several important features in this pericope.

Firstly, Jews contemporary with Jesus (and with Luke), especially those associated with the community at Khirbet Qumran and many of the revolutionaries, particularly if they were associated with the Hasmonean dynasty, expected a year of favor and political victory for the Jews and a year of defeat and retribution, often amounting to vengeance, for the Gentiles. These would include the Romans and compromising Jews. Galilee, in which region Nazareth was situated, had a special proclivity to apocalyptic hopes and revolutionary movements.

Secondly, perhaps the most important result of research on Luke 4:16-30 in the last two decades has been to find in it a reflection of the personage of Melchizedek and to reaffirm the importance of Isaiah 61 behind the text of Luke 4:18-19. The most pertinent text is 11 *Q Melch.* from Qumran.[2] The text runs about twenty-five lines and is a commentary on Isaiah 61, although there are allusions to this text throughout rather than direct quotations. It proclaims the eschatological Jubilee when, as well as the Jubilee precepts according to Leviticus 25:9-17 being fulfilled, Melchizedek, a supernatural figure, will come to inaugurate the Jubilee as a year of favor for the faithful Jews and of vengeance and slaughter for the enemy. Melchizedek's two functions are "to exact vengeance of the judgments of God" and to bring good news to the pious. He, or a prophet, is the one anointed by the Spirit (cf. Isa. 61:1ff). The Day of Vengeance is a prominent theme in the Scrolls (e.g., 1 *QS* 9:21-23; 10:19-21). What is arresting in Luke 4:18-19 is the omission of the Day of Vengeance which occurs in all the manuscripts of Isaiah 61:2. Further, if all of Isaiah 61:1-9 is read, one sees that Luke implies that Jesus omitted other material which was hostile to the Gentiles.

11 *Q Melch.* is probably dated around 50 C.E. In this case its influence on Luke 4 is redactional. Interest in Melchizedek is found in Christian circles in the second century C.E. but it occurs earlier in Philo and in rabbinical circles. Thus it is not impossible that Luke and John were influenced by this interest.

Thirdly, when Jesus announces that his Scripture is fulfilled "today" this gives rise to a fierce Christological debate, for people are amazed that the son of Joseph can make such egregious claims. Most interpretors would argue that Jesus' words first kindle admiration in the congregation and then anger develops and ends in an attempt to murder Jesus. One major difficulty which arises with this interpretation is that it seems strange that a congregation should change from great admiration to murderous intent in such a short time. Violet wanted to explain the dative after *emarturoun* (witness) as a dative of disadvantage.[3] Jeremias built on his thesis, remarked the omission of the Day of Vengeance, and concluded that the difficult verses should be translated: "they protested with one voice and were furious because he (only) spoke of God's year of mercy (and omitted the messianic vengeance)."[4]

Both Matthew and Mark report this hostility and they refer to Jesus as the son of Mary and to four of his "brothers" (cousins) by name. Luke calls Jesus "son of Joseph" and omits the names of Jesus' relatives. Probably he does this because at least three (Simon, James, and Judas) bear Maccabean or revolutionary names which were popular among the nationalist freedom fighters in the first century C.E.

The attitude of the congregation was aggravated when Jesus alluded to the miracles of Elijah and Elisha, which were performed for Gentiles, and implicitly referred to these prophets dining and even lodging with Gentiles.[5] Famine brings disparate people together. Jesus' words are pertinent to the problems of Luke's Christian communities as they respond to the question whether Jews and Gentiles should dine together and what relationship they will have in the new era.

Fourthly, Jesus may have been inaugurating or proclaiming a jubilee year in which, according to Jewish law, debts were cancelled, slaves (and prisoners) were released, and people returned to their own land and the land lay fallow but the poor were allowed to glean the fields and orchards of the crops or fruits which grew naturally. It is interesting to note that some of the revolutionary leaders had social programs. For example, Simon bar Giora attacked the rich, freed slaves, and offered rewards to the free (*B.J.* 4:508). Rhoads observes: "The religious rationale for Simon's social program may have come from Isaiah's call 'to bring good tidings to the poor . . . to proclaim liberty to the captives . . . to proclaim the year of the Lord's favor, and the day of vengeance of our God.' (Isaiah 61:1, 2). As such, the divine vengeance on the Roman enemy was to be accompanied by the freeing of slaves. If this was Simon's understanding he would have viewed himself in the messianic role of the liberator."[6]

One might ask whether Luke is contrasting Jesus with leaders like Simon bar Giora. The latter pursued strict and violent military discipline. He may have been seen within the tradition of the mighty warrior who was expected to wage holy war. However, Jesus seems to suggest that the Jubilee which he announces would benefit *both* Jews *and* Gentiles.

Isaiah 61 was used on the Day of Atonement and also to inaugurate the Jubilee year. There is some evidence that there was a sabbatical year about 26–27 C.E., that this particular year would be in the course of ten Jubilee periods and that, this being so, the apocalyptic hope with reference to Daniel 9:27 would be aroused. Strobel believes that in view of the dominant messianic week prophecy of Daniel 9:24ff., a failure to count up the Jubilee years would be highly unlikely.[7] The date of John the Baptist's ministry and the important sentence (Mk. 1:15) "the time is fulfilled" may point to a Jubilee year. Blosser concludes that Jesus commenced his public ministry "on a strong prophetic note."[8] Jesus announces a new age and he himself appears to be a prophet like Moses; both men proclaimed a new age and proclaimed Jubilee principles. Jesus has returned home just as every person is required to go to his own land in the Jubilee year. He conducted his ministry according to Jubilee principles. However, the fact that for Jesus the Jubilee year is shared by both Jews and Gentiles greatly angered the Nazareth synagogue congregation. Jesus' prophetic mission will not comprise urging and encouraging people to fight for religious freedom, like the leaders among the revolutionaries, but will be one of healing and forgiveness.

In this pericope Luke is able to foreshadow the major themes of Jesus' or his own theology, namely, Jesus speaks as an anointed prophet; his mission is directed to the poor and oppressed; his ministry is a healing and illuminating one not only on the physical level but on the psychological and spiritual dimension; he proclaims a year (time) of favor both for Jew and Gentile and he will repudiate hatred and vengeance. His ideology will be inimical to many of his contemporaries and will lead to continual rejection and, finally, a martyr's death. Thus the Nazareth pericope sets the stage for the public life of Jesus and prepares the reader for its unique character.

Although Luke 4:16–30 is an illustration of Jesus' ministry, it is also a dramatic portrayal of his rejection. Miyoshi finds a parallel between Jesus' rejection by the Samaritans and his rejection by his people at Nazareth.[9] The attitude of Jesus towards vengeance is similar in both passages, namely, a repudiation of it. The rejection at Nazareth is only the beginning of the rejection in all Judea. For Luke Jesus' opening words are those of forgiveness and healing, not wrath and destruction.

Luke 4:16–30 is the basis of Luke's entire Gospel and a prelude also to Acts, especially as regards the Gentile mission. Dillersberger, cited by Elias, states ". . . it is a stroke of genius on the part of St. Luke to put this event at the beginning, for it lets us see, as in a picture planned by a master, the whole revelation which Jesus made to men [sic] in this 'acceptable year of the Lord.' "[10]

For Luke, therefore, Jesus' ministry begins on a note of reconciliation vis-à-vis the enemy. He does not wholly espouse the theology of the role of Melchizedek but rather greatly modifies it.

TAX COLLECTORS IN PALESTINE

A second important insight into Luke's emphasis upon reconciliation is his attitude towards tax collectors, or, to be more precise, towards toll-collectors. These people, whether Jewish or pagan, were ostracized and hated by the Jews and would be regarded rather like a member of the mafia in contemporary society. They and their families and associates were not allowed to be witnesses in court and not permitted to give to the charity fund; a house into which they entered was declared unclean, and, of course, no orthodox Jew would dine in their homes because of infringement of the purity and dietary laws. Tax/toll/collectors were classed with thieves, extortioners, and murderers.

Although the Jews did not always resist taxation by a foreign government, taxation was a very vexed question among them. Tax relief was an important issue in the time of the Maccabees. Simon achieved tax exemption in 142 B.C.E. Bo Reicke comments: "For the first time since the fall of Jerusalem in 597 B.C., thanks to their exemption from taxes, the Jews in 142 B.C. constituted once more an independent state, although the great powers surrounding them could still exert pressure. A new period began, that of seventy-nine years of freedom under Hasmonean rule."[11]

This year began a new chronology (1 Macc. 13:42), and Simon issued coinage in Jerusalem with the new dates with Hebrew inscriptions. The Jews honored Simon for his deeds by making him high priest, general, and ethnarch for eternity. They engraved this on bronze tables upon Mt. Zion (1 Macc. 14:25–29). It was approved by the Roman senate (1 Macc. 15:15–24;

Josephus *Ant.* 14:145–148). A new dynasty had been established.

In view of these events the revolt of Judas the Galilean in 6 C.E. can be understood better. When Judaea became a province and, therefore, subject to taxation to Rome in 6 C.E. Judas revolted. Josephus states that he and his followers

> . . . said that the assessment carried with it a status amounting to downright slavery, no less, and appealed to the nation to make a bid for independence. They urged that in case of success the Jews would have laid the foundation of prosperity, while if they failed to obtain any such boon, they would win honor and renown for their lofty aim; and that Heaven would be their zealous helper to no lesser end than furthering of their enterprise . . . (*Ant.* 18:4–5).

In *B.J.* 2:118 Josephus describes Judas as follows:

> a Galilean, named Judas, incited his countrymen to revolt, upbraiding them as cowards for consenting to pay tribute, and tolerating mortal masters, after having God for their Lord. This man was a sophist who founded a sect of his own, having nothing in common with the others. . . .

This last statement is modified in *Ant.* 18:23, where Josephus says that this sect is a fourth philosophy and similar to the Pharisees. Kennard identifies this Judas with the one who seized the opportunity to aspire to kingship in Galilee (*B.J.* 2:56).[12] Josephus directly connects the revolt under Judas with taxation and the subsequent fall of Jerusalem in 70 C.E.

However, the revolt of Judas was not based on purely economic grounds. Firstly, taxation was seen as an infringement of the first commandment; tribute might be paid only to Yahweh as king, not to any earthly monarch. Secondly, taxation of Palestine was sacrilegious because the land belonged to Yahweh and the Jews themselves were only tenants. Thirdly, it was also sacrilegious to conduct a census. Only Yahweh had this prerogative and he would take a census in the last days. Judas' rebellion was due to the fact that living persons (not half shekels or Passover lambs) were counted in the census: it was equated with idolatry and aroused Messianic expectations. Fifthly, the taxation may have involved using foreign coins which bore pagan images and inscriptions which were offensive to the Jews. Sixthly, it has been suggested that one cause of the rebellion was a refusal on the part of Rome to recognize and give relief in the sabbatical years: these had been recognized in the days of Julius Caesar.

Seventhly, and lastly, Black remarks that, although Judas' rebellion was a single episode, two incidents throw light upon it: firstly, the capture of Hezekiah, the archbrigand, by Herod and, secondly, the smoking out of the brigands, also by Herod.[13] Dalman observes: ". . . in the Maccabean period these (caves of Rubela) were already places of refuge for the strict Jews who adhere faithfully to the Law. . . . In the year 38 B.C. the place was used, as Josephus put it, by 'robbers', whom Herod caused to be 'smoked out' . . . (and) who were certainly the remnant of the armies of the last Hasmonean prince, Antigonus. . . ."[14]

After the death of Herod, Judas seized the royal palace and the armory at Sepphoris in Galilee. Josephus says further that he aspired after royalty (*B.J.* 2:56): he could mean that the family of Hezekiah was a branch of the Hasmonean house. However, it is his rebellion against the census some years later which gave him a place in history. Farmer suggests that Judas might have been descended from the Maccabees and that this may account for his aspiration after royalty.[15]

If Black and Farmer are correct in their hypothesis, the descendants of Hezekiah carried on the resistance movement after Herod's conquest of Palestine and provided a "Hasmonean" opposition to the Herodian factor. If so, Judas, the Galilean, is an important link in the "dynastic" chain, and thus his rebellion is not only important as an anti-Roman demonstration but also as a Hasmonean, anti-Herodian one.

Yet the subject of taxation could have been a more inflammatory one among the Jews and Jewish Christians during the time Luke wrote his Gospel. After the fall of Jerusalem in 70 C.E., the half-shekel tax which every male Jew had paid yearly to the Temple was contributed to Rome and sent to the temple of Jupiter Capitolinus. This must have been a source of tremendous controversy among Jews and Jewish-Christians.

TAX COLLECTORS IN LUKE'S GOSPEL

In the light of these events and perhaps others similar to them, Luke's treatment of tax collectors is remarkably interesting. Mark refers only twice to tax collectors, one being the call of Levi. Matthew has nine references but, except for the call of Matthew, these are general statements. In Luke one finds singular and important narrative material about tax collectors.

Luke's references to tax collectors are carefully placed. Firstly, he reports that Joseph and Mary went down to register for the census (Luke 2:1-7). Thus Luke makes their conduct entirely different from that of Judas the Galilean and his followers. Secondly, Luke reports that John the Baptist gave special advice to tax collectors (Luke 3:12-13). He does not tell them to give up their occupation but merely to exact no more than that which was required. Not all Jews received converted tax collectors back into the community because it was so difficult for them to make adequate restitution to those whom they had wronged.

Thirdly, the calling of Levi in Luke is more elaborate than in Mark or Matthew. Luke appears to suggest that Jesus deliberately sought out Levi. Both Mark and Matthew say that Jesus was passing by (*paragōn*) but Luke omits this and uses *theaomai* instead of *eiden*. Luke's is a stronger verb (cf.

23:55 and three times in Acts). Whereas Mark and Matthew merely say that Matthew (Levi) arose and followed Jesus, Luke says that Levi left everything and rose up and followed. One may compare the conditions for discipleship in Luke 9:57–62.

In Mark and Matthew it is not clear who was the host of the meal, Jesus or Levi, but in Luke it is expressly said that Levi gave the banquet. Among even orthodox Jews one could dine with Gentiles in one's own home because the purity laws would be observed. Dining in the house of a sinner was an entirely different matter. One could not be certain that the ingredients of the meal had been tithed, the meat killed according to the purity laws, dishes for meat and dairy produce kept separate, and the persons who prepared the meal in a state of purity.

The meal with the tax collectors is described as a great banquet (*dochē megalē*). The great feast must be of religious significance, for every meal was so with a Jew. *Dochē* is used for a banquet in Genesis 21:8 (Isaac's weaning party), Genesis 26:30 (the covenant meal between Abimelech and Isaac), Daniel 5:1 (King Balshazzar's feast for a thousand of his lords), and Luke 14:7–14 (the parable about the seats at a feast).

Luke has also changed Mark and Matthew's "many" to a "large crowd of tax collectors and others." One notes that he replaces "sinners" with "others." It is interesting to speculate who these "others" might have been. As Mark and Matthew describe them as "sinners," they may be people in despised trades who were regarded as "sinners" by strict Jews. Jeremias gives lists of suspected or despised occupations which would ostracize those who practiced them and deprive them of civic and religious privileges.[16] They include: ass-drivers, camel-drivers, sailors, carters, herdsmen, shopkeepers, physicians, and butchers (*Kidd.* 4:14); dung collectors, copper-smelters, and tanners (*Ket.* 7:10); goldsmiths, flaxcombers, pedlars, weavers, barbers, launderers, blood-letters, bath-attendants (*Kidd.* 82a); and finally, gamblers, usurers, pigeon trainers, dealers in the produce of the sabbatical year, tax collectors, and publicans (*Sanh.* 25b). It is easy to understand that many belonging to these trades would be associated with a commercial center or travelling posts like Capernaum, where Levi had been taking tolls. Thus Jesus' fellow guests may have comprised a motley crowd. They would be the type of people with whom toll collectors came into frequent contact.

If these people were gathered around Jesus, then one can conjecture the enormous offense Jesus caused contemporary Jews. As Donahue observes, Jesus' fellowship with toll collectors could be interpreted as fellowship with virtual traitors.[17] Both this and the rebellion over taxation in 6 C.E. might well have been very important contributions to the hatred of Jesus which eventually led to his crucifixion.

Ellis may be right when he says that the feast may be a farewell dinner for Levi's colleagues.[18] On the other hand, it may have been an initiation feast for those colleagues to bring them into a close and formal relationship with Jesus' disciples, almost a covenant meal.

Levi's meal for Jesus is the first meal of many in Luke's Gospel. The Lukan meals have significant theological meaning. They comprise: the meal where the sinful woman enters (Luke 7:36–49); the feeding of the five thousand (9:10–17); Mary and Martha (10:38–42); denunciation of the Pharisees (11:37–54); seats at a banquet and the parable of the Great Supper (14:1–24); Zacchaeus (19:1–10); the passover (22:4–38); and the Emmaus meal (24:29–43). Thus all of them have their own contribution to make to Lukan theology and are of religious, social and political importance in view of the revolutionaries' and Qumran's separation from "perverse people."

Jesus began his ministry by dining wtih the dregs of society and thereby forming a brotherhood and sisterhood with them.

Fourthly, in Luke 15:1–7 the parable of the Lost Sheep is spoken in favor of tax collectors and sinners who drew near to hear Jesus (v. 1). Luke strengthens his point by adding two parables from his own material, namely, the Lost Coin and Prodigal Son.

Fifthly, in Luke 18:9–14 Luke tells the parable of the Pharisee and the tax collector. This comes as part of Luke's answer to the question "Who will be found faithful when the Son of Man comes?" It is a good example of his teaching concerning the qualifications for entering the kingdom and is an extension of his teaching on discipleship. It is a striking instance of faith and humility triumphing over legalism and piety. It stands as the climax of the journey section, the non-Markan section of Luke's Gospel. In the parable God justifies the publican, not the Pharisee. As Jeremias states: "Such a conclusion must have utterly overwhelmed its hearers. It was beyond the capacity of any of them to imagine. What fault had the Pharisee committed, and what had the publican done by way of reparation?"[19] The tax collector is like the repentant psalmist in Psalm 51, and God is the God of those in despair as in the same psalm.

Sixthly, in Luke 19:1–10 Luke relates the story of the conversion of the chief tax collector, Zacchaeus. It is the last story in the pre-Jerusalem ministry of Jesus. W. P. Loewe finds that this pericope condenses much that is peculiarly Lukan in the rest of the Gospel.[20] He singles out the vocabulary: "tax collectors" who appear in contrast to the self-righteous; the rich, who are indifferent to the poor; the theme of "seeking" (cf. 11:9,10; 12:31; 11:30; 9:9); of "seeing" (cf. 2:12, 29, 30; 3:6; 9:9; 19:3; 23:8); "today" (cf. 2:11; 23:43); *dei* (it is necessary) (2:49; 4:43; 9:22; 13:33; 17:25; 22:37; 24:7, 25–27, 44); son of Abraham (1:55, 73; 3:8–9); and the mission of the Son of Man to save what is lost.

Loewe finds the Zacchaeus pericope to be strategically placed, for it is associated with the healing of the blind man at Jericho, which Luke has moved so that it occurs as Jesus comes towards the city, not when he leaves it. Both the healing of the blind man and the conversion of Zacchaeus answer the question posed in 18:8, "But when the Son of Man comes, will he find any faith on earth?"

The Zacchaeus incident also brings the theme of toll collectors to a climax.

Jericho itself is a significant city for the conversion, for here tolls would be collected on goods coming to Judaea from Perea, and travellers to Jerusalem, Bethel, and the North could hardly avoid it. Zacchaeus was probably the head of a large group of toll collectors; as such his conduct would be highly influential.

He gave half his possessions to the poor, whereas the Rabbis advised that one-fifth was sufficient. He was also prepared to pay anyone whom he had deceived fourfold. This was the penalty imposed on robbers. Normally a collector, who confiscated anything wrongfully, was obliged to restore only double the value of the goods. Even if force were used only a threefold restitution was required. Zacchaeus, therefore, was going far beyond the demands of the law or duty.

So the Zacchaeus pericope forms a grand finale to the theme of tax collectors in Luke's Gospel, and Zacchaeus' hospitality is Jesus' last recorded meal before the Passover. It forms a magnificent prelude to Jesus' triumphal entry into Jerusalem.

Luke, by making his toll collectors both so prominent and so attractive, seeks to allay resentment, agitation, and rebellion over the question of taxes on the part of the first-century Jews and perhaps converts in his own church.

In view of the hatred of taxation and tax agents, particularly exemplified by Judas the Galilean and illustrated plentifully by the New Testament, it was a bold stroke for Luke to show a kindly disposition towards them and for Jesus to accept one among the twelve (and perhaps many among his disciples). It would be tantamount to declaring that Judas' revolt was not legitimate.

THE SAMARITANS

In Matthew 10:5f. Jesus charges the disciples, who are setting out on their first mission: "Go nowhere among the Gentiles, and enter no town of the Samaritans, but go rather to the lost sheep of the house of Israel. . . ."

Luke not only omits this statement, which may show racial prejudice, but he includes special material about Samaritans: Luke 9:51–56, Jesus refused hospitality by the Samaritans; Luke 10:29–37, the Good Samaritan; and Luke 17:11–19, the Samaritan leper. Finally, he recounts the conversion of the Samaritans by Philip the evangelist and their reception of the Holy Spirit through the imposition of hands by Peter and John from Jerusalem (Acts 8).

The above pericopes cannot be understood without a brief survey of the history of the hostilities between Jews and Samaritans throughout Jewish history but more particularly in the first century C.E., so that one realizes the provocative step Luke was taking in including this material.

The breach caused by the conquest of the Northern Kingdom by Assyria in the eighth century B.C.E. and the immigration of foreigners into the area with the consequent intermarriage and introduction of idolatry is well known. Equally well discussed is the conflict between the Jews and the Samaritans over the rebuilding of the Temple after the exile in the sixth century B.C.É. However, less frequently mentioned are the following conflicts.

Josephus reports that in the time of Alexander the Great the Samaritans, whose chief city was Shechem, courted his favor and asked for relief from tribute during the seventh year. Josephus remarks:

> For such is the nature of the Samaritans, as we have already shown somewhere above (*Ant.* 9:291 and note). When the Jews are in difficulties, they deny that they have any kinship with them thereby indeed admitting the truth, but whenever they see some splendid bit of good fortune with them, they suddenly grasp at the connexion with them, saying that they are related to them and tracing their line back to Ephraim and Manasseh, the descendants of Joseph.

Ant. 11:322–324 records the building of the temple for the Samaritans on Mt. Gerizim, a rival temple to the one in Jerusalem which would also divide the nation (*Ant.* 11:323). This was also in the time of Alexander.

When the Jews were suffering under the cruel persecution of Antiochus Epiphanes in 175 B.C.E. (1 Macc. 1:44), Josephus reports:

> . . . they [the Samaritans] would no longer admit that they were their kin or that the temple of Garizein [Gerizim] was that of the Most Great God, thereby acting in accordance with their nature, as we have shown (*Ant.* 9:291); they also said they were colonists from the Medes and the Persians, and they are, in fact, colonists from these peoples [*Ant.* 12:257–264].

They sent a letter to Antiochus stating that they were not Jews and asking him that their temple should be known as that of Zeus Hellenios. Antiochus granted their request.

Matters were not improved in the days of the Maccabees. Apollonius, the governor of Samaria, took his soldiers and set out against Judas Maccabeus. But Judas defeated him in battle (1 Macc. 3:10; cf. *Ant.* 12:287).

The vital break between the Samaritans and the Jews came in 129 B.C.E. John Hyrcanus marched against Samaria, attacked and besieged it vigorously "because of the injuries which, in obedience to the kings of Syria, they had done to the people of Marisa, who were colonists and allies of the Jews. . . ." Hyrcanus captured the city of Samaria after besieging it for a year "but not content with that alone, he effaced it entirely and left it to be swept away by the mountain-torrents, for he dug beneath it until it fell into the beds of the torrents, and so removed all signs of its ever having been a city" (*Ant.* 13:280). The temple was destroyed.

In Roman times Pompey rebuilt several cities, including Samaria (*Ant.* 14:75). Indeed, Josephus lists Samaria as one of the towns liberated by Pompey from the rule of the Jews (*B.J.* 1:156). Colonists gladly flocked to this city (*B.J.* 1:166). Samaria declared itself in favor of Herod the Great and sent supplies of corn, wine, oil, and cattle to him (*B.J.* 1:299). In 37 B.C.E., three years after he had been proclaimed king in Rome, Herod besieged Jerusalem. He added insult to injury "leaving his most efficient lieutenants to superintend these works, he went off himself to Samaria to fetch the daughter of Alexander, son of Aristobolus, who . . . was betrothed to him. Thus so contemptuous was he already of the enemy, he made his wedding an interlude to the siege" (*B.J.* 1:342–344). Later Herod founded Sebaste in Samaria and also built a temple to Caesar. He considered making a third rampart against the entire nation out of Samaria. He fortified it and brought settlers there (*Ant.* 15:296–8). Thus Samaria was placed in a position of antagonism vis-à-vis the anti-Herodian Jews.

When Varus quelled disturbances in Palestine, he spared the city of Samaria because it had taken no part in the general tumult (*B.J.* 2:66–71). This was another sign that Samaria was pro-Roman.

However, two further incidents in the first century aggravated Jewish-Samaritan relationships. In the procuratorship of Coponius (6–9 C.E.) the Samaritans secretly joined the Jewish Passover pilgrims in the Temple and committed an egregious sacrilege. They placed human bones in the porticoes and in the sanctuary and defiled the whole Temple. Josephus remarks that the priests excluded everyone from the Temple, an action which was quite unprecedented (*Ant.* 18:29–30).

The second incident was even more volatile and most probably one of the major causes of the Jewish-Roman war (66–74 C.E.). In *B.J.* 2:232–235 Josephus reports that during the time of the Roman governor Cumanus (48–52 C.E.) at a village called Gema, which was situated in the great plain of Samaria on the borders between Galilee and Samaria, the Samaritans of the village murdered one of a large company of Jews on their way to Jerusalem for the festival of the Passover. Enraged by this incident a great crowd of Galileans assembled intending to make war on the Samaritans. The Jewish authorities, however, tried to negotiate with Cumanus and beseeched him to punish the murderers in order to avoid the fighting. Cumanus, however, belittling their cause, dismissed the leaders. When intelligence of the murder reached Jerusalem, the masses abandoned the Passover feast and hurried to Samaria without any generals in command and without listening to the magistrates. They chose as their leaders Eleazar, a "bandit," and Alexander. The Jewish crowds massacred the inhabitants of Ginae (Gema) without distinction of age and burnt down their village.

Cumanus, taking with him a troop of cavalry known as Sebastians from Caesarea, went to avenge the Samaritans. He imprisoned many of Eleazar's followers and also slaughtered a considerable number. The magistrates of Jerusalem, still hoping to avert war, hastened to the Jewish insurgents and, dressed in sackcloth and with ashes upon their heads, implored them to return home and not to bring down "the wrath of the Romans on Jerusalem, but take pity on their country and sanctuary, on their own wives and children; [for] all these were threatened with destruction merely for the object of avenging the blood of a single Galilean." If Josephus be correct, it is very important to note that the Jewish leaders predicted dire consequences if the masses continued their fight. Eventually Quadratus, the governor of Syria, came to the rescue and after considerable difficulty the Jews were exonerated and the emperor condemned the Samaritans and ordered three of the most prominent men to be executed. Cumanus was banished.

Josephus gives another account of this event in *Ant.* 20:118–136 in which he elaborates some details, e.g., that a number of Galileans (not one) were slain and that Cumanus was bribed by the Samaritans. The controversy lasted a whole year from one Passover to the next, and Rhoads rightly observes: ". . . this incident, which took place around 51 C.E., was a turning point in Jewish relationship to Rome, for the assertion of liberty and the direct clash with Roman soldiers in Judea stirred up all the dissatisfied elements throughout the countryside."

In the light of these continual and bitter conflicts between the Samaritans and the Jews it is understandable that only Luke and John speak in favor of the Samaritans. The Lukan communities could also be affected by the last two events mentioned.

LUKE'S INTRODUCTION OF THE SAMARITANS

The Samaritans are introduced at a key point in Luke's narrative, namely, Luke 9:51f., when Luke leaves his Markan source and begins the long section of the Travel Narrative when Jesus goes from Galilee to Jerusalem. There is the solemn announcement of his *analēmpsis*, that is, his going up to Jerusalem, his being raised up on the cross, and his being exulted in glory.

Of prime importance is the fact that our pericope, which is peculiar to Luke, records Jesus' attitude towards the inhospitable Samaritans. One notes that he is accompanied by James and John, the "sons of thunder" or "sons of rage," who may be described as religious zealots. When the Samaritans refuse Jesus, these "zealots" innocently ask the Lord whether they are to bid fire to come down from heaven and to consume them. Some ancient authorities add "as Elijah did." Obviously the disciples are still thinking of Jesus in the character of Elijah, who called down fire three times upon the Samaritans (2 Kings 1:9–16). According to the best manuscripts Jesus merely turned and rebuked them but some ancient manuscripts add: "And he said, 'You do not know what manner of spirit you are of; for the Son of Man came not to destroy men's lives but to save them.'"

Flender argues that this rejection of the spirit of Elijah also contains a rejection of the political messiahship which accompanied the concept of Elijah *redivivus*.[21] Further, he observes that, by introducing the heavenly exaltation (*analēmpsis*), Luke removes the political associations in the tradition which he is using. Jesus' destination is still Jerusalem, but he will receive a heavenly exaltation, not an earthly kingdom.

So the solemn journey to Jerusalem begins with an explicit and active denial of the *lex talionis* (Exod. 21:23–25). The supercession or reversal of the *lex talionis* will be elaborated in Jesus' teaching, especially in the parables during this journey. His own death according to Luke is also a dramatic reversal of the *lex talionis* (*vide infra*). The verses about the Samaritans are significant because they show the spirit in which Jesus deals with hostility, they foreshadow his passion, especially the Lukan passion, and portray an open rejection of the spirit of the zealous actions of Elijah. The opposition of the Samaritans is typical, and Jesus' response and the material in 10:30–37 and 17:11–19 are, on the whole, atypical of the average response of Jesus' Jewish contemporaries toward the Samaritans. More especially the whole pericope is a challenge to the Lukan church who may well have had vivid reminiscences of the incident at Ginae, the governorship of Cumanus and the year long struggle with the Samaritans. After Quadratus had controlled the conflict between the Samaritans and the Jews he went to Antioch (*B.J.* 2:224). Luke was probably in communication with the Christians at Antioch and may have been informed accurately about Cumanus' actions. Thus Jesus in Luke 9:51–56 forms a vivid contrast to the action of the Jewish masses over the incident at Ginae.

THE GOOD SAMARITAN (LUKE 10:25–37)

Enslin sees the Samaritan mission as the beginning of the Gentile mission and part of the divine plan.[22] It may be "intended as deliberate and conscious answer to Matt. 10:5." It is a prelude to the mission of the seventy which is also in the Central Section and which is a "deliberative counterfoil to the sending of the Twelve in Galilee."

The pericope of the Good Samaritan appears to be Luke's redaction of the question of the lawyer found in Mark 12:28–34 and Matthew 22:23–40. The story of the Good Samaritan is not said to be a parable and, indeed, it may relate a real incident or be representative of similar incidents which did occur on that road (cf. *B.J.* 4:475 and Strabo 16.2:41).

Sellin thinks that the story should be considered from an ethnological point of view, not an ethical or Christological one.[23] He believes that Luke 10:25–37 is a completely Lukan composition.[24] The vocabulary and style are Lukan although some phrases come from the LXX.

G.V. Jones states: "The parable is not a pleasant tale about the Traveller who did his good deed: it is a damning indictment of social, racial and religious superiority."[25]

Thus Luke's narrative of the Good Samaritan marks a significant, highly provocative, and novel step in the mission of Jesus. Luke's teaching, which commands a new attitude towards the Samaritans, must have been a progressive step which the early Christians found difficult to embrace. In the light of the defiling of the Temple and the Cumanus' incident preceding the war the narrative dramatically illustrates Jesus' command to love one's enemies and to do good to them. Indeed, the whole story illustrates Jesus' teaching in the Sermon on the Plain (Luke 6:27–49).

THE SAMARITAN LEPER (LUKE 17:11–19)

Luke records another incident which occurred as Jesus was traveling to Jerusalem between Samaria and Galilee. It is the curing of the ten lepers, one of whom was a Samaritan. If Luke has redacted—or if one compare—the healing of the leper reported in Matthew 8:1–4 and Mark 1:40–45 (cf. Luke 5:12–16), then his addition of the Samaritan is very striking.

In the texts relating the cure of one leper Jesus bids the patient to report to the priests and also to offer the prescribed sacrifice which, presumably, would take place in the Temple. In Luke 17:11–19 there is no mention of the sacrifice. One may ask whether this was out of courtesy and sympathy for the one Samaritan. His temple had been brutally destroyed by a Jew, John Hyrcanus, in 129 B.C.E. Therefore, he could not offer sacrifice, although he could show himself to priests. His nine companions go to Jerusalem to Herod's temple. The Samaritan returns to give thanks vis-à-vis the new temple, namely, Jesus. This pericope, therefore, shows some affinity to John 4 (the only other pro-Samaritan text in another canonical Gospel). On that occasion Jesus declares:

> But the hour is coming, and now is, when the true worshippers will worship the Father in spirit and truth, for such the Father seeks to worship him [John 4:23].

For Luke, the grateful Samaritan leper is one of these true worshippers.

THE CONVERSION OF THE SAMARITANS IN ACTS

Luke brings his Samaritan theology to a close in Acts 8 where he shows the conversion of the Samaritans and their reception of the Holy Spirit through the Jerusalem apostles. The unique aspect of this text is that the Holy Spirit is not given with the reception of baptism. It is perhaps best to explain this in the words of F. E. Bruner:[26]

> It was evidently not the divine plan, according to Luke's understanding, that the first church outside Jerusalem should arise entirely without apostolic contact. . . . The Samaritans were not left to become an isolated sect with no bonds of union with the apostolic church in Jerusalem. If a Samaritan church and a Jewish church had arisen indepen-

dently, side by side, without the dramatic removal of the ancient and bitter barriers of prejudice between the two, particularly at the level of ultimate authority, the young church of God would have been in schism from the very inception of its mission.

THE WAY TO THE CROSS (LUKE 23:26–32)

Matthew and Mark devote only one verse to the way to Golgotha. Luke has six. Luke makes an important change with reference to Simon of Cyrene. In Mark 15:21 and Matthew 27:32 he is forced into service (*aggareuō*), but Luke uses *epilambanomai* (catch, take hold of). Luke avoids the provocative reference to pressing into service. As a result Simon appears as a concrete example of a disciple taking up his cross and following Jesus. The technical word "follow" for discipleship is employed of the great crowd of people who accompany Jesus. Thus in Luke the people are not only relieved of the guilt of condemning Jesus but they accompany him to the cross as disciples. The wailing women are especially pointed out. These take the place of the mockers in Mark and Matthew.

This scene of the wailing women brings to a climax Luke's theology of the people. In contrast to the chief priests and leaders they do not condemn Jesus but rather remain faithful to him in his final trial. Manson says that they raise "the death-wail over Him in anticipation."[27] Jesus replies with a similar dirge. This is Luke's third lamentation over Jerusalem (Luke 13:34–35; 19:41–44; and 23:28–31; cf. 11:49–51 and 21:41–44).

When Jesus speaks to the wailing women he means if you knew what was to happen to Jerusalem you would wail for yourself rather than for me. Jesus uses the formula of prophetic oracles in the Old Testament. Jesus' words to the wailing women reflect Hosea 10:7–8, which are spoken about Samaria. This is a bold stroke. Luke, or Jesus, takes a text which originally condemned Samaria and uses it as a prophetic warning against Jerusalem. This would have been a scandal to contemporary Jews.

Jesus speaks of the childless being blessed. This may be seen in light of traditions reflected in the text of *B.B.* 60b where one finds the Rabbis discussing the appropriateness of sexual abstinence and refraining from begetting of children in view of catastrophes overcoming Jerusalem. This asceticism, unusual for Jews, might have influenced Luke but could hardly influence Jesus.

Thus in the beginning of the Lukan passion Jesus' disposition is entirely different from the revolutionaries who hoped for the divine deliverance of Jerusalem even as the Romans entered the city (*B.J.* 6:73; cf. 98). Towards the end they averred ". . . it [the Temple] would yet be saved by him who dwelt therein and while they had Him for their ally they would deride all menaces unsupported by action; for the issue rested with God" (*B.J.* 5:459).

THE CRUCIFIXION (LUKE 23:32-43)

The first important difference in the scene of the crucifixion in Luke is the report that Jesus was crucified between two "evildoers" (*kakourgoi*), not, as in Mark and Matthew, two "robbers" or "revolutionaries." The Greek of Mark and Matthew is *lēstai*, the very word which Josephus uses so very frequently for the social bandits and/or revolutionaries. At this supreme moment of the Master's death Luke does not want to associate him with revolutionaries. However, perhaps there is a deeper meaning; not only does Luke avoid revolutionaries but "evildoers" could comprise the classes of "sinful" people with whom Jesus had identified himself from the very beginning of his ministry, tax and toll collectors, traders, merchants, usurers, gamblers, adulterers, etc. Thus Jesus died in the company of those to whom he had had a special ministry.

Further, Jesus is portrayed as praying for the forgiveness of his enemies, once again implementing his own teaching in the Sermon on the Mount and the Sermon on the Plain and reversing the *lex talionis*. One notes, however, that some early and important manuscripts and versions omit this verse (v. 34). Metzger believes that the omission cannot be explained as a deliberate deletion from the original text by those who thought that the fall of Jerusalem showed that Jesus' prayer had not been answered.[28] He concludes that, although the logion probably was not part of the original Gospel, it "bears self-evident tokens of its dominical origin. . . ."

Daube has, perhaps, given the best interpretation of this verse, which is so characteristic of the Gospel and Acts written by Luke.[29] Daube notes that Harnack thought that the prayer was offered on behalf of the Romans, but that later it was misinterpreted as a prayer for the Jews.

An obvious parallel is the first part of Stephen's prayer in Acts 7:60, but the second part of Jesus' oration finds no echo in Stephen's prayer. Nevertheless, it is very Lukan. The evangelist is interested in the relationship between sin and ignorance, continues Daube. The theme occurs five times in Acts (3:17; 13:27; 14:16; 17:30; 26:9). It can also be compared to Luke 12:47f., where the servant, who did not know the master's will, received fewer stripes.

Daube argues that the prayer for forgiveness could be offered also for the Jews, for in vv. 28ff. Jesus points to the "fearful consequences which even those among the crowd who weep cannot foresee, and where the verb 'do' is used of the conduct of Jesus' adversaries 'for it they do these things in a green tree. . . .' "[30] Further, ignorance or unwitting sin of the Jews is emphasized in Acts. Both in Jewish and Gentile sources there are precedents for forgiving unwitting sin.[31] Unwitting sin is contrasted with "sin committed with a high hand" in the Old Testament (Numb. 15:9; Deut. 17:12; cf. *P. Sheb.* 33a and *Bab. Yoma* 36b). In Leviticus 16:21 there is a discussion of three types of sin, sin through presumption, sin through rebellion, and sin through ignorance.

B.B. 60b says: "It is better that the Israelites should transgress in ignorance than wilfully." *Makk.* 2:5 and 10b speak of the difference between murder and homicide. The sinner who does not know the Torah is less culpable.[32] *B.M.* 33b states "a student's unwitting sin counts as intentional, an ignoramus' intentional sin counts as unwitting: the latter is not informed."

However, the theology of unwitting sin is understood clearly from the Day of Atonement. On this day Numbers 15:26 is used: "And it shall be forgiven all the congregation of the children of Israel and the foreigner who sojourns among them, seeing that all the people were in ignorance." In fact this sentence was taken out of its context and placed at the beginning of the twenty-four hour service for the Day of Atonement.[33] It seems to have been inserted into the liturgy of the Middle Ages but it can be traced back to Eleazar the Great (first century) who thought that this sentence also covered presumptuous sin.

Yoma 36b also refers to forgiving iniquity with reference to Exod. 34:7, God's compassion after Israel's sin over the Golden Calf. Daube observes: "It is noteworthy that the topic of this Baraitha is the High Priest's confession of sins on behalf of Israel on the Day of Atonement."[34] One may compare also the high priest in Hebrews who has compassion on the weak and ignorant (Heb. 5:2). Daube states: "Considering a doctrine like that of Eleazar the Great and an intercession like that of Moses for his backsliding people, . . . it would be unreasonable to deny the possibility of Luke 23:34 being a prayer for the Jews and having a thoroughly Jewish background."

Yoma 36b distinguishes between "wrongs" and "deliberate misdeeds"; "transgressions" as "rebellious deeds" and "sins" as "inadvertent omissions." Thus the high priest on the Day of Atonement prays, "I have sinned, I have done wrong, I have transgressed before Thee, I and my house," etc. In this way he covers all sin, witting and unwitting.

Daube also adds that from a baraitha we are virtually certain that Jonah was used as an afternoon reading on the Day of Atonement.[35] This is appropriate for the book ends thus: "And should I not spare Nineveh that great city wherein are more than six score thousand persons that do not know their right hand from their left hand, and also much cattle?" The Ninevites were Gentiles who had not heard of Yahweh. Thus Daube shows that Luke 23:24, Acts 3:17 and 13:27, and James' prayer in Hegesippus are consonant with a Jewish environment for Jesus' prayer as he was fastened to the cross is like that of the high priest on the Day of Atonement.[36]

The present writer, however, would add one point to Daube's thesis. If scholars who argue that Jesus' homily at Nazareth (Luke 4) inaugurated a Jubilee Year, are correct, that Jubilee Year, eschatological or not, would commence on the Day of Atonement. Jesus' ministry is one of atonement for religious and social outcasts. It is, therefore, fitting that Luke should portray Jesus on the cross as the new high priest on a new Day of Atonement who intercedes at his own most traumatic hour for all sinners.

The climax of the crucifixion according to Luke is the part played by the two evildoers and by Jesus in relationship to them. Only Luke records the words of the repentant criminal and Jesus' response. From the beginning of the crucifixion scene Luke has emphasized the criminals. They do not mock Jesus, as in Matthew and Mark. Their dialogue with Jesus is given considerable space. Luke alone recounts the words of the criminal who defended Jesus against the taunt of the other one and his appeal to Jesus to remember him when he comes into his kingdom and Jesus' reply that "today" he will be with him in paradise. Obviously Luke believes in the efficacy of a martyr's intercession.

This pericope is the climax of Jesus' ministry with "tax collectors" and "others," the climax of his ministry of forgiveness and reconciliation. With the word "today," Jesus indicates that the new time of salvation which was predicted on the occasion of the birth of the Savior (2:11) and proclaimed at the commencement of his ministry (4:21, cf. 5:26) has now been fully implemented.

NOTES

1. One notes how relatively late this occurs in Matthew and Mark.

2. For a full discussion of the text see Fred H. Horton, *The Melchizedek Tradition* (Cambridge University Press, 1976).

3. B. Violet, "Zum rechten Verständnis der Nazareth-Perikope," *ZNW* 37 (1938): 251–271.

4. J. Jeremias, *Jesus' Promise to the Nations* (London: SCM Press, 1958), pp. 44ff.

5. L. Crockett, *The Old Testament in the Gospel of Luke: With Emphasis on the Interpretation* (Ann Arbor: University Microfilms, 1966), pp. 138, 283, 294–99, 320.

6. David M. Rhoads, *Israel in Revolt 6-74 C.E.* (Philadelphia: Fortress Press, 1976), p. 142. He cites C. Roth, "Simon bar Giora, Ancient Jewish Hero," *Commentary* 29 (1960): 54–55.

7. A. Strobel, "Die Ausrufung des Yobel jahres in der Nazareth-predigt Jesus: zur apocalyptischen Tradition, Lc. 4:16–30," in W. Eltester, ed., *Jesus in Nazareth* (Berlin: De Gruyter, 1972), p. 44.

8. D. W. Blosser, "Jesus and Jubilee, Luke 4:16–30," Ph.D. diss. (St. Andrews University, Scotland, 1979), see especially pp. 105–113, 114–117, and 254–273.

9. M. Miyoshi, *Der Anfang des Reiseberichts, Lk. 9:51–10:14* (Rome: Biblical Institute Press, 1964), p. 18.

10. J. W. Elias, "The Beginning of Jesus Ministry in the Gospel of Luke: A Redaction-Critical Study of Luke 4:14–30", Th.D. diss. (Toronto School of Theology, 1978).

11. Bo Reiche, *The New Testament Era* (Philadelphia: Fortress Press, 1968), p. 62.

12. J. S. Kennard, "Judas of Galilee and his Clan," *JQR* 36 (1945): 281–286.

13. M. Black, "Judas the Galilean and Josephus' Fourth Philosophy," *Josephus Studien*, ed. O. Betz, K. Haacker, and M. Hengel (Göttingen: Vanderhoech und Ruprecht, 1974), pp. 45–47.

14. G. H. Dalman, *Sacred Sites and Ways* (London: S.P.C.K., 1935), p. 119, cited by Black, pp. 46–47.

15. W. R. Farmer, "Judas, Silas and Athronges," *NTS* (1958): 151.

16. J. Jeremias, *Jerusalem in the Time of Jesus* (London: SCM Press, 1969), p. 304, cf. also J. Jeremias, "Zollner und Sunder," *ZNW* (1931): 293–300.

17. John R. Donahue, "Tax Collectors and Sinners," *CBQ* 33 (1971): 57.

18. E.E. Ellis, *The Gospel of Luke* (London: Oliphantes, 1974), p. 107.

19. J. Jeremias, *The Parables of Jesus* (London: SCM Press, 1963), p. 144.

20. W. P. Loewe, "Towards the Interpretation of Lk 19:1–10," *CBQ* 36 (1974): 321–331.

21. H. Flender, *St. Luke Theologian of Redemptive History* (London: S.P.C.K., 1967), p. 34.

22. M. Enslin, "Luke and the Samaritans," *HTR* 36 (1943): 281.

23. G. Sellin, "Lukas als Gleichniserzahler: Die Erzahlung vom barmherzigen Samariter (Luke 10:25–37)," *ZNW* 66 (1975): 37–38.

24. Ibid., p. 31.

25. G. V. Jones, *The Art and Truth of Parables* (London: S.P.C.K., 1964), p. 115.

26. F. D. Bruner, *A Theology of the Holy Spirit* (Grand Rapids: Eerdmans, 1970), p. 176.

27. T. W. Manson, *The Sayings of Jesus* (London: SCM Press, 1949), p. 343.

28. B. M. Metzger, *A Textual Commentary on the Greek New Testament* (London: United Bible Societies, 1971), p. 180.

29. D. Daube, "For They Know Not What They Do," *Texte und Untersuchungen (Studia Patristica)* 79 (1961):58–70.

30. Ibid., p. 59.

31. Ibid., p. 61.

32. Ibid., p. 62.

33. Ibid., p. 65.

34. Ibid., p. 67.

35. Ibid., pp. 67–68.

36. Ibid., p. 69.

7

Martyrdom in Luke-Acts and the Lukan Social Ethic

CHARLES H. TALBERT

In Luke-Acts the deaths of Jesus and Stephen are portrayed as martyrdoms.[1] When we focus on the Lukan Jesus' death, two things need to be said. On the one hand, in contrast to other New Testament witnesses like Paul (e.g., 1 Cor. 15:3; 2 Cor. 5:21; Rom. 3:25) and Matthew (e.g., 26:28), Luke avoids any connection between Jesus' death and the forgiveness of sins.[2] In the speeches of Acts, both Peter (Acts 2:38; 3:19; 5:31; 10:43) and Paul (Acts 13:38; 17:30; 26:18) preach the forgiveness of sins as the risen Christ directed (Luke 24:47). Yet neither combines the forgiveness of sins with the death of Jesus on the cross. In contrast to Mark 10:45 ("For the Son of man also came . . . to give his life as a ransom for many"), Luke 22:27b ("I am among you as one who serves") avoids any mention of an atoning death. In Luke 22:37 (Isa. 53:12) and Acts 8:32–33 (Isa. 53:7–8), although Isaiah 53 is quoted, there is no mention of the sacrificial death of the servant. In Luke-Acts, neither baptism (Acts 2:38, 41; 8:12, 13, 16; 8:37–39; 9:18; 10:47–48; 16:15; 19:5; 22:16) nor the Lord's Supper (Luke 22:16–20; 24:30ff.; 24:41ff.; Acts 2:42–46; 20:7, 11; 27:35) is connected with Jesus' death (contrast Rom. 6:3ff. and 1 Cor. 11:23ff.). In Luke-Acts forgiveness of sins flows from the earthly Jesus, especially at mealtime (Luke 5:29–32; 15:1ff.; 19:7f.), and after the resurrection from the exalted Lord (Acts 2:38; 4:11; 5:31—"God exalted him at his right hand as leader and savior, to give repentance to Israel and forgiveness of sins").[3]

On the other hand, Luke portrays the death of Jesus as a martyrdom, the unjust murder of an innocent man by the established powers due to the pressure of the Jewish leaders. Jesus is innocent of the charges against him (Luke 23:4, 14, 15, 22, 41, 47). He is delivered up by the Jewish chief priests and scribes (Luke 22:66 and 23:1–2; 23:13 and 18, 21, 23, 24; cf. Acts 5:27, 30; 13:27) and executed by Gentiles (Luke 23:24; Acts 4:27). His death is parallel to the sufferings of the prophets of old at the hands of the Jews (Luke 13:33; Acts 7:52—"which of the prophets did not your fathers persecute? And they killed those who announced beforehand the coming of the Righteous One, whom you have now betrayed and murdered"). So Jesus stands at the end of a long line of martyrs. Like the martyrs in 2 Maccabees 7:2, 11 and 4 Maccabees 6:1 and 10:23, Jesus is silent before his accusers (Luke 23:9). As in the martyrdom of Isaiah, Jesus' martyrdom is due to the Devil (Luke 23:3, 53). As in the case of the martyrs slain by Herod (Josephus, *Ant.*, 17:6: 2–4§149–67), there is an eclipse at Jesus' death (Luke 23:45). His demeanor in martyrdom leads to the conversion of one of the thieves crucified with him (Luke 23:40–43). Jesus' death as a martyr is a fulfillment of Old Testament prophecies (Luke 24:25–27, 46; Acts 13:27–29), a part of God's plan (Acts 2:23).

When we focus on the Lukan picture of Stephen's demise, we find that the story of Stephen parallels that of Jesus. Both are tried before the Council (Luke 22:66f.; Acts 6:12f.). Both die a martyr's death. Acts 7:59, "Lord Jesus, receive my spirit," echoes Luke 23:46, "Father, into thy hands I commit my spirit." Acts 7:60, "Lord, do not hold this sin against them," echoes Luke 23:34, "Father, forgive them; for they do not know what they are doing."[4] Both stories contain a Son of man saying: Luke 22:69 and Acts 7:56. This is remarkable since Acts 7:56 is the only occurrence of the title Son of man outside the Gospels and on any lips except those of Jesus. Both men's deaths issue in evangelistic results (Luke 23:39–43; Acts 8:1ff.; 11:19ff.). Moreover, the story of Stephen's martyrdom fulfills Jesus' words: Luke 21:12–19, especially v. 16 ("some of you they will put to death"; cf. also Luke 12:1–12). The deaths of both Jesus and Stephen are portrayed as martyrdoms in Luke-Acts. Having noted this fact, it is now necessary to focus on two facets of the Lukan theology of martyrdom.

MARTYRDOM AS REJECTION

These martyrdoms are understood by the Evangelist in the first instance as the *rejection of God's spokesmen* which results in the rejection of the rejectors by God. This aspect of the Lukan mind can be grasped if we look at those martyrdoms in the context of the Evangelist's understanding of Israel. This understanding may be set forth in five summary statements.

1. Before Israel's refusal of the gospel, Luke regards her as a reality existing on two levels: first, as an historical people defined by race and nationality, the Jewish nation (e.g., Luke 7:5; 23:2; Acts 10:22; 24:10, 17; 26:4; 28:19); and second, as the people of God (e.g., Luke 1:68; 2:32; 7:16; Acts 7:34; 13:17).[5] Recognition of this fact is crucial to further discussion.

2. The third Evangelist makes a great deal of the Jewish rejection of Jesus and the Christian message (e.g., Luke 2:34; 4:28–29; 13:34; 19:14; 19:39;

19:44; 20:13-16; 23:1-2; 24:20; Acts 4:1-2, 17-18; 5:17-18, 40; 7:58; 13:45; 14:19; 17:5-9; 17:13; 18:5-6, 12-17; 19:8-9; 20:3; 21:27-30, etc.). At the same time, he makes clear the fact that the earliest believers were Jewish (Acts 1:13-14, 21) and that there were many Jewish converts to Christianity (Acts 2:41, 47; 4:4; 5:14; 6:7; 13:43; 17:4; 21:20, etc.) both in Jerusalem and elsewhere. Hence the Lukan narrative shows how the Christian movement divided Israel into two groups: the repentant and the unrepentant. Israel did not reject the gospel but became divided over the issue.

3. In the Lukan perspective the repentant portion of the Jewish nation is Israel, the people of God. It is to them and for them that the promises have been fulfilled. This restored Israel is the presupposition of all the missionary work that follows to the Gentiles (Acts 15:15-18). God first rebuilds and restores Israel and then as a result the Gentiles seek the Lord. The unrepentant portion of the nation, however, has forfeited its membership in the people of God (Acts 3:23). A formal statement of the rejection of the unrepentant portion of the Jewish nation is delivered three times, once in each main area of missionary activity. Acts 13:46 has Paul and Barnabas say to the unbelieving Jews in Antioch of Pisidia: "It was necessary that the word of God should be spoken first to you. Since you thrust it from you, and judge yourselves unworthy of eternal life, behold, we turn to the Gentiles." In Acts 18:6 the scene is Corinth. Here, when the unbelieving Jews opposed him, Paul said: "Your blood be upon your heads! I am innocent. From now on I will go to the Gentiles." Finally, in Acts 28:25-28 Paul says to the unbelieving Jews in Rome: "Let it be known to you then that this salvation of God has been sent to the Gentiles; they will listen."

4. It is incorrect to say *only* that for Luke it is when the Jews have rejected the gospel that the way is open to the Gentiles.[6] It is equally incorrect to say *only* that when Israel has accepted the gospel that the way to the Gentiles is opened.[7] Both, indeed, are parts of the total view of Luke.[8] That is, both Acts 15:15-18 on the one hand and Acts 13:46; 18:6; and 28:25-28 on the other are parts of the total perspective of the third Evangelist. In the first place, the Jewish Christian community in Jerusalem, as the restored Israel, is the means through which salvation comes to the Gentiles (Acts 15:15-18). The Gentiles are incorporated into believing Israel. They are, however, incorporated without circumcision and the law, that is, without first becoming proselytes (Acts 15). In the second place, the explanation why the Lukan church feels no obligation to evangelize the national-racial entity of Israel is that these unrepentant ones have excluded themselves from Israel, the people of God (Acts 13:46; 18:6; 28:25-28). Hence, in Luke's view, by the end of Acts the people of God are no longer a race or a nation but those who believe (Luke 20:9-18). The unbelieving Jews remain an historical people who experience the fall of Jerusalem and the destruction of the temple (Luke 13:35a; 19:41-44; 21:20-24; 23:27-31), but they do not belong to Israel, the people of God. The destruction of the temple and of the holy city, moreover, are understood as the consequences of the rejection of Jesus by the racial-national Israel.[9]

5. The question whether Luke, like Paul in Romans 9–11, envisioned a final conversion of the entire Jewish people prior to the parousia, prompted by the inclusion of the Gentiles in the people of God, is debatable. Most scholars think that the Lukan Paul of Acts 28:25–28, unlike the historical Paul of Romans 11, seems resigned to a Gentile church.[10] A few Lukan scholars think that Luke, like Paul in Romans 11:20, looked forward to a time when the Jews as a people would be reinstated.[11] Acts 1:6; Luke 21:24, 28; and Luke 22:28–30 are about the only supports for this stance that are not simply too far-fetched. There is enough question about even these texts, however, to make it improbable that the Gentile Christian community from which Luke-Acts came expected any final conversion of the nation as a whole before the parousia. The Evangelist would not have ruled out the conversion of any individual Jew, but as far as the direction of the church's mission was concerned, it was to Gentiles. In this Luke is akin to Justin Martyr, who believed that a remnant of Jews was still being saved by conversion to Christianity in his own day (*Dialogue with Trypho*, 32; 55; 64). Justin, furthermore, allowed these Jewish Christians who lived within the church to practice the law (*Dialogue*, 47:2).

In the Lukan narrative we note that those responsible for the deaths of Jesus and Stephen are the chief priests and their associates, not the Pharisees. On the one side, in the third Gospel the Pharisees vanish as soon as Jesus enters Jerusalem in 19:45 (The last we hear of Pharisees is in 19:39 on the outskirts of the city.). The opponents in the passion narrative are the chief priests, rulers, Sadducees, and the Council (Luke 19:47; 20:1, 19, 27; 22:4, 50, 52, 54, 66; 23:1, 10, 13; cf. 24:20—"how our chief priests and rulers delivered him up to be condemned to death, and crucified him"). On the other side, in Acts 1–5 the enemies of the church are all associated with the temple (Acts 4:1, 5–6, 8, 15, 23; 5:17, 21, 22, 24, 26, 27, 34, 41). Likewise, Stephen in Acts 6:12 is brought before the Council, where he is interrogated by the high priest (7:1).

If the clear sense of language is followed in Acts 7:54ff., then the Council members must have participated in the death of Stephen. In the Lukan perspective, therefore, it is the rulers of the nation and the administrators of the temple, that symbol of Jewish national identity, who are portrayed as the instruments behind Jesus' martyrdom and as agents involved in Stephen's death. This is the Evangelist's way of saying that it is the racial-national entity that has rejected God's messengers, not once but twice. What could be attributed to ignorance the first time (Acts 3:17) is clearly deliberate the second time. If the martyrdom of Jesus symbolized the first rejection of God's messenger, the martyrdom of Stephen symbolized the second. The racial-national Israel twice rejected God's messenger. The result is spelled out clearly by Luke. Luke 20:9–18 and Acts 3:23 make it plain. Those who have rejected Jesus have been rejected by God. The first dimension of the Lukan understanding of martyrdom, therefore, is that such a death represents the *rejection of God's messenger* by those supposed to be God's people.

MARTYRDOM AS LEGITIMATION

A second dimension of the Lukan understanding of martyrdom is that *such deaths serve to legitimate* Jesus and the Christian cause and to function as *catalysts for evangelistic outreach*. This aspect of the Lukan mind can be grasped if we look at these martyrdoms in the context of the understanding of martyrdom in Graeco-Roman, Jewish, and early Christian thinking.[12]

Graeco-Roman Views of Martyrdom

We may begin with a look at the Graeco-Roman view of martyrdom. On the one hand, martyrdom was regarded positively in many circles in antiquity. It was a commonplace that true philosophers lived their doctrine as well as expounding it. The philosopher's word alone, unaccompanied by the act, was regarded as invalid (e.g., Seneca, *Epistle* 52:8-9; Dio Chrysostom, *Discourse*, 70:6). Some very harsh things were said about philosophers' sincerity—or lack of it—in antiquity. Josephus (*Against Apion*, 1:8) exaggerated when he said that no Greek philosopher would ever die for his philosophy. The same sentiments are found, however, in Lucian (*The Fisherman*, 31): "in their life and actions . . . they contradicted their outward appearance and reversed (philosophy's) practice." Epictetus (*Discourses* 1:29:56) says: "What, then, is the thing lacking now? The man . . . to bear witness to the arguments by his acts." Seneca (*Epistle* 24:15) joins the chorus: "There is a very disgraceful charge often brought against our school—that we deal with the words, and not the deeds, of philosophy." In view of this cynicism about philosophers' sincerity, sometimes only the willingness to die or actual death could validate a philosopher's profession.

Several examples of philosophers sealing their profession with either their deaths or their willingness to die illustrate this fact. Tertullian (*Apology* 50) tells us that Zeno the Eleatic, when asked by Dionysius what good philosophy did, said it gave contempt of death. When he was called on to prove it, given over to the tyrant's scourge, he was unquailing as he sealed his opinion even to death. In the *Life of Secundus the Silent Philosopher*, Secundus, because of an incident that had caused his mother's suicide, put a ban on himself, resolving not to say anything for the rest of his life—having chosen the Pythagorean way of life. The Emperor Hadrian arrived in Athens and sent for Secundus to test him. When Secundus refused to speak, Hadrian sent him off with the executioner with instructions that if he did speak his head should be cut off. If he did not speak, he should be returned to the Emperor. When he was returned to Hadrian after having been willing to die for his vow of silence, Secundus was allowed to write answers to the twenty questions asked by the Emperor—which answers were put in the sacred library. His willingness to die had validated Secundus' philosophy. Origen (*Against Celsus*, 8:66) commends Celsus when the pagan says: "If you happen to be a worshipper of God and someone commands you either to act blasphemously or to say some other disgraceful thing, you ought not to put any trust in him at all. Rather than this you must remain firm in face of all tortures and endure death rather than say or even think anything profane about God."

The sealing of one's profession in death as a martyr sometimes issued in furthering the cause of the philosopher. Plato's *Apology* tells the story of Socrates' death. In chapter 39 Socrates says: "I fain would prophesy to you; for I am about to die, and that is the hour in which men are gifted with prophetic power. And I prophesy to you who are my murderers, that immediately after my death punishment far heavier than you have inflicted on me will surely await you." What is meant in this context is that there will be more accusers than there are now. His position vindicated by death, Socrates' disciples will attack the Athenians as never before.

On the other hand, however, Graeco-Roman teachers gave two serious cautions about martyrdom. Martyrdom is not to be sought. Seneca (*Epistle* 24:25) says: "Above all, he should avoid the weakness which has taken possession of many—the lust for death." Martyrdom does not provide certain results. That is, it does not guarantee the furtherance of one's cause. It may win some but not necessarily others (Lucian, *Peregrinus* 13; Marcus Aurelius, 11:3:2).

Jewish Tradition Regarding Martyrdom

The view of martyrdom in ancient Judaism has similarities to this Graeco-Roman stance but there are also differences. On the one side, there was a positive attitude toward martyrdom. Two streams of thought ran alongside one another. One stream spoke of the prophets dying as martyrs at the hands of God's people (e.g., Jer. 2:20; Neh. 9:26; 1 Kings 10:10, 14; 2 Chron. 24:20-22; Jubilees 1:12; Lives of the Prophets; Martyrdom of Isaiah; cf. also Matt. 23:31-39; Heb. 11:36ff.; 1 Thess. 2:15; Mark 12:1-12). Here the emphasis is on the sinfulness of God's people (cf. Luke 13:33-34; Acts 7:52). The other stream spoke of the faithful among God's people dying as martyrs at the hands of the Gentiles. Here, as in Graeco-Roman paganism, it was believed that the true prophet sealed the truth of his testimony with death. In 4 Maccabees 7 the aged scribe Eleazar refused to eat swine's flesh as demanded by the Syrians or even to pretend to eat it (cf. 2 Macc. 6:18ff.). Instead he endured willingly the scourge, the rack, and the flame (2 Macc. 7:4). In 4 Maccabees 7:15 the author cried out: "O life faithful to the Law and perfected by the seal of death." It was also believed that such martyrs gained thereby the resurrection from the dead (2 Macc. 7:9, 14, 23, 28-29—the seven brothers and their aged mother; Josephus, *War* 1:33:3§651f.—those who tore down the golden eagle Herod the Great had erected over the gate of the Temple; 4 Macc. 9:18; 16:25; b. Ber 61b—Akiba). Such martyrs' deaths moreover were believed to benefit the nation (2 Macc. 7:37-38; 4 Macc. 6:27-29; 17:22), effecting a new relationship between God and the people.

Sometimes the martyrs' actions made converts to Judaism. For example, b. Abodah Zarah 18a, tells of R. Hanina b. Teradion who in the time of Hadrian was arrested for teaching Torah to groups. He was burned to death. After watching, the executioner then threw himself into the fire. Whereupon a *bath qol* (voice from heaven) exclaimed: R. Hanina and the executioner have been assigned to the world to come.

On the other side, we find the same two cautions among Jewish teachers that we found in the pagan world. Overeagerness for martyrdom is denounced as self-annihilation (e.g., Genesis Rabbah 82).[13] Martyrdom is no guarantee of another's conversion (e.g., 2 Macc. 6:29).

Martyrdom in Early Christianity

Ancient Christianity was deeply indebted to the pagan and Jewish views about martyrdom in defining its own stance. On the one hand, there was a positive attitude toward martyrdom. Like pagans and Jews, most Christians believed that the truth of their profession must be sealed in blood if it came to that (e.g., Revelation; Justin, *Apology,* II, 12). It is, of course, true that some Gnostics refused to undergo martyrdom (cf. Irenaeus, *Against Heresies,* 1:24:3–6—Basilides; Tertullian, *Against All Heresies,* 1—Basilides; *Scorp.,* 1—Valentinians and other Gnostics). Christians also believed, like the Jews, that martyrdom benefited the martyr (Revelation; 2 Tim. 4:6–8; Matt. 10:32–33; cf. the *Martyrdom of Apollonius,* where Apollonius says: "Proconsul Perenius, I thank my God for this sentence of yours which will bring me salvation."). Christians also believed, like the Jews, that martyrdom benefited the community of Christians (e.g., Martyrdom of Polycarp 1:1; Eusebius, *Church History,* 4:15:3, who says Polycarp put an end to the persecution by his martyrdom.). Christians, even more than pagans and Jews, believed that martyrdoms had "evangelistic" benefits. They helped spread the gospel. For example, Justin, *Dialogue,* 110, says: "The more we are persecuted, the more do others in ever-increasing numbers embrace the faith." Tertullian, *Apology,* 50, says: "We conquer in dying. . . . The oftener we are mown down by you, the more in number we grow; the blood of Christians is seed." The Epistle to Diognetus 6:9 says: "Christians when they are punished increase the more in number every day." In 7:7–8, it says: "Can you not see them thrown to wild beasts, to make them deny their Lord, and yet not overcome? Do you not see that the more of them are punished, the more numerous the others become?" Compare also the Martyrdom of Apollonius and the Martyrdom of Potamiaena and Basilides. Lactantius (d. A.D. 325), *Divine Institutes* 5:19, says: "It is right reason, then, to defend religion by patience or death in which faith is preserved and is pleasing to God himself, and it adds authority to religion."

On the other hand, Christians shared the pagan and Jewish reservations about martyrdom. An overeagerness for martyrdom is denounced (e.g., Martyrdom of Polycarp, 4: "We do not approve those who give themselves up, for the gospel does not teach us to do so"; the *Acts of St. Cyprian* says: "Since our discipline forbids anyone to surrender voluntarily."). Martyrdom was not regarded as a certain proof.[14]

SUMMARY OF LUKE'S ATTITUDE TOWARD MARTYRDOM

When we compare Luke-Acts with its environment we find many points of contact. Like pagans and Jews, as well as later Christians, Luke-Acts assumed that martyrdom legitimated a philosopher's/prophet's profession, and that such a death might very well issue in the conversion of others to the innocent one's cause, though Christian emphasis is more often here than in pagan or Jewish circles (cf. Luke 23:42–43; Acts 8:1b, 4ff; 11:19ff). In Luke-Acts, the two Jewish streams of martyrology flow together in the picture of Jesus' death. Jesus is a prophet rejected and killed by God's people (cf. Luke 13:33 ff.; Acts 7:52); he is also a devout Jew executed unjustly by the Gentiles (Acts 4:25–28). Stephen's death reflects only the first of three streams— prophetic martyrdom at the hands of God's people. Further, Luke-Acts agrees with Jewish thought in the belief that by martyrdom the man of faith gains eternal life (so Jesus and Stephen—cf. Luke 21:19), and the belief that the martyrdom of a righteous man benefits the community (so Luke 22:19–20 says that Jesus' blood sealed the new covenant).

Luke shares with the milieu generally the two main reservations about martyrdom. On the one hand, martyrdom is not to be sought (cf. Luke 22:42— "Father, if thou art willing, remove this cup from me; nevertheless not my will, but thine, be done."). Jesus did not have a lust for death but sought to avoid it, if God would permit it. On the other hand, martyrdom is not proof of the truth of one's cause and does not lead to the conversion of everyone (cf. Luke 23:39–43, where only one of the two thieves crucified with him is converted; the other rails at Jesus).

How then would Luke's first readers/hearers have perceived his account of the martyrdoms of Jesus and Stephen? Three things would likely have stood out. First, neither man died because of a lust for death. Both were healthy selves. Second, both legitimated their profession as they sealed it with their blood. Both were sincere in their stands. Third, this legitimation is evidenced in the conversion of others as a result of their deaths. Martyrdom has an evangelistic function. In the ancient world this Lukan motif would have served as part of the confirmation of the Christian message. Its persuasiveness was that of a selfless commitment on the part of stable persons.

THE SOCIAL IMPLICATIONS OF LUKE'S VIEW

What are the *implications* of this view of martyrdom for our understanding of the Lukan social ethic? What kind of political and social stance does Luke attribute to Jesus? This question is prompted by *Jesus, Politics, and Society*, by Richard Cassidy.[15] Cassidy argues that the Lukan Jesus is portrayed as a Gandhi-like figure advocating nonviolent resistance. Is this position tenable in light of our previous discussion? I think not.

Cassidy works with three possible stances:[16] (a) nonresistance (where people refrain not only from physical violence but also from directly confronting those responsible for existing ills; they identify with those suffering from such evils; they offer no defense if they themselves are subjected to violence by those who have power; their hope is that their example will eventuate in changes in the attitudes and actions of others); (b) nonviolent resistance (where people avoid violence to persons but confront in a nonviolent way those responsible for existing social ills; their hope is that the challenge will serve to create a dialogue that may eventually result in a favorable change of behavior); and (c) violent resistance.

These or similar stances had their representatives among Jewish people at the time of Christian origins. The Zealots were the advocates of armed revolution against Rome. Josephus gives us at least two examples of nonviolent resistance in Jesus' time. The first is found in *Antiquities* 18:3:1 § 261–309 and *War* 2:9:3 § 184–203. This is an account of a five-day sit-in to protest Pilate's introduction of images into Jerusalem. When threatened with death if they did not end their protest, the Jews cast themselves on the ground and bared their throats, declaring that they gladly welcomed death rather than violate their law. The protest caused Pilate to remove the offensive images from the city. A second is found in *Antiquities* 18:8 § 244–272 and *War* 2:10 § 184–198. This tells of a general strike by Jews that left fields untilled in the sowing season for more than a month. The protest prevented Caligula's statue from going up in the temple.

Although during the Hasmonean rule at least some of the Pharisees functioned as a political party, from the rise of Herod the Great until the end of the first Jewish revolt against Rome, the Pharisees seem to have moved away from direct political involvement and to have adopted an attitude of indifference regarding rulers and the forms under which they ruled. It seems likely that the Pharisees did not oppose Roman rule in Judea.[17] Their concern in this period was with the proper ordering of the life of God's people according to the law.

The Lukan Jesus' stance is more complex than Cassidy's description allows. Two components must be recognized in Luke's picture of Jesus' social and political stance. First, although the Lukan Jesus shows no deference toward political rulers (e.g., Luke 13:31–33), this does not mean that he is involved, Gandhi-style, in a nonviolent resistance to them. Like the Pharisees, the Lukan Jesus manifests an *indifference* to the political rulers. For someone who believed that all power and authority resided with God and all history unfolded according to his purpose, human rulers were of little consequence. Since the rulers shared no common assumptions that would facilitate dialogue with him, the Lukan Jesus opted for silence in their presence. Second, toward the Jewish structures (the church), however, the Lukan Jesus showed no indifference. Here he was involved in *nonviolent resistance*. Confrontation between the Lukan Jesus and the Jewish leaders was frequent (e.g., Luke 5:12–6:11; 11:37–54; 13:10–17; 14:1–24; 16:14–15; 19:47–20:47). Only at Luke 19:45 is there any hint of possible violence. The Evangelist has so shaped the cleansing story, however, that it becomes merely Jesus' entry into the site of his subsequent teaching (Luke 19:47–21:38). Moreover, Luke 22:49–51 has Jesus explicitly reject violence against Jewish authority. Non-violent confrontation aimed at dialogue and hoping for a change of behavior seems the best description of the Lukan Jesus' stance toward the Jewish structures. This was doubtless due to the fact that Jesus and the Jews shared common assumptions about God and values. With such a people dialogue could be profitable.

The Lukan view of martyrdom offers specific support to this correction of Cassidy's thesis. Were the deaths of the Lukan Jesus and Stephen designed by either to influence the political structures of the times (that is, Roman political structures)? Were their deaths the result of Rome's resistance to their political agitation? The answer to both questions must be in the negative. In Luke-Acts these deaths were the outcome of a struggle within the people of God, which at that time was also a racial-national entity. The deaths, moreover, had their positive influence on those within the people of God: the thief converted on the cross was almost certainly a Jew, and the spread of the gospel in Acts 8 and 11 was by Christians (cf. Phil 1:12–14, where Paul's imprisonment and threatened martyrdom caused most of the Christians to be bold in preaching). The Lukan Jesus and his followers, like the Pharisees of Jesus' time, had as their concern the proper ordering of the life of God's people.[18] If the Lukan Jesus adopted an attitude of indifference regarding rulers and the forms under which they ruled, the Christians in Acts basically looked with favor on the Roman structures because, when they worked at their best, they protected the preachers of the gospel from attack (e.g., Acts 17:1–9; 18:12–17; 19:23–41; 21:30–32; 23:12–35), and, even when they were flawed (e.g., Acts 24–28), they facilitated the preaching of the gospel.

The Lukan Jesus' primary vehicle for social change—if such language is even legitimate in describing Lukan thought—was the structure of life in the community of his disciples. Among his followers the Lukan Jesus sought a revolution in social attitudes. His disciples were to live in the present in light of God's reversal of all human values in the Eschaton. Such a stance, of course, was regarded by some as "turning the world upside down" (Acts 17:6), even if that was not a primary or even a conscious intention of the Christians. By embodying structures of social relationships that reflected the new life in the Spirit under the Lordship of Jesus, the Christian community functioned in the larger society as an agent of social change.

It would be improper, I think, to close without at least raising the question of the relevance of the Lukan perspective for modern life. Two contemporary Christian ethicists reflect the stance we have found in Luke-Acts: John Howard Yoder[19] and Stanley Hauerwas.[20] Yoder's thesis is that the first duty of the church for society is to be the church. That means to be a society which through the way its members deal with one another demonstrates to the world what love means in social relations. In this way the church fulfills its social responsibility by being an example, a witness, a creative minority formed by obedience to nonresistant love. From this point of view, the church does not attack the social structure of society directly, as one power group among others, but indirectly by embodying in its life a transcendent reality. Hauerwas acknowledges both his debt to Yoder and to the Gospel of Luke. The Lukan Jesus, he argues, did not go to the top (to Caesar or to Pilate) to get something done. Nor did he go to the Left (the Zealots). He went instead to the poor and the sinners. He established a community to embody God's grace. By insisting on being nothing less than the community of love, moreover, the church forces the world to face the truth of its own nature. "The most vital form of Christian social ethics must actually be a concern about the kind of community that Christians form among themselves."[21]

To conclude: The Lukan Jesus is no more a social activist of the Gandhi variety than of the Zealot type. Like the Pharisees of the historical Jesus' time, he is preoccupied with the ordering of the life of the people of God. It is through the leaven of the life of the community of the Lukan Jesus' disciples that the world is turned upside down. This Lukan perspective on social ethics, moreover, is now incorporated in at least one stream of contemporary Christian theological ethics. The advisability of basing contemporary Christian ethical thought on Lukan perspectives is a matter for Christian ethicists to decide after debate. What the Lukan point of view is with regard to social ethics, however, seems to me beyond debate.

NOTES

1. C. H. Talbert, *Luke and the Gnostics* (Nashville: Abingdon Press, 1966), chapter 5; Gerhard Schneider, *Die Passion Jesu nach den Drei Alteren Evangelien* (Munich: Kösel, 1973), p. 167.

2. Luke 22:19-20 and Acts 20:28 are often cited as exceptions to this claim. Neither actually is. Both speak about the death of Jesus as the seal of the new covenant.

3. Richard Zehnle, "The Salvific Character of Jesus' Death in Lucan Soteriology," *TS* 30 (1969): 420-44; I. H. Marshall, *Luke: Historian and Theologian* (Grand Rapids, Mich.: Zondervan, 1970), p. 169.

4. This verse is textually questionable. It is omitted by such witnesses as P[75] and B. It is included by such witnesses as X*. The language and thought are Lukan (Father— Luke 10:21; 11:2; 22:42; 23:46; forgive because of ignorance—Acts 3:17; 13:27; intercede for executioners—Acts 7:60). Sayings of Jesus are found, moreover, in each of the main sections of the crucifixion narrative (23:28-31, 43, 46). If one is missing here the pattern would be disturbed. It could have been omitted either because it was believed to have conflicted with vs. 28-31 or because the events of A.D. 66-70 were thought to show that it was not answered. The probabilities are that it is an integral part of the Third Gospel.

5. A. George, *Etudes sur l'oeuvre de Luc* (Paris: Gabalda, 1978), pp. 87-125.

6. Hans Conzelmann, *Die Apostelgeschichte* (Tübingen: J.C.B. Mohr, 1963), p. 78; Ernst Haenchen, *The Acts of the Apostles; A Commentary*, trans. B. Noble (Philadelphia: Westminster, 1971), pp. 100ff.

7. Jacob Jervell, *Luke and the People of God* (Minneapolis: Augsburg, 1972), pp. 41–74.

8. S. G. Wilson, *The Gentiles and the Gentile Mission in Luke-Acts* (Cambridge: Cambridge University Press, 1973), pp. 231–233.

9. This became standard Christian argument. Cf. Eusebius, *Church History*, 3:5:3–6.

10. E.g., Marshall, *Luke: Historian and Theologian*, pp. 186–187.

11. A. W. Wainwright, "Luke and the Restoration of the Kingdom of Israel," *Expository Times* 89 (1977): 76–79; Robert Karris, "Missionary Communities: A New Paradigm for the Study of Luke-Acts," *CBQ* 41 (1979): 80–97.

12. On the general topic of martyrdom, cf. W. H. C. Frend, *Martyrdom and Persecution in the Early Church* (Oxford: Blackwell, 1965); Norbert Brox, *Zeuge und Märtyrer* (Munich: Kösel, 1961); H. A. Fishel, "Martyr and Prophet," *JQR* 37 (1947): 265–280, 363–386.

13. Stanley Hauerwas in a private conversation suggested that Jews and Christians would have reservations about an overeagerness for martyrdom because they believed that life belonged to God. Therefore, one is not free to dispose of it at will. For the Jewish casuistry developed to help Jews avoid martyrdom, see David Daube, *Collaboration with Tyranny in Rabbinic Law* (New York: Oxford University Press, 1966).

14. H. Musurillo, *The Acts of the Christian Martyrs* (Oxford: The Clarendon Press, 1972), passim.

15. Richard Cassidy, *Jesus, Politics, and Society: A Study of Luke's Gospel* (Maryknoll, N.Y.: Orbis Books, 1978).

16. Ibid., pp. 40–41.

17. Ibid., pp. 122–123.

18. H. C. Kee, *Christian Origins in Sociological Perspective* (Philadelphia: Westminster, 1980), p. 42.

19. Yoder is known to a wide reading audience by his *The Politics of Jesus* (Grand Rapids: Eerdmans, 1972). There he argues that "a social style characterized by the creation of a new community and the rejection of violence of any kind is the theme of New Testament proclamation from beginning to end" (p. 250). He has strong support from Jacques Ellul, *Violence* (New York: Seabury Press, 1969), who shows the fallacy of the logic of the assumption that violence, while wrong in the oppressor, becomes right when used by Christians for desirable social change. The best summary of Yoder's position is found in Stanley Hauerwas, *Vision and Virtue* (Notre Dame, Ind.: Fides, 1974), in a chapter entitled, "The Nonresistant Church: The Theological Ethics of John Howard Yoder," pp. 197–221.

20. Stanley Hauerwas, "The Politics of Charity," *Int* 31 (1977): 251–262.

21. Hauerwas, *Vision and Virtue*, p. 216.

8

Luke's "Innocent" Jesus: A Scriptural Apologetic

DARYL SCHMIDT

One of the distinctive features about the Lukan passion narrative is the threefold set of charges brought against Jesus by the chief priests and scribes (23:2), followed by Pilate's triple profession of Jesus' innocence (23:4, 14f, 22).[1] Long before the advent of redaction criticism, Henry J. Cadbury claimed that "Luke appears to be interested in the charges, but he is more interested in the verdict."[2] What Cadbury attributed to Luke can just as appropriately be said of Cadbury and of redaction critics since Conzelmann: they appear to be interested in Luke's charges, but they are much more interested in the verdict of innocence professed by Pilate. Cadbury saw in Luke's statement of political charges and declaration of innocence the basis for discerning Luke's apologetic,[3] which Conzelmann later formulated in explicitly political terms: "To be a Christian implies no crime against Roman law," but rather demands "loyalty to the State."[4]

Richard Cassidy is among those who have challenged Conzelmann's arguments for a Lukan political apologetic.[5] Even though Cassidy seeks to "underscore the great contrast between Conzelmann's findings" and his own, especially regarding the political apologetic, he nevertheless agrees with Conzelmann that Jesus is innocent of the threefold set of political charges and that the charges must be seen as false.[6]

We propose to take a closer look at the bases for the charges in Luke and to challenge the judgment that they are blatantly false. We will contend, rather, that they are to be regarded as Luke's summary of how the chief priests and scribes understood Jesus, and that the "innocence" has to do with a scriptural, not a political, apologetic.

111

THE ACCUSATIONS AGAINST JESUS

The trial before Pilate begins with the chief priests and scribes stating, "We have found this man perverting our nation, and forbidding us to give tribute to Caesar, and saying that he himself is Christ a king" (23:2 RSV). The second charge in the accusation, forbidding payment of tribute, appears to be a perversion of the earlier incident which provoked the saying, "Render to Caesar the things that are Caesar's, and to God the things that are God's" (20:25). Since Conzelmann interprets this as a "demand of loyalty" to Rome, it demonstrates that "the Jews are lying in their accusation," that they offer "a deliberate lie," which justifies labeling them as "liars."[7] Cassidy is less harsh on the accusers, but he basically agrees with Conzelmann.[8]

Any judgment made about the veracity of the accusations must be done in the larger context of the trial scene. The second accusation is never brought up again anywhere in the trial. Rather, Pilate immediately asks Jesus about the third accusation: "Are you the king of the Jews?" Even though Jesus' response: "You have said so," is less than unequivocal, Pilate claims to have found no crime in him. Then the accusers repeat the first charge in even more explicit terms: "He stirs up the people, teaching throughout all Judea, from Galilee even to this place" (23:5). After the scene with Herod, Pilate calls together all the involved factions and repeats: "You brought me this man as one who was perverting the people" (23:14). This is now the third time that this charge has been made against Jesus. What, if any, basis is there in Luke's story for this accusation?

The three versions of the charge are:

v. 2: perverting our nation *(diastprephonta to ethnos hēmōn)*
v. 5: he stirs up the people *(anaseiei ton laon)*
v. 14: perverting the people *(apostrephonta ton laon)*

The second version also adds the important explanation, "teaching throughout all Judea from Galilee even to this place." So the cumulative accusation is that, in the perspective of the chief priests and scribes, Jesus' teaching had perverted and stirred up the people. There are three different verbs used by Luke. The two verbs translated "pervert" are *diastrephō* and *apostrephō*. The first one suggests "misled" and the second is more "lead away from." The third verb is *anaseiō*, which suggests "arouse" or "incite." It is used only one other time in the New Testament, in Mark's passion story, where the chief priests are said to incite the crowd to prefer Barabbas to Jesus (15:11). In Luke the chief priests accuse Jesus of inciting the people with his teaching, which from the perspective of the Jewish leaders would indeed be to mislead them, or to lead them away from their leaders. The question then becomes: did Luke actually present Jesus' teaching as having such an effect on the relationship of the people to their leaders?

ANALYSIS OF THE FIRST ACCUSATION

The initial Lukan summary of Jesus' ministry was in terms of his teaching: "A report concerning him went out through all the surrounding country. And he taught in their synagogues, being glorified by all" (4:14b–15). An example of such a synagogue-teaching scene follows in his home-town of Nazareth, but he is hardly "glorified by all." Instead, "when they heard this, all in the synagogue were filled with wrath" (4:28), and they chased him out of town. Not deterred, "he went down to Capernaum . . . he was teaching them on the sabbath; and they were astonished at his teaching, for his word was with authority" (4:31f). Soon afterward, in a story unique to Luke, Simon is called to discipleship after Jesus has used his fishing boat as a teaching-platform, because "the crowd was pressing upon him to hear the word of God" (5:1–3). After the subsequent healing of the leper, "the report went abroad concerning him, and great multitudes gathered to hear and to be healed" (5:15). The healing of the paralytic, which follows, is introduced by Luke as taking place while Jesus was teaching in a setting that included Pharisees and law-teachers "from every village of Galilee and Judea and from Jerusalem" (5:17). Not much later Luke again has Jesus teaching in the synagogue, being watched by scribes and Pharisees, as the setting for the healing of the withered hand (6:6f). They respond in fury and begin discussions of what to do with Jesus (6:11).

After a night of prayer, Jesus chooses the Twelve and then delivers a speech on the plain to "a great multitude of people from all Judea and Jerusalem and the seacoast of Tyre and Sidon, who came to him to hear him and to be healed" (6:17). At the end of the speech Luke again emphasizes that "all his sayings" were "in the hearing of the people" (7:1). The healing of Nain, another story unique to Luke, provokes a response of "God has visited his people," followed by a typical Lukan summary: "this report concerning him spread through the whole of Judea and all the surrounding country" (7:16f).

We see that Luke has presented the ministry of Jesus as having its crucial locus in his teaching, which was directed primarily to the people.[9] Even when the occasion is a healing, Luke places it as an incident during Jesus' teaching. When the crowds gather it is to hear and to be healed. From the beginning this was not confined to people from Galilee, but the crowds were attracted from throughout Judea. Luke also gave a foretaste of things to come when he indicated that the Jerusalem leadership was threatened by the impact of Jesus' teaching.

In his special central section featuring Jesus "on the way" to Jerusalem, Luke continues to develop these emphases. He summarizes the journey as a teaching one: "he went on his way through towns and villages, teaching, and journeying toward Jerusalem" (13:22), and he characterizes people as saying that Jesus "taught in our streets" (13:26). The few healing stories in this section are given a teaching setting or are important for the observing audience. The first is set typically while "he was teaching in one of the synagogues on the sabbath" (13:10); the second is in the presence of lawyers and Pharisees and raises the issue of what is lawful on the sabbath (14:13); the last is in Jericho where "all the people" saw it and praised God.

As the journey gets closer to Jerusalem, the tension builds between leaders and people. Luke notes: "the crowds were increasing" (11:29) and "many thousands of the multitude had gathered together" (12:1), while "the scribes and Pharisees began to press him hard and to provoke him to speak of many things, lying in wait for him, to catch at something he might say" (11:53f). It is the things he says that, on the one hand, attract the crowds of people, and, on the other hand, cause growing alarm on the part of the leaders. As Jesus journeys to Jerusalem "great multitudes accompanied him" (14:25) and "the tax collectors and sinners were all drawing near to hear him" (15:1), while various leader-types became indignant (13:14) and murmured (15:2) and scoffed (16:14).

Most of Jesus' interactions on the way are with representative individuals from the crowds: a man (9:38), a woman (10:38; 11:27; 13:11), a lawyer (10:25; 11:45), a Pharisee (11:37), a ruler (14:1; 18:18), or just one of the crowd (12:13; 13:1, 23). While some teachings are directed specifically to the disciples, in preparation for their role as apostles (17:5), they are never the ones who address Jesus as "teacher." All eleven times Jesus is addressed as *Didaskale* in Luke, it is by someone other than a disciple: by a Pharisee (7:40; 19:39), by a lawyer (10:25; 11:45), by a ruler (18:18), by someone from the crowd (9:38; 12:13), and in Jerusalem three times by opponents (20:21, 28, 39), and once by someone in the temple crowd (21:7). Luke's focus on Jesus' teaching is even more striking after he arrives in Jerusalem. He directly enters the temple and makes it his place of teaching,[10] as Luke summarizes at the beginning of his days in Jerusalem: "he was teaching daily in the temple. The chief priests and the scribes and the principal men of the people sought to destroy him; but they did not find anything they could do, for all the people hung upon his word" (19:47f). We notice that in Jerusalem the scribes have been joined by other groups of leaders and the Pharisees are not involved.[11]

The first incident described "one day as he was teaching the people in the temple" has the leaders coming to ask by what authority Jesus was acting. He shifts the burden of response to them and they are afraid to answer because, they say, "all the people will stone us" (20:6). Jesus then tells the people a parable directed at the leaders. In response, "the scribes and the chief priests tried to lay hands on him at that very hour, but they feared the people" (20:19), so they send spies "to take hold of what he said, so as to deliver him up to the authority and jurisdiction of the governor" (20:20). The Jerusalem leaders' fear of the people has driven them to want to find evidence against Jesus that could be brought before the Roman governor. However, Luke states that "they were not able in the presence of the people to catch him by what he said" (20:26), referring to "Render to Caesar . . . and to God. . . ." After Jesus silences the scribes (20:40) and denounces them "in the hearing of all the people" (20:45), Luke presents the final temple teaching of Jesus, and then summarizes again at the end of Jesus' days in Jerusalem: "every day he was teaching in the temple . . . and early in the morning all the people came to the temple to hear him" (21:37f). The two summaries, 19:47f and 21:37f, form the framework for the whole section.[12] In this way Luke has emphasized that Jesus' teaching stands between the people and their leaders.[13] As a result, "the chief priests and the scribes were seeking how to put him to death, for they feared the people" (22:2). Whereas earlier their fear of the people kept them from seizing Jesus (19:48; 20:19, 26), it now becomes the basis for their desire to do so.

When the chief priests and scribes aided by temple assistants (22:52), finally arrange to seize Jesus, their hearing before the council (22:66) does not have false witnesses (Matt. 26:60// Mark 14:56f) nor any verdict of blasphemy (Matt. 26:65//Mark 14:64; Luke 22:65 instead has them blaspheming Jesus). They only want to inquire about his possible role as the Christ and the Son of God. When he does not deny either one they claim to have all the evidence they need and are ready to present charges before Pilate (22:67–23:1).

The accusations are strong: first, "We found this man perverting our nation." Is this a deliberate falsehood, a lie? When they restate the charge, "he stirs up the people, teaching throughout all Judea, from Galilee even to this place," the reader recognizes that Luke is not presenting a deliberate lie, but a realistic appraisal of the effect of Jesus' teaching on the people, as experienced by the chief priests and scribes. Luke had emphasized the people as the audience of Jesus' teaching, and the resulting fear the leaders have of their people. Therefore, to charge that as a result of Jesus' teaching the people had been estranged from their leaders is surely not a fabrication. Jesus had indeed diverted the people from their leaders, and done so by taking over the temple.

THE SECOND AND THIRD ACCUSATIONS

When we consider the other two accusations now, they are less obviously lies. The second charge was that they found him forbidding tribute to Caesar.[14] To be sure, there is nothing approaching a direct statement in Luke to validate that.[15] However, it is important here to be cautious regarding the conventional treatment of "Render to Caesar" and "render to God" as an endorsement of two separate obligations.[16] As part of Jesus' teaching on the way to Jerusalem he had emphasized the no-compromise approach required of any follower (9:57–62; 13:22–30), summarized in 16:13, "No servant can serve two masters. . . . You cannot serve God and mammon," and restated in Acts (5:29), "We must obey God rather than men." So when crafty spies came looking for evidence to take to the governor, which implies that Jesus was vulnerable on this issue,[17] they do not get a "yes" or "no" answer to their question, but rather one that qualifies Caesar's claims by God's claims. In the spirit of "obey only God" the reminder of Caesar's image and inscription on the coin is hardly an appeal to loyalty to the claims of Caesar. The chief priests and scribes interpret Jesus' refusal to singularly endorse Caesar as an act of defiance. We can label that a misinterpretation, but not a deliberate falsehood.

The third charge was that they found him saying that he himself is Christ, a king. They had just directly asked him the Messiah-question and he refused to deny it (22:67–70). Again, the refusal to make an unequivocal response is interpreted by the chief priests and scribes in the affirmative. Again Luke has provided evidence that there is some legitimate basis for this. He had anticipated the role of Jesus in the opening chapter in very kingly terms (1:32f), and had given the baptism story a focus on the words of royal identification (3:21f). The crowds call him king when he approaches Jerusalem and the rulers and soldiers mock him respectively, as Messiah and King (23:36f). So the third charge also results from the misinterpretation of the chief priests and scribes, and thus it too can hardly be called a lie.

We must conclude that in Luke's presentation the chief priests and scribes are indeed threatened by the way Jesus' teaching has captivated the people, they misinterpret the political implications of his conduct, and when they are finally driven to do something about it only a drastic measure will do. Even when they fail to convince Pilate of their interpretation of Jesus' activity they persist until they have their way (23:18–25).

PILATE'S VERDICT

It is in this context, then, that Luke has Pilate proclaiming Jesus "innocent." He does so, however, after asking Jesus only one question: "Are you the king of the Jews?" and not receiving any kind of denial: "You have said so" (23:4). In fact, it was just such an open-ended answer that the chief priest and scribes had earlier chosen to interpret in the affirmative. It is their word against Pilate's. When they expand the first accusation to include teaching in Galilee, Herod gets a chance to question him, but gets no answer (23:9). When Pilate reiterates his finding of innocence a second and third time, it is without additional evidence (23:14, 22). This declaration can hardly serve as proof, then, that Jesus was indeed not guilty of any of the charges against him, since Luke has already provided a legitimate basis for each of the charges. Even if we insist that the chief priests and scribes are wrong in their interpretation, that only makes Pilate's verdict of innocence technically correct; it does not make the accusers into liars.

LUKE'S SCRIPTURAL APOLOGETIC

What main purpose, then, is served by this declaration of innocence? Since the political apologetic often attributed to Luke has been called into question, another direction must be pursued. We propose that the motif of Jesus' innocence is integral to the scriptural apologetic which Luke develops regarding the death of Jesus.[18] The apologetic is given its most explicit expression in the Gospel in the Emmaus story.[19] The disciples had hoped that Jesus, a mighty prophet before all the people, would redeem Israel, until the rulers crucified him (24:19–21). The disciples failed to understand because they were slow "to believe all that the prophets have spoken," namely, that it was "necessary that the Christ should suffer these things and enter into his glory." Then "beginning with Moses and all the prophets," the resurrected Christ "interpreted to them in all the Scriptures the things concerning himself" (24:26f). He reinforced this later in Jerusalem: " 'These are my words which I spoke to you while I was still with you, that everything written about me in the law of Moses and the prophets and the psalms must be fulfilled.' Then he opened their minds to understand the scriptures and said to them, 'Thus it is written, that the Christ should suffer. . . .' " (24:44–46). The only thing the disciples had not understood in Luke's Gospel was the saying that the Son of Man would suffer (9:45; 18:34). Now it is explained to them as a necessity, based on Scripture. The apologetic regarding the cross is that it was necessitated by Scripture. Luke had indicated this already in 22:37: "For I tell you that this scripture must be fulfilled in me. 'And he was reckoned with transgressors'; for what is written about me has its fulfillment." The scriptural text here is from Isaiah 53, where the one who suffers is innocent (*dikaios*). In fact, this becomes the centurion's confession in Luke: "Certainly this man was *dikaios*" (23:47).[20] Just as it was necessary for the Messiah to suffer, Scripture also required that it be innocent suffering.

Luke develops this apologetic further in Acts. Peter addresses all the people who come to the temple portico, reminding them that they had denied the innocent (*dikaios*) one, out of ignorance, as did the rulers, "But what God foretold by the mouth of all the prophets, that his Christ should suffer, he thus fulfilled" (3:14, 17f). The next day Peter speaks again, this time to the rulers and elders, of the Jesus "whom you crucified" (3:10). When the rulers question Peter and seek to quiet him and John, Luke says, "they let them go, finding no way to punish them, because of the people" (4:21), reminding us of the role of the people in Luke's Gospel. In the joy of their release the apostles call to mind the opening of Psalm 2: "Why did the Gentiles rage, and the peoples imagine vain things? The kings of the earth set themselves in array and the rulers were gathered together, against the Lord and against his Anointed" (4:25f). This is interpreted as the rationale for the scenario of Luke's passion story: "Truly in this city there were gathered together against thy holy servant Jesus, whom thou didst anoint, both Herod and Pontius Pilate, with the Gentiles and peoples of Israel" (4:27).[21]

These same themes are reinforced elsewhere in Acts. Jesus is called *dikaios* by both Stephen (7:52) and Paul (22:14). Philip explicitly connects Isaiah 53 with Jesus (8:32–35). Paul argues from the Scripture that the Christ must suffer (17:2f), and he proclaims that the Jerusalemites and their leaders were fulfilling the prophets when they condemned Jesus (13:27). The early Christian preaching presented in Acts thus makes clear Luke's position: the circumstances of Jesus' death must be understood in the light of Scripture. The extent of this scriptural apologetic is more than adequate to account for the Lukan passion scenario of the rulers causing the suffering of one, who by scriptural necessity, must be innocent. It may indeed be the case that this apologetic was also in the service of a more political interest on the part of the evangelist, such as countering the political implications of Jesus' death at the hands of the Romans,[22] or recommending Christianity as nonpolitical and unthreatening.[23] However, the resulting pictures of a quietist Jesus that are often credited to Luke hardly do justice to the evidence. Here we substantially concur with Cassidy.[24]

One further question remains to be addressed: Why then did Luke present political charges against Jesus that have some plausibility? One factor that must be taken into account is how much those charges are echoed in the trial scenes in Acts.[25] In Philippi Paul and Silas are dragged before rulers and charged with disturbing the city and advocating unlawful practices (16:19–21); in Thessalonica their host is dragged before city authorities to hear the charges against Paul and Silas: they have turned the world upside down, acted against the decrees of Caesar and said that Jesus is a king (17:6f), remarkably parallel to Luke 23:2. Especially when translated more adequately, "These men who have stirred up sedition throughout the empire act contrary to the decrees of Caesar, saying that there is another king, one Jesus." This becomes "the damning charge of disloyalty to the Roman Emperor."[26] When Paul reaches Jerusalem the accusations focus on his teaching (21:21). He is charged with "teaching men everywhere against the people and the law and this place," the temple (21:28). In the resulting uproar he is dragged out and arrested. Eventually he is taken before the governor and, in a scene structured very much like Luke 23:2, "they began to accuse him, saying . . . we have found this man a pestilent fellow, an agitator among all the Jews throughout the world, and a ringleader of the sect of the Nazarenes" (Acts 24:2, 5).

The main charge that emerges from all these incidents is that Paul's activity had led to unrest among the Jews. As in the case of Jesus so here also there is legitimate basis for the accusation. Paul's presence had in fact stirred up crowds in Philippi (16:22), in Thessalonica (17:5), in Corinth (18:12), in Ephesus (19:40) and in Jerusalem (21:27, 30). Even though he too is declared innocent three times (23:9; 25:25; 26:31), the charges against him are clearly not mere fabrication.

When we consider the charges against Jesus in the light of Paul's trials in Acts, we note especially the second version of the main accusation in 23:5: he "stirs up the people, teaching throughout all Judea." This could well be another instance where "Luke in the interest of his Jesus-Paul parallelism conformed his gospel accounts to Acts,"[27] making Luke 23:5 anticipate the nature of the charges against Paul in Acts. Jesus' teaching had stirred up people throughout Judea; Paul's teaching stirred up people throughout the world (Acts 17:6; 24:5). In both cases this kind of activity leads to Jerusalem, where both men are seized (Luke 22:54; Acts 21:30). Their teaching had indeed been provocative.

We must finally return to Luke's original formulation of the main charge against Jesus, perverting the nation (23:2). This goes beyond the parallels between Jesus and Paul. Here the charge is much stronger. Jesus is accused of misleading his own people, a charge that is especially fitting to make against a prophet. Luke's language is the same as Exodus 5:4, where the King of Egypt responds to Moses and Aaron's divine message calling for freedom by accusing them of turning the people (*diastrephete ton laon*) from their work for the Pharaoh, and also 1 Kings 18:17, where King Ahab responds to Elijah's divine message of judgment by accusing him of being the one who perverts Israel (*ho diastrephōn ton Israēl*). Jesus, like Moses and Elijah, is accused of having diverted the people away from the governing authorities, as a result of his teaching activity. Therefore, the motif of misleading the people is but another part of Luke's scriptural apologetic: the innocent one who suffers is "the prophet like Moses."[28]

In response to this main charge of misleading the people, repeated three times, comes the declaration of innocence, repeated three times. Both the accusation and the declaration must be seen in the light of Luke's scriptural apologetic. Jesus' teaching activity had indeed led to the estrangement of the people from their leaders. They claim that he has been misleading the people. What results is a miscarriage of justice, a typical outcome in the life of a prophet. Though "innocent," he suffers at the hands of kings and rulers, again in accordance with Scripture.[29]

NOTES

1. For a discussion of the trial scene in Luke see Paul W. Walaskay, "The Trial and Death of Jesus in the Gospel of Luke," *JBL* 94 (1975): 81–93. For two very different ways of reading the evidence see Gerard S. Sloyan, *Jesus on Trial* (Philadelphia: Fortress Press, 1973), pp. 89–109, and S. G. F. Brandon, *The Trial of Jesus of Nazareth* (New York: Stein & Day, 1968), pp. 116–125.

2. Henry J. Cadbury, *The Making of Luke-Acts* (London: SPCK and Naperville, Ill,: Allenson, 1958, 1927), p. 305.

3. Ibid., p. 311.

4. Hans Conzelmann, *The Theology of St. Luke* (New York: Harper & Row, 1961), pp. 138–140. See also Helmut Flender, *St. Luke: Theologian of Redemptive History* (Philadelphia: Fortress Press, 1967), p. 61.

5. Richard Cassidy, *Jesus, Politics, and Society: A Study of Luke's Gospel* (Maryknoll, N.Y.: Orbis Books, 1978), pp. 128–130. See also Jacob Jervell, *Luke and the People of God* (Minneapolis: Augsburg, 1972), pp. 155–158; and Ray Barraclough, "A Re-Assessment of Luke's Political Perspective," *Reformed Theological Review* 38 (1979): pp. 10–18.

6. Ibid., pp. 65, 128.

7. Conzelmann, *Theology,* pp. 140, 85.

8. Cassidy, *Jesus*, pp. 106 n.21, and 167 n.8.

9. See Jerome Kodell, "Luke's Use of *Laos*, 'People,' Especially in the Jerusalem Narrative," *CBQ* 31 (1969): 327–343.

10. Conzelmann, *Theology*, pp. 75–78, focuses on the cleansing as an act of "taking possession," and while he notes the importance of the teaching, it does not figure significantly in his treatment of the material.

11. Ibid., p. 329. See also Joseph B. Tyson, "The Opposition to Jesus in the Gospel of Luke," *Perspectives in Religious Studies* 5 (1978): 144–50; and J. A. Ziesler, "Luke and the Pharisees," *NTS* 25 (1978/79): 146–157.

12. See Arland J. Hultgren, "Interpreting the Gospel of Luke," *Int* 30 (1976): 353–365, especially p. 360.

13. See David L. Tiede, *Prophecy and History in Luke-Acts* (Philadelphia: Fortress Press, 1980), pp. 87f.

14. Brandon, *Trial*, p. 146, wants to see this as a "general feature of his teaching."

15. Sloyan, *Jesus*, p. 107, regards it as the main charge and as baseless.

16. See the summary of the problem in D. R. Griffiths, *The New Testament and the Roman State* (Swansea, Wales: John Penry Press, 1970), pp. 56–62; and Charles H. Giblin, " 'The Things of God' in the Question Concerning Tribute to Caesar," *CBQ* 33 (1971): 510–527.

17. See John Howard Yoder, *The Politics of Jesus* (Grand Rapids: Eerdmans, 1972), p. 53; and Joseph B. Tyson, "The Lukan Version of the Trial of Jesus," *NovT* 3 (1959): 249–258, especially p. 255.

18. See Tiede, *Prophecy*, p. 121: "The death of Jesus, the destruction of Jerusalem, and the rejection of Christian preaching were three mysteries of a cry requiring scriptural interpretation, and they all came to expression in the passion story."

19. See Paul Schubert, "The Structure and Significance of Luke 24," in *Neutestamentliche Studien für Rudolf Bultmann* (Berlin: Alfred Töpelmann, 1957), pp. 165–186, e.g., p. 176: "Luke's proof-from-prophecy theology is the heart of his concern in chapter 24."

20. See William J. Larkin, "Luke's Use of the Old Testament as a Key to His Soteriology," *Journal of the Evangelical Theology Society* 20 (1977): 325–335; and George D. Kilpatrick, "A Theme of the Lucan Passion Story and Luke xxiii. 47," *JTS* 43 (1942): pp. 34–36.

21. See Tiede, *Prophecy*, p. 102 and p. 109. The fulfillment of this text also accounts for the scene in Luke 23:13, where the people and rulers are together before Pilate, in contrast to the division between the people and rulers in the rest of the passion story, as noted above.

22. See Ellis E. Jensen, "The First Century Controversy over Jesus as a Revolutionary Figure," *JBL* 60 (1941): 261–272.

23. Conzelmann, *Theology*, pp. 138–140.

24. See Cassidy, *Jesus*, pp. 77–79 and pp. 82–84.

25. See Charles H. Talbert, *Literary Patterns, Theological Themes and the Genre of Luke-Acts* (Missoula, Mt.: Scholars Press, 1974), p. 17; and A. J. Mattill, Jr., "The Jesus-Paul Parallels and the Purpose of Luke-Acts: H. H. Evans Reconsidered," *NovT* (1975): 15–46, especially p. 33.

26. H. U. W. Stanton, "Turned the World Upside Down," *Expository Times* 44 (1932/33): 526–527.

27. Mattill, "Jesus-Paul," p. 37. See also Walaskay, "Trial," p. 89.

28. See Tiede, *Prophecy*, pp. 40–47, 53–55, 124.

29. A corollary to the argument that Luke is engaged in a scriptural apologetic is that it is not an anti-Jewish polemic. Tiede, *Prophecy*, argues forcefully that Luke is a participant in an ongoing, intra-Jewish hermeneutical debate over faithfulness to Jewish Scripture, which presupposes the election of Israel (see especially pp. 47–51, 59, 66, 84, 118–120, 127–132).

9

According to Luke, Who Put Jesus to Death?

E. JANE VIA

In his book *Jesus, Politics, and Society,* Richard Cassidy attempts to identify Luke's understanding of Jesus' social and political stance.[1] As part of this endeavor, Cassidy analyzes the trial narrative of Luke's Gospel.[2] He considers the major figures present at Jesus' trial, their attitudes and evaluations of Jesus, and Jesus' response to them. He concludes that Jesus' stance toward Pilate and Herod at his trial is substantially the same as that which he adopted during his ministry: Jesus neither cooperates with nor defers to religious or political authorities.[3]

Although Cassidy's basic conclusion can be applauded, his summary of the evidence involved in his study, and some of the specific conclusions he draws, are arguably inaccurate. A more thorough and detailed consideration of the evidence, while modifying some of Cassidy's more specific conclusions, gives greater support to the basic conclusion Cassidy draws about Jesus' stance toward religious and political authorities.

OVERVIEW OF THE TRIAL NARRATIVE

Cassidy selects the chief priests, Pilate, Herod, and Jesus as the main figures present at Jesus' trial. He then analyzes the trial narrative, scene by scene, focusing on the interaction between Jesus and these other figures: the hearing before the Sanhedrin is the result of the chief priests' and their allies' joyful reception of Judas' offer to betray Jesus. According to Luke, Judas,

I wish to accord special thanks to Mary Theresa Nuesca, a senior student in Religious Studies and Psychology at the University of San Diego, San Diego, California. Her critical editorial skills enhanced the final version of this article.

122

the chief priests, the elders, and some of the high priest's servants seized Jesus at the Mount of Olives. From there they took him to the courtyard of the high priest's house where he was beaten and mocked. At daybreak, a session of the Sanhedrin was convened.[4] Before the Sanhedrin, according to Luke, Jesus is asked by the council members whether he is the Christ and whether he is the Son of God. Cassidy describes Jesus' responses to both questions as searing, terse, and noncommittal.[5]

In his review of Jesus' first appearance before Pilate, Cassidy considers the charges the Sanhedrin members bring against Jesus: he perverts the nation, forbids Jews to give tribute to Caesar, and says he is Christ, a king. Cassidy considers whether the charges are true, based on Luke's account of Jesus' ministry; and, with many other scholars, concludes that the charges are false.[6] Pilate asks whether Jesus is king of the Jews. Cassidy concludes that Jesus' reply is again noncommittal, showing no deference to Pilate; but Pilate declares to those present: "I find no crime in this man."[7]

Cassidy accurately reports that when Jesus appeared before Herod, Herod questioned Jesus at some length. Jesus answers none of Herod's questions. Although it is suggested earlier in Luke's Gospel that Herod wanted to kill Jesus, at this meeting he is merely interested in Jesus performing some sign. Cassidy finds that since Herod held some power over Jesus and since Pilate's apparent interest in Herod's judgment suggests that Herod's judgment would have some influence over whether Jesus lived or died, "it is striking that Jesus refuses to cooperate with him."[8]

Cassidy then considers Jesus' second appearance before Pilate, in which Pilate completely exonerates Jesus, implies that Herod is qualified to judge whether Jesus is dangerous to Roman rule and conveys that Herod has agreed with Pilate that there is no crime in Jesus. In the next six verses, Pilate reaffirms his initial decision twice. In this section, Cassidy attacks the political apologetic theory of Conzelmann.[9] Cassidy interprets that theory to hold that Luke was concerned with establishing Jesus' "loyalty and submission" to the Roman Empire.[10] Cassidy argues that this is not Luke's concern; but it *is* Luke's concern to "indicate in unmistakable terms that the chief priests and their allies were the ones primarily responsible for Jesus' ultimate fate."[11] He then systematically and correctly reviews all the incidents in which the chief priests express an intention to kill Jesus or participate in action to have him killed. Cassidy concludes from his review of the chief priests' role that "Luke shows quite precisely and specifically that it was the chief priests and their allies who brought about Jesus' death, but he (Luke) does not in any way infer that the Jewish people as a whole were involved or even that the chief priests were the representatives of the Jewish populace."[12]

Next Cassidy analyzes Luke's description of Jesus' crucifixion. He describes Roman soldiers who, acting on Pilate's orders, took Jesus outside the city and crucified him but argues that Luke's description of Jesus' execution "does not diminish the responsibility of the chief priests and their allies for Jesus' death."[13] In fact, Luke's account indicates that "the chief priests and their allies played the leading role in bringing about Jesus' death.''[14]

Cassidy's attention then turns to a summary of Jesus' responses to his accusers and to a reconsideration of Pilate's and Herod's verdicts. He argues that a general pattern emerges in Jesus' responses: he did not cooperate with or defer to the authorities who judged him. He points out that Jesus' failure to do so is especially obvious in his appearances before Pilate and Herod: since neither expressed an interest in seeing Jesus killed, it seemingly would have been in Jesus' best interest to cooperate with them.[15]

Cassidy reminds the reader of his conclusion regarding Jesus' social stance: Luke's Jesus was deeply committed to establishing social relationships based on service and humility; he contrasted his own service-oriented practices with those based on domination and withheld his approval from rulers whose practices were not based on service and humility during his ministry and trial. Cassidy repeats that Jesus' stance toward Pilate and Herod at his trial is not a stance of cooperation or deference.[16]

In this same section, Cassidy again rejects the political apologetic theory, on the basis that in spite of Pilate's and Herod's verdicts that Jesus was innocent, their reasons for so finding are not explained. Cassidy argues that Pilate and Herod could see Jesus had done something to earn himself the chief priests' enmity but that they saw this as an affair in which they should not become entangled. Their main objective was to safeguard the Roman sway over Palestine and it was clear that Jesus did not pose that kind of threat to the Roman rule.[17]

There are four basic weaknesses in Cassidy's interpretation of the trial narrative as a reflection of Jesus' social and political stance according to Luke: (1) Cassidy sometimes seems to historicize what may have been literary and/or redactional material in the trial narrative. This is a problem throughout the book in spite of Cassidy's clear statement of purpose to the contrary at the beginning of the book.[18] Cassidy frequently drifts into a way of speaking about the narrative that implies he is speaking of the stance of the historical Jesus rather than that of Luke. That is, at least, confusing to the reader. (2) His focus on four major figures present at Jesus' trial (whom Cassidy selects), neglects the roles of other groups present at Jesus' trial and crucifixion. As a result, Cassidy may have exaggerated the role of the chief priests. (3) Cassidy fails to treat relevant passages in Acts necessary to confirm, if not elaborate on, Jesus' social and political stances according to Luke, and whom Luke blames for Jesus' death. This investigation would help distinguish Luke's views from supposed views of the historical Jesus. (4) Cassidy's absolute rejection of the "political apologetic theory" is unnecessary. It is based on an overestimation of the role of the chief priests and an underestimation of Pilate's and Herod's exoneration of Jesus.

OBJECTION 1: HISTORICIZATION

There are several places throughout Cassidy's book in which he seems to historicize Luke's account, including several in Chapter 5. It is undeniably difficult for any scholar to write so that the distinction between Luke's interpretation of Jesus and the historical Jesus is always clear. Redaction critics, in particular, face this problem. And yet, it is methodologically crucial that the distinction consistently be made. Cassidy is very clear about this distinction at the outset, but as the reader progresses she/he has the impression Cassidy is discussing social and political attitudes of the historical Jesus rather than Luke's understanding of Jesus' view. Perhaps this is merely an unintended implication of convenient language; but if Cassidy *does* historicize the text in places, one must inquire to what extent Cassidy's conclusions about Jesus' social and political stance were based on these hypothetical historical events.

An example of this tendency is Cassidy's discussion of Jesus' appearance before Herod. Cassidy considers Herod's historical power over Jesus' life or death in interpreting Jesus' refusal to cooperate with Herod. Cassidy seems to assume that the historical Jesus knew Herod's power over him and that, because he knew this, his refusal to cooperate with Herod is dramatic, or as Cassidy puts it, "striking."[19] Cassidy does not treat the possibility that, apart from *any* historical basis, Luke chose to portray Jesus as one who did not defer to political rulers. This is a redactional possibility since only Luke, of all the evangelists, tells of Jesus' appearance before Herod. This renders the historical character of the narrative questionable and simultaneously raises the important question of why Luke would want to write this episode into his version of the trial narrative. Perhaps Cassidy's implied treatment of the episode as historical explains his lack of attention to this redactional question and his ready dismissal of Conzelmann's political-apologetic theory. Whatever the reason, Cassidy does not adequately emphasize that, although Luke's Jesus does not defer to or cooperate with Herod, neither does he *actively* defy Herod. Herod questioned Jesus; and, Luke says, Jesus did not answer him (Luke 23:9).

In a similar way, Cassidy seems to historicize Luke's account of Pilate and Herod's verdicts about Jesus.[20] Cassidy speculates regarding what would have been in Jesus' best interest under circumstances such as those Luke describes. He postulates that, since neither Herod nor Pilate expressed an interest in seeing Jesus killed, it would have been better for Jesus to cooperate with them. He argues that Jesus' refusal to cooperate, given their power over him and attitudes toward him, reflects the degree to which Jesus, implicitly the historical Jesus, was committed to relationships based on service and humility: Jesus withheld his approval from rulers whose practices were *not* based on service and humility.[21] These conclusions may be drawn accurately about Luke's Jesus; but whether and to what extent Luke's Jesus mirrors the historical Jesus in these respects is another question. Even if Cassidy *is* analyzing the portrait Luke draws, Cassidy again overemphasizes Jesus' refusal to cooperate. Jesus' answer to Pilate's questions is indirect (Luke 23:3); but he does not actively defy Pilate either. It is also important to note that Jesus, in Luke's Gospel, does not subject either Herod or Pilate to the severe criticism he levels at some.[22]

In one final place in Chapter 5, Cassidy again seems to historicize Luke's account. Luke, Cassidy argues, gives no explanation for Herod and Pilate's verdicts that Jesus was innocent.[23] For Cassidy, Luke's silence on this matter is related to Luke's effort to lay primary responsibility on the chief priests for Jesus' execution. He bases this conclusion on what he speculates Herod and Pilate understood about the chief priests' enmity toward Jesus and what their political motives might have been: "Their main objective was to safeguard the Roman sway over Palestine."[24] Once more, Luke's interpretation of Jesus may accurately reflect the historical Jesus and his circumstances; but Cassidy's speculation about the understanding and motives of Herod and Pilate seems to treat Luke's account as factual, without accounting for redactional motifs. Cassidy thereby detracts from the meaning and emphasis of Luke's perspective, the explanation for which arguably lies in *Luke*'s *Sitz-im-Leben* rather than that of the historical Jesus. Cassidy again neglects the important redactional question: Why would *Luke* emphasize Herod and Pilate's verdicts that Jesus was innocent? This question needs to be answered directly and clearly.

OBJECTION 2: "THE CHIEF PRIESTS AND THEIR ALLIES"

One of the difficulties with Cassidy's analysis of the trial narrative is his use of the phrase "the chief priests and their allies."[25] Although Note 9 to Chapter 4 identifies the allies as the scribes and the elders[26] and Note 22 of Cassidy's chapter on the trial narrative refers the reader to Chapter 4 for more information,[27] only Herod Antipas and the Romans are discussed explicitly in Chapter 4 in addition to the chief priests. The use of this phrase lacks precision and makes it difficult for Cassidy's reader to evaluate the role of "the allies" in comparison to the role Cassidy assigns the chief priests in Luke's version of Jesus' trial narrative.

The Trial Narrative Reconsidered

An examination of the trial narratives of all four Gospels indicates that the magnitude Cassidy assigns to the role played by the chief priests and his minimization of the role of Pilate and Herod's exoneration of Jesus for Luke's purposes is misstated.

Mark

In Mark's account of Jesus' trial, there are eight basic characters who oppose Jesus. They are Judas, the chief priests (including the high priest), the scribes, the crowd (*ochlos*), which includes the servant of the high priest at 14:47, the elders, the Sanhedrin, captains, and Pilate. The scribes appear six times, the crowd four times, the elders three times, the Sanhedrin twice, Judas twice, and the captains once. Pilate appears in one long scene (15:2–15). In Mark's version, the chief priests take precedence. They are mentioned almost as frequently as all of the other characters put together, and they appear more than twice as often as any other character.

It is important to note, however, that the same Greek word in the singular refers to the high priest as refers in the plural to the chief priests as a group.[28] Out of fourteen references to chief priests, seven refer to the high priest.[29] It was to the chief priests that Judas went to betray Jesus and it was they who "rejoiced" at Judas' proposal and promised to pay him (14:10). The armed crowd which accompanied Judas to arrest Jesus was sent from the chief priests (and the scribes and elders) (14:43). Jesus was taken first to the high priest, who was meeting with the chief priests and scribes and elders (14:53). The chief priests, with all the council, sought for a witness against Jesus to put him to death, but did not find anyone (14:55). The high priest questioned Jesus (14:60–64). The chief priests called a meeting of themselves, the elders and scribes, and all the rest of the council to deliver Jesus to Pilate (15:1). It was the chief priests who accused him before Pilate (15:3). Pilate knew, Mark says, that the chief priests had delivered Jesus to Pilate out of envy (15:10). It was the chief priests who "stirred up the crowd" to ask for the release of Barabbas rather than Jesus (15:11). At the foot of the cross, the chief priests, with the scribes, mocked Jesus (15:31–32).

In Mark's passion narrative, the scribes and elders appear as co-conspirators with the chief priests in arranging Jesus' death; but the chief priests take the lead in it. They plan for it, convene the necessary meetings to condemn Jesus, interrogate Jesus in the person of the high priest, accuse Jesus before Pilate, stir up the crowd to release Barabbas, and mock Jesus on the cross. The statement that Pilate knew the chief priests had delivered Jesus to him out of envy is redactional to Mark's account and clearly confirms Mark's intention to emphasize the chief priests' responsibility for Jesus' death, while simultaneously disclosing their motive.

Matthew

Matthew's trial narrative follows Mark's with some modifications and additions. In Matthew, there are nine basic characters who oppose Jesus. They are the same characters who appear in Mark with the addition of the Pharisees. Matthew's emphasis is similar to Mark's but distinctive. References to the chief priests (including references to the high priest) appear nineteen times in Matthew. The elders appear nine times; the crowd, five times; the scribes, the captains, and Judas, twice each; and there is one reference each to the Sanhedrin and the Pharisees. Pilate appears in one scene (27:2–26). Simple mathematics make it clear that Matthew's account gives the chief priests prominence. The chief priests appear twice as often as the elders, almost four times as often as the crowds, and as often as all other characters mentioned put together. This presentation conforms to the accusations which were made of Jesus according to Matthew,[30] to the emphasis on teaching in Matthew's Gospel and to his resulting de-emphasis of cult in general and the temple cult in particular.[31]

It is the chief priests who assemble with the elders to consult how to seize and kill Jesus in the courtyard of the high priest Caiaphas (26:3–5). The armed crowd which accompanies Judas to arrest Jesus comes from the chief priests and "elders of the people," as Matthew says (26:47).[32] The scribes are not involved here as they were in Mark. As in Mark, it is the chief priests, with the help of the whole council, who seek false witnesses in order to put Jesus to death (26:59). As in Mark, the high priest questions Jesus (26:62–65). It is the chief priests in counsel with the "elders of the people" who agree to put Jesus to death (27:1), and deliver Jesus to Pilate (27:2). It is the chief priests and the elders who pay Judas for betraying Jesus (27:3). The chief priests, and the elders with them, accuse Jesus before Pilate (27:12). It is the chief priests, but again the elders with them, who "persuade the crowds" to ask for Barabbas' release rather than Jesus' (27:20). The chief priests, with the scribes and elders, mock Jesus at the cross (27:41–43). In Mark's account, the elders are not part of this scene. It is the chief priests, with the Pharisees, who ask Pilate to have Jesus' grave guarded until the third day (27:62).[33] Likewise it is the chief priests and the Pharisees who seal the grave with a stone (27:66). It is the chief priests who receive word of Jesus' resurrection appearance to Mary Magdalene (28:11) and who, with the elders, pay the soldiers who guard the tomb to say that Jesus' disciples stole the body when they were sleeping (28:12–15).

As in Mark's passion narrative, the chief priests plot to kill Jesus, arm the crowd that arrests Jesus, seek false witnesses to testify against Jesus, in the person of the high priest question Jesus, agree to have Jesus put to death, deliver Jesus to Pilate, accuse Jesus before Pilate, persuade the crowds to release Barabbas, mock Jesus at the cross, ask Pilate to have Jesus' grave guarded and pay the guards to falsely tell how Jesus' disciples stole his body. But, except in seeking the false witnesses to testify against Jesus (when the chief priests act in conjunction with the whole council), and in asking to have the grave guarded (when they act together with the Pharisees), the chief priests are with "the elders of the people," usually referred to simply as "the elders." The elders are never mentioned in Matthew's passion narrative without the chief priests, but the chief priests never act alone. The chief priests are always mentioned first, the elders second; but they are co-conspirators together in Jesus' death and even in the suppression of the news of the resurrection (Matt. 28:12) along with the Pharisees. Unlike Mark's account, the scribes are noticeably absent, except—presumably—when the council meets, of which they were a part, and except at the cross, where they also mock Jesus. For Matthew, then, it is the chief priests *with the elders* who put Jesus to death supported by the council, the crowds, the soldiers, and Pilate.

John

John's passion narrative is quite distinctive. Apart from Jesus and his disciples, the characters in John's account are the chief priests (including the high priests), the captains or soldiers, the officers (of the chief priests and

Pharisees [18:3], or of the Jews [18:12]), Judas, the Jews,[34] and Pilate. The chief priests, the soldiers and officers are impliedly included in the group referred to as "the Jews," in the passion narrative. The chief priests are mentioned thirteen times (including references to the high priest), the captains or soldiers six times, the officers six times, and the Jews nine times, only two of which are relevant to this study. (Other uses include John's use of the noun in 18:33: "Are you the king of the Jews?") Judas' name appears three times. Pilate appears in one long scene (18:28–19:16). The Pharisees appear once.

The band of soldiers and officers sent to the garden to arrest Jesus are sent from the chief priests and the Pharisees (18:3). Jesus is taken first to Annas, the father-in-law of the high priest, Caiaphas (18:13). The high priest Caiaphas, in the high priest's courtyard, counsels the Jews that Jesus should die (18:14–15). It is the chief priest Annas who questions Jesus and then sends him to Caiaphas (18:19, 24). It is not clear from John's account whether it is the chief priests, the soldiers, or both who send Jesus to Pilate (18:28) and accuse Jesus before Pilate (18:30). It is clear from John's narrative that the chief priests *know* Jesus is sent to Pilate and permit it (18:24–28), but the reference at this point of the narrative is to "the Jews" (18:31). However, when Pilate questions Jesus he tells Jesus that Jesus' own "nation" and the chief priests have handed him over to Pilate (18:35).

It is not clear who demands that Barabbas be released instead of Jesus (18:39–40). When Pilate presents Jesus flogged, crowned with thorns, and dressed in purple, it is the chief priests, with the soldiers, who call for Jesus' crucifixion (19:6). In Pilate's conversation with Jesus, Jesus explicitly tells Pilate that Pilate's sin is not as great as the sin of those who delivered Jesus to him (19:11). Then "the Jews" call for Jesus' crucifixion (19:12) and, presumably, the chief priests are among them. When Pilate refers to Jesus as "your king" before "the Jews," it is the chief priests who shout "We have no king but Caesar" (19:15). It is the chief priests who argue with Pilate that the sign he placed on Jesus' cross, "King of the Jews," should read "The one *who claimed* to be King of the Jews" (19:21).[35] It is the soldiers who actually crucify Jesus and cast lots for his garments (19:23–25a). It is one of the soldiers who pierces Jesus' side (19:34).

In John's account, it is the chief priests—working consistently with and through the soldiers and officers—who arrest Jesus, interrogate Jesus, and deliver him to Pilate. The soldiers mock him. The chief priests and officers, who are among and are supported by the nebulous group John calls "the Jews," demanded that Pilate crucify him, gamble for his garments, and pierce his side. "The Jews" effect Jesus' death but they do so through the machinations of the chief priests carried out by the soldiers and officers. Although the Pharisees are mentioned, their role is minor.

Luke

With these Gospel accounts, we can now compare Luke's account. In Luke's account there are more characters than in any other passion narrative of the Gospels: the chief priests (including the high priest), the scribes, the elders, the captains of the temple, Judas, the Sanhedrin, the multitudes, and the crowd (including the servant of the high priest at 22:50), the soldiers, the people, the rulers, Pilate, and Herod. Except for the Pharisees (who appear in Matthew's account of the chief priests' attempt to suppress the news of Jesus' resurrection), and "the Jews" and the officers of John's account, Luke's version involves all of the characters of every other version. Only Luke adds to the already long list of participants the person of Herod, the multitudes, and the rulers.

In Luke's version, as in those of Matthew, Mark, and John, the chief priests appear more frequently than other characters. The chief priests appear ten times, Judas three times, the scribes three times, the elders twice, the captains of the temple twice, the multitudes twice, the crowd twice, the rulers twice, the people twice, the council once, and the soldiers once. Pilate appears in two scenes (23:1-7 and 23:13-25), both before and after Jesus appears before Herod (23:9-12). As noted above, it is only in Luke's version that Jesus appears before Herod. It is only Luke, therefore, who makes passing judgment on Jesus the event which creates a bond of friendship between Pilate and Herod who, according to Luke, were formerly enemies. In Luke's Gospel, the chief priests appear less than half as often as all of the other characters put together.

It is the crowd (22:47), among whom are the servant of the high priest (22:50), the chief priests, the captains of the temple, and the elders (22:52) who arrest Jesus in the garden. In Matthew and Mark's accounts, the armed crowd that arrests Jesus was sent *from* the chief priests and the elders (and the scribes in Mark) but did not include them. John's version is that soldiers and officers were sent *from* the chief priests and Pharisees. Only Luke makes the chief priests, the temple captains, and the elders present and participants of Jesus' arrest. The scribes are not implicated in Luke's account of Jesus' arrest. It is this same *group* who take Jesus to the high priest's house. It is the elders of the people *with* the chief priests and scribes who take Jesus to appear before the Sanhedrin (22:66); and it is "they" (the elders, chief priests, and scribes) who interrogate Jesus (22:67-70). It is "they" (the elders, chief priests, and scribes) who condemn Jesus (22:72), take him to Pilate (23:1), and accuse him before Pilate (23:2). This same group becomes "the chief priests and the crowds [*ocheous*]" (23:4) whom Pilate informs he finds no crime in Jesus; and "they" further accuse Jesus of inciting people with his teaching (23:5).

Although it is Pilate who sends Jesus to Herod because he discovers Jesus is a Galilean, it is the chief priests *with* the scribes who accuse Jesus before Herod, while the soldiers (Herod's) treat Jesus with contempt and mock him (23:11). When Herod returns Jesus to Pilate, Pilate calls together the chief priests *with* the rulers and the people (*laon*) to pronounce his verdict of Jesus' innocence. He then interprets Herod's return of Jesus as evidence of Jesus' innocence and announces that he plans to flog Jesus and release him (23:13,

16), whereupon "they all" (chief priests, rulers, and people) cry out for Barabbas' release (23:18–19). When Pilate *again* expresses his desire to release Jesus, the same *group* (chief priests, rulers, people) demand Jesus' crucifixion (23:20–21). Yet a third time Pilate proclaims he finds no crime in Jesus, and wants to flog him and release him, but "they" (chief priests, rulers, people) call with even louder cries for Jesus' crucifixion. It is to *"their will"* that Pilate delivers Jesus up (23:25). Later, on the road to Emmaus, Cleopas tells the risen Jesus, whom he does not recognize, that the chief priests *and rulers* condemned Jesus to death and crucified him (24:20). Thus, in Luke's account, "they," who are apparently the same *group* (chief priests, rulers, people), lead Jesus away (23:26), crucify him (23:33), and cast lots for his garments (23:34).

The multitudes and crowds, however, are sometimes against Jesus and sometimes for Jesus. The chief priests, leaders, and the people together with a multitude demand his crucifixion (23:18), but another multitude of people follow him on the road to Golgatha, wailing and lamenting him (23:27). Although the crowd (*ochlos*) sometimes participates in Jesus' death, other crowds (*ochloi*) gather at the cross, and return home beating their breasts after Jesus dies (23:48). In this way, Luke conveys that the attitudes of the multitudes and crowds toward Jesus are divided. The people (*laos*) watch him on the cross; but it is the rulers who scoff at him, challenging him, if he is Messiah, to save himself (23:35). Likewise, the soldiers—not the multitudes and crowds—mock him, telling him to save himself if he is King of the Jews (23:38).

So it is that in Luke's Gospel, too, the chief priests are participants in every phase of Jesus' arrest, "trial," and crucifixion. They *never* appear alone, however, and they are not always mentioned first. In Jesus' arrest, the captains of the temple and the elders are co-conspirators with the chief priests. At Jesus' trial, the chief priests are present to lead Jesus to the Sanhedrin but they are present with the "elders of the people" and the scribes. All of these people together interrogate Jesus, bring him to Pilate, and accuse him. It is the chief priests, this time with the multitudes, who respond to Pilate's first judgment that Jesus is innocent. It is the chief priests, with the scribes, who accuse Jesus before Herod. The chief priests *with* the rulers and the people are those Pilate summons to announce his verdict of Jesus' innocence and the ones who cry for Barabbas' release and Jesus' crucifixion. Luke implies that it is the chief priests with the rulers and the people who lead Jesus away, crucify him, and cast lots for his garments. At the foot of the cross, the chief priests are silent while others (the rulers and soldiers) mock him.[36]

Here Luke diverges from Matthew and Mark, in whose accounts the chief priests also revile Jesus.[37] The chief priests are more consistently involved in Jesus' death than others are, but always in conspiracy with someone else (Judas, the captains of the temple, the elders, the scribes, the Sanhedrin, Pilate, the hostile crowd, the rulers, the people, soldiers). Luke's use of pronouns ("they," "all of them," etc.) lessens the prominence of the chief priests and increases the participation of these other groups beyond their explicit mention.

Summary

The results of this Gospel comparison of the trial narratives show that, although Luke consistently involves the chief priests in Jesus' trial and death, he does *not* give their role the emphasis that Mark, Matthew, and John's accounts do. There are fewer explicit references to them in Luke than in Mark and Matthew. In Luke, they never act alone (i.e., are always mentioned as part of a group) and are not always mentioned first among a group. Luke introduces more additional characters than the other evangelists, thereby mitigating the chief priests' role. Luke's frequent use of verbs without named actors (translated "they" in English) fuses the chief priests' role with that of everyone else. The high priest does not interrogate Jesus at all; the elders of the people, with the chief priests and scribes, interrogate Jesus before the Sanhedrin. In Matthew and Mark, the chief priests appear approximately twice as often as all of Jesus' other opponents put together. In Luke, the chief priests are explicitly mentioned less than half as often as all of Jesus' opponents put together. In John's Gospel, the chief priests are explicitly mentioned as many times as in Luke; but in John, the cast of additional characters is so small that the activity of the chief priests stands out.

In summary: It is primarily the chief priests, with the scribes and elders, who accomplish Jesus' crucifixion in Mark's Gospel. It is primarily the chief priests, with the help of the elders, who do so in Matthew's account. It is the chief priests, working through the soldiers and officers, who achieve Jesus' death in John's Gospel. By contrast, in Luke's Gospel, it is various individuals and groups, among whom the chief priests consistently appear, who put Jesus to death.

Luke's use of the term "rulers" at 23:13 and 23:36 captures the idea Luke strives to convey in distributing responsibility for the crucifixion among so many people. It simultaneously refers to almost everyone involved, Jew and Gentile alike: the chief priests, the high priest, the scribes, the elders, the Sanhedrin, the soldiers or captains, Pilate, and Herod. The only participants in Luke's passion narrative who do not come within this broad classification are Judas, the crowd, the multitude, and the people. The crowd, the multitude, and/or the people (which usually include one or more of these "rulers"), include by implication the masses gathered in Jerusalem for the Passover festival. Each of these terms functions synonymously for the other.

The result is that two main categories of participants emerge in Luke's passion narrative: (1) the rulers, among whom the chief priests consistently appear; and (2) the crowds, multitudes, and people. Taken together, there are far more references to those among the former category than there are references to the latter. This indicates that Luke places primary responsibility on the rulers and secondary responsibility on the crowds, etc.

One final factor merits attention. Because the rulers are those who put Jesus to death, Jerusalem takes on a special significance. Jerusalem is the place where "the rulers" of the Jews dwell. Luke has alluded to the importance of Jerusalem in other ways throughout his Gospel, especially in 13:33-35 where Jesus explains that he must go to Jerusalem to die because no prophet can perish outside of Jerusalem. This thought, in the same passage, prompts Jesus to mourn Jerusalem who has previously killed the prophets and "stoned those sent to her."[38] Other passages suggest the same,[39] as other scholars have noted.[40]

Thus it is not other rulers, but primarily the Jewish rulers of Jerusalem who put Jesus to death with the help of Pilate.

OBJECTION 3: CONFIRMATION IN ACTS

Inserted into several of the speeches of the first half of Acts, speeches commonly referred to as the missionary speeches,[41] are kerygmatic summaries of the life, death, and resurrection of Jesus. Each of these Jesus narratives[42] functions as part of the speech to which they belong and, therefore, shares the broad functions of the speeches themselves within the book of Acts.[43] Luke's format for the speech is to precede it with some event which evokes a response in a crowd, either positive or negative, which requires an explanation from Jesus' disciples.[44] The opportunity to explain is also the occasion to preach the gospel to the audience in six of the major speeches in Acts.[45] In the course of preaching the gospel, the disciples must explain who Jesus was, how he died, and what the meaning of his death, and in some instances, his resurrection, is understood by them to be. In doing so, Luke identifies those who were responsible for Jesus' death. The consensus of modern Acts critics is that the speeches of Acts were either entirely composed by Luke or were composed from pre-Lukan traditions heavily edited by Luke for Lukan literary and theological purposes. Therefore, the identification of those who are responsible for Jesus' death is redactional to Luke and should contribute to the reader's understanding of Luke's views on this subject.

In Peter's speech on Pentecost in Acts 2,[46] Peter addresses a "multitude" of "devout Jews from every nation" (2:5-6). This description makes clear that among those present are both Hellenistic Jews from all over the world and Judean Jews, as well as, presumably, Jerusalem Jews.[47] This is important because when, in the Jesus narrative, Peter identifies those responsible for Jesus' death, he says: "*You* killed this man who was given up through the fastening hands of lawless men by the fixed plan and foreknowledge of God" (2:23). "You" refers to the *multitude (plēthos)* of 2:5, 6. The multitude appeared in Luke's crucifixion narrative although its character was dichotomized.[48] Here the multitude is referred to by Peter during the course of his speech as "Men of Judea and all those inhabiting Jerusalem" (2:14b) and as "Men of Israel" (2:22). They are those who gave up Jesus. The lawless men through whose hands he was given up are not identified.

In Peter's speech of Chapter 3,[49] the audience is the people (*laos*) (3:9, 11, 12). In this Jesus narrative, when Peter describes how Jesus was killed, he says: ". . . *you* delivered [Jesus] and denied [him] in the presence of Pilate when he [Pilate] had decided to release him" (3:13). Peter continues: "*You* denied the holy and just one and *you* asked a murderer to be granted to you and *you* killed the author of life whom God raised from the dead" (3:14–15). Peter continues by saying "And now, *brothers*, I know that *you* acted through ignorance as did your rulers *(archontes)* (3:17)." It is the people, with their rulers, who delivered Jesus, denied him in Pilate's presence, requested that Barabbas be released instead of Jesus, and killed him. This is consistent with Luke's Gospel account in which the multitude (*plēthos*) leads Jesus before Pilate and accuses him.[50] The multitude there consists of the elders of the people (*laos*), the chief priests, the scribes, and the Sanhedrin members.[51] When Pilate sees Jesus the second time, he calls together the chief priests, the leaders (*archontas*), and the people (*laos*) who shout for Barabbas' release instead of Jesus' and who shout for Jesus' crucifixion.

The Jesus narrative of Peter's speech of Chapter 4[52] is addressed to the rulers (*archontes*) of the people (*laon*) and the elders (4:8). Included are the scribes in Jerusalem, Annas the high priest, Caiaphas, John, Alexander, and "as many as were of the high-priestly class" (4:5–6). ". . . *You* crucified (Jesus) whom God raised from the dead . . . ," Peter accuses them. All of these individuals and groups were referred to directly or indirectly in Luke's trial narrative.

The commandant of the temple (5:24, 26), the high priest, the ones with him, the Sanhedrin, and all the senate of the children of Israel (5:27) are the audience of Peter and the apostles' speech in Chapter 5.[53] The Sadducees are also implicated (5:17). ". . . *You* killed [him], hanging him on a tree . . . ," Peter and the apostles preach. Except for "the Senate" and the Sadducees, all of these appeared in Luke's trial narrative.

Peter's speech of Chapter 10[54] is addressed to a distinctive audience, Cornelius and his household (10:24), who are Gentile.[55] Peter is there because he and Cornelius have had concurrent visions directing them to one another. It is this episode in Acts which, according to Luke, inaugurates the Gentile mission; and it is Peter's vision (10:9–16), amplified by his experience with Cornelius, which provides the rationale for the inclusion of the Gentiles in the Gospel. When Peter describes to Cornelius who put Jesus to death, he simply says "they killed [him] hanging [him] on a tree" (10:39). In this context, "they" refers to the Jews (10:39) in whose country Jesus went about doing good and curing all those oppressed by the devil (10:38), and the Jews in Jerusalem (10:39). From the point of view of a Gentile like Cornelius, perhaps a more detailed explanation would not have been understood. Cornelius (Luke might have imagined), like many Gentiles in Luke's own audience, would not have understood the differences among various types of Jews (e.g., scribes and Sadducees).

The last Jesus narrative appears in what is usually identified as the last missionary discourse of Acts, Paul's speech at Psidian Antioch in Chapter 13.[56] Here Paul is presented by Luke as addressing the members of a Hellenistic synagogue gathered to worship on a Sabbath (13:14). As Hellenistic Jews living outside of Jerusalem, they would not have participated in Jesus' death in any way. The words of this sermon reflect this presumption because, when Paul describes Jesus' death he says: ". . . the ones dwelling in Jerusalem and *their* rulers . . . condemned him, and finding no cause of death in him, they asked Pilate to destroy him" (13:27-28). This designation makes more specific the descriptions Luke has provided up to now in the speeches. The multitude who opposed Jesus, the rulers, certainly the chief priests and the high priest, the elders of the people, the Sadducees, the Sanhedrin, even the people (*laos*) who were present at Jesus' trial and crucifixion were Jews in Jerusalem. The speeches taken together convey that it was Jerusalem Jews, both Hellenistic and Judean in background, but especially their rulers, who put Jesus to death. They put him to death even though they knew he was innocent; but they did so, Luke says, out of ignorance (3:17).

Other Relevant Passages in Acts

Other passages in Acts shed light on Luke's views about who put Jesus to death. It is part of Luke's literary and theological intent to show that what happened to Jesus happened to the great leaders and saviors of Israel before Jesus.[57] Likewise, Luke shows that what happened to Jesus also happened to Jesus' disciples. This Lukan theme and literary technique suggests that the same persons portrayed as responsible for Jesus' death in the Gospel will appear in Acts as opponents of Peter, Paul, and the early church. Relevant passages include the prayer of Chapter 4, the story of Stephen (6:1-7:60), Peter's imprisonment (12:4-19), and Paul's many troubles on his missionary journeys.

In the prayer of Jesus' disciples which follows Peter and John's release from prison (4:24b-30), Luke shows how Ps. 146:6 is fulfilled in Jesus' death.[58] The raging of the nations, of which the Psalm speaks, is fulfilled in the assembling of "the kings of the earth" and "the rulers" against the Lord and Christ who Luke's readers know from 2:36 to be Jesus. Luke then interprets those who assembled against God's holy servant Jesus to be Pilate and Herod with the Gentiles and the peoples (*laois*) of Israel. The association of Pilate and Herod with the Lukan passion narrative is obvious. As noted above, these two "kings of the earth" also come within the meaning of the word "ruler," as Luke elsewhere employs it. The presence of Pilate in Luke's passion narrative is symbolic of the participation of the Gentiles in Jesus' death, which Luke foretold in the passion predictions. The people (*laos*) were explicitly involved in Jesus' crucifixion in Luke, although their role is secondary to that of the rulers. The prayer confirms that Luke sees the rulers and people as responsible for Jesus' death.

Stephen's death is a result of some false witnesses stirring up the people (*laos*), the elders, and the scribes who seized Stephen and led him before the council and the high priest (6:12). It is this entire group who eventually rushes on Stephen "and casting him outside the city, stoned him" (7:57-58). Commentators frequently note the similarities and relationships between Jesus' trial and death and Stephen's trial and death.[59] Like Jesus, Stephen is accused by witnesses who are false. All those who participate in Stephen's death were explicit participants in Jesus' death: the people, the elders, the scribes, the Sanhedrin, and the high priest.

In Chapter 12, just after Luke's reader is informed that Herod put James, the brother of John, to death with a sword, and that Herod was ill-treating some of the ones of the church (12:1-2), Herod arrests Peter during the Passover holidays and puts him in prison (12:3-4). Peter is released by an angel who comes to him during the night (12:7-11). Although Herod searches for Peter after his miraculous release, he is unable to find him to imprison him again (12:19).

Herod was also part of Luke's trial narrative. His role in Jesus' death has its parallel in his treatment of Jesus' disciples: Herod could find nothing in Jesus for which to punish him, but allowed him to be crucified; he killed James and put Peter in prison simply because he saw that it pleased "the Jews" when he ill-treated Christians.[60]

Paul, in his missionary journeys, faces one opponent after another. In Chapter 13, Paul and Barnabas were chased out of Psidian Antioch by Jews who were jealous of the crowds Paul's preaching drew (13:45) and who urged "the honorable and worshipping women along with the chief men of the city" to persecute them (13:50).[61] At Iconium, "disobedient Jews," not the great multitude (*plēthos*) of Jews who did believe (14:1), "excited and embittered the minds of the nations against the brothers" (14:2). When they finally rushed Peter and Barnabas, insulting them and stoning them (14:5), the rulers were explicitly among them. At Philippi, the presumably Gentile owners of a maiden possessed by a spirit who recognized Peter and his friends as "servants of the most high God who announce a way of salvation" (16:16-17), have Paul and Silas dragged to the marketplace to appear before the rulers (*archontas*) and the praetors (*stratēgois*) because they have lost their economic interest in the maiden (16:19).[62]

At Thessalonica, some jealous Jews took aside some wicked men, loafers of the marketplace, and gathered a crowd (*ochlopoiēsantes*) to persecute Paul (17:5). At Beroea, the same Thessalonian Jews troubled the crowd (*ochlous*) over Paul and Silas (17:13). At Corinth, although some Jews believed (18:4-5), some resisted and eventually set on Paul, bringing him to the tribunal to accuse him before the Gentile ruler Gallio. He refused to hear the case but not before the synagogue ruler struck Paul in the face (18:6-17). At Ephesus, those who opposed Paul were some Jews who were "hardened and disobeyed, speaking ill of the way," and a mob of Gentile silversmiths who were incited against Paul by accusations that Paul would destroy their business (19:9, 24-28).

There was a plot against Paul in Greece, which caused him to leave Greece (18:3); but Luke does not say who plotted. In Jerusalem, Asian Jews stirred up the crowd (*ochlon*), causing the people (*laon*) to come together to try to kill him (21:27-31). Soldiers took care of the incident (21:32);[63] and Paul had to appear before the chief priests and Sanhedrin (22:30), a multitude (*plēthos*) (23:7) consisting of Sadducees who opposed Paul, and Pharisees who ended up defending Paul (23:8-10).[64] In still another incident some Jews plotted to kill Paul and appealed to the chief priests and scribes for help (23:12-16). Gentile rulers, warned of the plot, enabled Paul to escape their machinations (23:16-33).[65]

At Caesarea, Paul was accused before the Gentile governor by the high priest, some elders, and an orator named Tertullus, all of whom were later referred to as "the Jews" (24:1, 9). Later, the chief priests and "the first ones of the Jews," a synonym in Hellenistic Judaism for the "rulers" of Jerusalem, informed Festus against Paul (25:2). When Festus heard Paul's case, Paul was accused by "Jews who came down from Jerusalem" (25:7). Because Festus wanted to "show the Jews favor," he asked Paul if he wanted to appeal to Caesar (25:9). Paul did appeal to Caesar and, as a result, remained a prisoner, even though Festus, along with Bernice and King Agrippa, later agreed that Paul "has done nothing worthy of bonds or death" (26:30-32). During Paul's shipwreck, the soldiers (*stratiōtōn*) wanted to kill Paul but the Gentile centurion came to his rescue (27:42-43). To the very end, even in Rome, Paul continued to preach. There "some first ones of the Jews" believed, but some of these did not (28:24-25), and once again Paul vowed to commit his mission to the Gentiles.

This survey of those who oppose Paul on his missionary journeys shows that the individuals and groups, in their identity and function, parallel those whom Luke associates with Jesus' death. Differences between the opponents of Jesus in the passion narrative and the opponents of Paul in Acts have their source in the Gentile context in which Paul's missionary journeys are set. The jealous or disobedient Jews, for instance, become an appropriate designation of those Jews in a Gentile city who reject Paul, in contrast to the "believing Jews" of a Gentile city who accept the gospel Paul preaches. Likewise, the term "ruler" no longer accurately designates the Jewish leaders of a Gentile city where prominent Jewish citizens achieved roles of leadership occupied by chief priests, scribes, and other religious leaders in Jerusalem. "Chief men and women" is more appropriate. And if even the differences were significant, the similarities outweigh the differences.

Those who opposed Jesus are basically the same as those who oppose Paul: (1) Some Jews (13:45, 14:2, 17:5, 19:9, 21:27-31, 23:12-16, 24:19, 28:24-25) whose roles parallel those of the people (*laos*) in the passion narratives; (2) the rulers (*archēchois*) (14:5, 16:6-7) who parallel the rulers of the passion narrative; (3) Gentiles whose interests are threatened by Paul's preaching (16:16-17, 19:24-28, 23:16-33); they are reminiscent of Pilate, whose personal and political interests are threatened by Jesus' teaching; (4) the crowds (*ochlous*) (17:5, 13; 21:27-31) who parallel the crowds in the passion narrative; (5) Gentile rulers like Gallio and Festus who always find Paul innocent of charges his fellow Jews make against him, as Gentile ruler Pilate found Jesus innocent (18:6–18, 25:9); (6) Synagogue leaders (18:6–17) who had their counterparts among those who served on the Sanhedrin; (7) soldiers (21:32, 27:42–43) who appeared in the passion narrative; (8) the chief priests (20:30, 23:12–16), the Sanhedrin (22:30), and the scribes (23:12–16), all of whom appeared in Luke's passion narrative; (9) some Sadducees (23:8–10) who are not mentioned in Luke's passion narrative, but whose counterpart may be found in the chief priests; (10) the people, who are incited to violence (21:27–31); (11) the high priest (24:1, 9) and the elders (24:1, 9); (12) King Agrippa, whose Jewish contacts and awareness make him reminiscent of Herod.

Summary: Acts

One of Luke's important literary techniques in Acts is to refer several times in different ways to the same event(s). The Jesus narrative which appears in six different speeches is an example of this technique.[66] Luke intends the various references to a single event to be read cumulatively. No one passage provides the complete picture of the event Luke is interpreting; but the picture which emerges in the reader's mind from having read several different descriptions of one event is fuller than any one description could be. This literary principle is at work in all the passages in Acts which refer to Jesus' death: they are to be read cumulatively in order to discover Luke's full perspective.

The overall perspective provided by Luke in the Jesus narratives of the speeches in Acts and by those passages in which the opponents of Jesus' disciples are identified, supports the conclusion drawn from the trial narrative: according to Luke, many people were responsible for Jesus' death; but primarily responsible were the rulers (Jewish and Gentile). The people (and crowds and multitudes) are also implicated, although their opposition is sometimes incited by the rulers.

OBJECTION 4: REJECTION OF
THE POLITICAL-APOLOGETIC THEORY

A careful reading of Conzelmann's political-apologetic theory reveals that Cassidy has misconstrued Conzelmann's position. Conzelmann does speak of Luke's attempt to depict Jesus as loyal to the Roman government;[67] but the overall point of Conzelmann's theory is not this. Rather, Conzelmann means to say that Luke—living in an age when the church was suffering from its increasingly separate existence from Judaism and, therefore, from its status as an illegal religion—desired to show readers, Jewish and Gentile alike, that neither Jesus nor his disciples were ever judged guilty of crime against the Roman government or of anything deserving imprisonment or death.[68] Luke tries to show that, like Jesus and the disciples of the early church, the church of Luke's time has troubles because of its theological differences with Jews who do not accept Jesus as Messiah.

The church remains part of Israel, though in theological dispute with "some" of Israel. As such, it is entitled to the same legal status as Judaism. This theme constitutes a plea (or if one prefers, an apology) on Luke's part for the end of persecution of Christians by Rome based on Jewish accusations against them. It simultaneously explains the origins of Jewish complaints against Christians (jealousy, theological differences, etc.). This purpose is entirely consistent with Luke's portrayal of who put Jesus to death in the Gospel and Acts. It is consistent with Luke's redactional emphasis on the official judgments of Gentile rulers that Jesus, and his disciples after him, were innocent of any crime against Rome.

Cassidy rejects Conzelmann's hypothesis without providing a substantive explanation of these redactional patterns in Luke. Cassidy should have used his research to modify, refine, and clarify Conzelmann's thesis rather than to reject it. Conzelmann was misguided in some of the elements which characterize his thesis;[69] e.g., Cassidy is right to argue that Luke did not portray Jesus as loyal and subservient to Rome. Cassidy is correct in his description of Jesus' attitude toward rulers, Roman or otherwise. Jesus rejected the premise of their rule and did not defer to their authority or cooperate with them. But this is not incompatible with the main thrust of Conzelmann's thesis. It is, rather, complementary to it.

Jesus had values which contradicted the foundations of the Roman political system; yet Rome did *not* find Jesus an intolerable threat, according to Luke. The *religious* authorities of Jesus' time *did* find Jesus an intolerable threat; and the Roman authorities put Jesus to death to please, or appease, Jesus' Jewish opponents, according to Luke.

In a world in which Christians were suffering persecution frequently, Luke's thesis maintained Jesus' integrity without making Jesus' followers the inevitable and irreconcilable enemies of the world in which they struggled to exist. Luke, as far as we know, did not compromise Jesus; nor should modern commentators compromise Luke. While it is profoundly important that modern Christians, and perhaps especially Americans, come to terms with the social and political views of Jesus; and while it is important that we understand how alien Jesus' values are to the foundations of the political, economic, *and religious* systems of which we are a part, it is also important that we not distort the evangelists' attempts to preach to the church of their time by forcing a message which is not there. Cassidy's thesis is a basis for revision of Conzelmann's thesis, not for its rejection.

The redactional emphasis on Pilate's triple declaration of Jesus' innocence, coupled with responses of Gentile rulers to Christians of the early church, calls for a change of emphasis in Cassidy's thesis too. Jesus did not defer to nor cooperate with the religious or political authorities of his time; but, according to Luke, Jesus' real enemies were *not* the political authorities.

They were the religious authorities. The courage Jesus displays in Luke's account of Jesus' trial and death is most evident in his refusal to cooperate with the religious authorities. They, above all, according to Luke, could have spared Jesus' life. It was Jesus' refusal to defer to or cooperate with them which cost him his life.

CONCLUSION

Richard Cassidy has made an important contribution to Lukan exegesis in his book *Jesus, Politics, and Society*. His basic thesis, that, according to Luke, Jesus did not defer to nor cooperate with religious or political authorities, stands firm. It was not the chief priests "and their allies" who put Jesus to death, however. The trial narrative in the Gospel and relevant passages in Acts make clear that it was the religious and political authorities who put Jesus to death, with the support of the multitudes, crowds, or people (as Luke chooses to say). The chief priests are prominent among the leaders; but other authorities are included in Luke's account in a way that merits explicit mention: the scribes, the elders, the Sanhedrin, Roman Pilate, half-Jewish Herod, who ruled Galilee under Roman authority, and soldiers, all of whom Luke refers to as "rulers" in 23:13 and 23:25. Irrespective of the actual events which surrounded the death of the historical Jesus, this is Luke's theological interpretation of those events and the persons they involved. To what extent Luke's interpretation reflects the actual, historical circumstances is yet another question.

Luke's portrayal of Jesus' social, political, *and religious* stance stands side by side with Luke's effort to portray Jesus and his church as worthy of legal status in Rome, an important social, political, and theological task in its own right. To give credibility to this position, Luke lays the responsibility for Jesus' death primarily on the Jerusalem rulers (leaders) of the Jewish people. To strengthen this position, Luke explains that the Gentile rulers who put Jesus to death did so *not* because they found him guilty of any crime, although he died a criminal's death, but to gain the favor of the Jews, especially their leaders. In this way, Luke removes theoretical obstacles to the legalization of Christianity as a religion in the Roman Empire and undermines rationales for Roman persecution of Christians.

One might say that Luke's perspective is summarized in the saying: Render to Caesar what is Caesar's; render to religious authorities what is theirs; but render to God what is God's. Luke's political apologetic, so important to the first-century church, does not have the same significance to the modern Western church; but the meaning of Luke's message remains the same. Were Luke with us today, s/he would no doubt remind us to render to political authorities what is theirs, to religious authorities what is theirs, but above all, to render to God what is God's; and the meaning of all these would be as radical now as it was in the time of Jesus or Luke.

NOTES

1. *Jesus, Politics, and Society* was published by Orbis Books, Maryknoll, New York, in 1978.

2. Ibid., Chapter Five, "The Trial and Death of Jesus," pp. 63–76.

3. Ibid., p. 75.

4. Cassidy correctly draws attention to the important difference between Luke's account of the hearing of the Sanhedrin and Matthew and Mark's accounts. In Luke, the focus is on whether Jesus claimed to be Messiah. Luke does not even mention the charge which dominates Matthew and Mark's accounts: that Jesus boasted of destroying and rebuilding the temple. Later, in Acts, a version of this accusation is falsely made against Stephen that he "does not cease to speak words against this holy place" (Acts 6:13).

5. Cassidy, *Jesus, Politics, and Society*, p. 64.

6. Cassidy also states that "The basic thrust of the charges is that Jesus had adopted a stance similar to the Zealots" (p. 65). This is, perhaps, an overstatement. Because Jesus was seen by the chief priests as someone who wanted to throw off Roman rule would not in itself make Jesus seem like a Zealot. Many Jews who were not Zealots as Josephus describes them longed for the throwing off of Roman rule. This longing is reflected in the popular hatred among Jews of Jesus' time for fellow Jews who collected taxes from Jews to pay Rome. A clear distinction between Jesus and the Zealots, presumably clear to the Jews of Jesus' time, was that Jesus did not take up arms against Roman rule as Zealots did.

7. Ibid., p. 66.

8. Ibid., p. 67.

9. Hans Conzelmann, *The Theology of St. Luke* (New York: Harper & Row, 1961), pp. 137–148.

10. Cassidy, *Jesus*, p. 69.

11. Ibid. Why an effort to show certain Jewish leaders responsible for Jesus' death is incompatible with some version of the political-apologetic theory is unclear. It is not logic which stands in the way of these two ideas functioning simultaneously in Luke in a complementary way.

12. Ibid., p. 70. To dissociate completely the chief priests from the people, as Cassidy does, misrepresents the evidence. Pilate calls the chief priests and the leaders (*archontas*) and the people (*laon*) together after Herod returns Jesus to Pilate, to inform them as a group that Pilate has found "no crime" in Jesus (23:13–14). "They" (the chief priests [*archontas*] and [*laos*]) *together with* the whole multitude (*pamplēthei*) shout for Barabbas' release (23:18) and Jesus' crucifixion (22:21–23). At 23:1 the multitude (*plēthos*) includes the chief priests by reference to 22:66 where they are not mentioned first. At 23:4, the chief priests are with the crowds (*ochlous*). Cassidy's assertion that the chief priests do not *represent* the people seems accurate. That the Jewish people as a whole were in *no* way involved in Jesus' death simply does not stand up in light of the evidence of these passages.

13. Ibid., p. 71. The participation of Roman soldiers in Jesus' crucifixion does diminish, however little, the responsibility of the "chief priests and their allies" for Jesus' death by introducing one more distinctive group of participants.

14. Ibid., p. 72.

15. Ibid., pp. 71–75.

16. Ibid., p. 75.

17. Ibid., p. 76.

18. Ibid., pp. ix, 7.

19. Ibid., p. 67

20. Ibid., pp. 72–75.

21. Ibid., p. 75.

22. For example, Jesus' violent outburst at the money changers in the temple, although—as is often forgotten—they were at the temple for the convenience of worshippers so that they could buy their offerings at the temple. Their presence was helpful, for instance, to pilgrims who travelled long distances to worship at the temple and could not carry their offerings with them (Luke 19:45–46). Another example of Jesus' active defiance is his outspoken criticism of the scribes, which, presumably, as far as many Jews of Jesus' time were concerned, was unfair, uncalled for, and disrespectful (Luke 11:47–52, 20:45–47). Likewise, Jesus was outspokenly critical of what he called, in Luke's version, the "hypocrisy" of some Pharisees. Neither Herod nor Pilate is subjected to such criticisms.

23. Ibid., pp. 75–76.

24. Ibid., p. 76.

25. Ibid., p. 63.

26. Ibid., p. 156.

27. Ibid., p. 76.

28. *ho archiereus* = the High priest; *hoi archiereis* = the chief priests.

29. The chief priests appear at 14:43, 14:55, 15:1, 2, 10, 11, 31. The high priest is referred to in 14:47, 53, 54, 60, 61, 63, 66.

30. The accusation made of Jesus in Matthew's account (26:61), like that in Mark's account (14:58), is that Jesus said he would destroy God's temple and rebuild it in three days.

31. In Matthew, Jesus is portrayed as the scribe par excellence; cf. Norman Perrin, *The New Testament: An Introduction* (New York: Harcourt Brace Jovanovich, 1974), ch. 8. Jesus' Sermon on the Mount is the perfect scribe's true interpretation of the law of Moses and the customs. Jesus' disciples must be "scribes for the kingdom of heaven" (Matt. 13:52). Jesus' declaration in the Sermon on the Mount that he has not come to destroy the law but to fulfill the law (Matt. 5:17) echoes throughout the Gospel. The amount of teaching material in Matthew, the longest Gospel, exceeds that of any other. Note that the stories about Jesus being taken to the temple (Luke 1–2) are absent from Matthew. The last command of the Risen Lord to his disciples is that they go to the nations, baptizing and teaching (Matt. 28:19–20). Hosea 6:6, which Matthew has Jesus quote on two occasions (9:13, 12:7), summarizes Matthew's critical attitude toward cult: "It is mercy I desire, and not sacrifice."

32. Matthew also refers to the "elders of the people" at 27:1. Mark does not use this expression, nor does John. Luke employs it at 22:66.

33. This passage is redactional to Matthew, as is the narrative that the chief priests and elders pay the soldiers who guarded the tomb to say someone stole Jesus' body while they slept (28:12–15).

34. The collective noun "the Jews" appears not only in John's passion narrative, but throughout the Gospel (c. 70 times). The noun is not necessarily derogatory in use. If John was a Hellenistic Jewish writer as modern commentators suggest, e.g., Perrin, *The New Testament*, pp. 249–250 (or, perhaps, Gentile) addressing a predominantly

Gentile-Christian audience, the collective noun "the Jews" would be an ethnically appropriate designation without being necessarily anti-Semitic.

35. Here the chief priests are referred to as "the chief priests of the Jews," a phrase which does not appear in the Jewish Scriptures.

36. The best reading of Luke 23:35b is that the rulers, also with them (the people), scoffed at Jesus while the people stood watching, not that the rulers also scoffed with the people.

37. Cf. Matthew 27:41–43, Mark 15:31–32. Note that in John's account (19:20–30), no one reviles Jesus on the cross.

38. Jerusalem, who "stones the one sent to her," foreshadows the stoning of Stephen in Jerusalem, which Luke narrates in Acts 7.

39. It is Luke, and only Luke, who makes Jerusalem prominent in Jesus' infancy. Although Jesus is born in Bethlehem, he is taken one week later to Jerusalem to be presented at the temple and, presumably, circumcised (2:22–39). On this occasion, two important prophecies are made about Jesus' future by Simeon and Anna (2:25–39), one of which foresees Jesus' death (2:34b–35). Only Luke alludes to Jesus' bar mitzvah in Jerusalem (2:41–50). The temptation narrative explicitly makes Jerusalem and the temple a temptation to Jesus (3:9–12). The devil's taunt, "If you are the Son of God, throw yourself down" because God's angels will preserve him, alludes to the taunts of those at the cross. In the transfiguration narrative, Luke—and only Luke—speaks of Jesus' exodus which he is about to accomplish in Jerusalem (9:30–31). The journey narrative, redactional to Luke, begins with Luke's statement that ". . . when the days of Jesus' assumption were approaching, he set his face to go to Jerusalem" (9:51). The passion predictions point to Jerusalem, explicitly in 18:31. In contrast to the other Gospels, the resurrection appearances occur in or near Jerusalem in Luke. Acts scholars note the importance of Acts 1:8 as a structural outline for Acts in which the starting place is the nascent church at Jerusalem. Jerusalem is the setting for the first seven chapters of Acts, the "first council" of the church (ch. 15) and Paul's final arrest (chs. 21ff.).

40. Conzelmann, *Theology of St. Luke*, pp. 73–93.

41. Martin Dibelius, *Studies in the Acts of the Apostles*, ed. Heinrich Greeven (London: S.C.M. Press, 1956); Ulrich Wilckens, *Die Missionsreden der Apostelgeschichte*, WMANT 5 (1963).

42. I chose this phrase to describe this kerygmatic substructure in the speeches of Acts in my dissertation "Moses and Meaning in Luke–Acts" (Ph.D. Diss., Marquette University, 1976); pp. 77–80 treat the characteristic components of this substructure and its function in Acts. One of the components isolated in that study, the culpability of "the Jews," does not survive the detailed analysis of this study. Other comments and conclusions made there withstand the test of this analysis.

43. Dibelius, "The Speeches in Ancient Historiography," *Studies in the Acts of the Apostles,* pp. 138–156. Via, "Moses and Meaning," pp. 91–97, 101–107.

44. Via, "Moses and Meaning," pp. 67–73, 75–77.

45. Chs. 2, 3, 4, 5, 10, and 13.

46. Acts. 2:14b–36, 38–39.

47. Acts 2:9–11.

48. The multitude appears in Luke's passion narrative at 23:1, 18, and 27, in the first two instances as collective opponents of Jesus, in the latter instance in support of Jesus.

49. 3:12b–26.

144   *E. Jane Via*

50. 23:1.
51. 23:13.
52. 4:8b–12.
53. 5:29b–33.
54. 10:34b–43.
55. As a centurion in the Roman army, Cornelius was clearly a Gentile. At 10:1, Luke describes him as a devout, God-fearing man, and at 10:22, as a just, God-fearing man, which might imply that Cornelius was interested in the synagogue. This whole episode, beginning at 10:1 and extending through 11:18, takes its premise from Cornelius' Gentile character, representative of all that which was traditionally unclean in Judaism, now "made clean" in Peter's eyes by his vision.
56. 13:16b–41.
57. E. J. Via, "An Interpretation of Acts 7:35–37 from the Perspective of Major Themes in Luke-Acts," *Seminar Papers*, Vol. 2. (Missoula: Scholars Press, 1978).
58. As is typical of Luke's style, there are allusions to several other Scripture passages in the prayer: Judith 9:12, 2 Macc. 15:22, Exod. 20:11, Isa. 42:5, and Ps. 2:1–2; but Ps. 146:6 is the primary focus of Luke's exegesis. There are also echoes of early Christian documents in this passage, *Didache* 10:3, 1 Clement 59.4, 60.3, 61.1, etc.
59. In Acts, Stephen (and later Paul) are falsely accused of the charge made of Jesus in the other Synoptics (Matt. 26:60–61, Mark 14:57–58). I. H. Marshall, *The Gospel of Luke* (Grand Rapids: Eerdmans, 1978), p. 850. H. O. Owen, "Stephen's Vision in Acts," *NTS* (1955): 224–226. R. Pesch, "Der Christ als Nachamer Christi: Der Tod des Stephanus (Apg 7) im Vergleich mit dem Tod Christi," *Bibel und Kirche*, 24 (1969): 10–11; and "Die Vision des Stephanus (Apg 7.55–56), im Rahmen der Apostelgeschichte," SBS 12 (Stuttgart: Kath. Bibelwerk, 1966).
60. Herod's involvement in John the Baptist's death should not be forgotten.
61. This is the first hint of any women, Jewish or Gentile, being persecutors of either Jesus or the church. In Gentile cities, however, the wealthy women may well have fallen among those who could properly be referred to as "rulers." "Chief men" certainly comes adequately under this category. Notice that the Jews involved are a limited group: the ones who were jealous of Paul's success as a preacher. This may reflect Luke's perception that the rulers who put Jesus to death were motivated by jealousy of Jesus' popularity as a preacher.
62. The *stratēgoîs*, here praetors, correspond to the *stratēgous tou hierou kai presbyterous* (22:52).
63. The *stratiōtas* correspond to the *stratiōtai* who offered Jesus vinegar on the cross, challenging him to save himself if he were King of the Jews.
64. The Pharisees, who are absent from the crucifixion narrative, are Paul's defenders here, as Gamaliel defended Peter and the apostles earlier in Acts.
65. This is consistent with Pilate's legal judgment that Jesus is innocent.
66. Another important example of this technique is Luke's composite story of Israel's past, of which Jesus is shown to be the fulfillment in the speeches of Chapters 7 and 13. They are meant to be read cumulatively. Via, "Moses and Meaning," pp. 145–160.
67. Conzelmann, *Theology of St. Luke*, pp. 139–140.
68. Ibid., pp. 137, 141–144.
69. The weakest link in Conzelmann's political-apologetic theory is his treatment of the Jews. He claims Luke wants to show that Jews are lying in their accusations against Christians (p. 140). The word "lying" does not accurately portray Luke's

view since, on more than one occasion in Acts, it is clear that an authentic theological dispute arose in Judaism over the meaning of Jesus (5:26–40, 23:1–10). Conzelmann does not distinguish among various groups of Jews as Luke does (believing Jews, disobedient Jews, jealous Jews, rulers of the people, etc.) but lumps them all together as "the Jews, . . . who are continually causing public disturbances" (p. 140). He sees the use of *Ioudaîos* as the birth of a collective polemic without considering its descriptive meaning in a Gentile cultural context. In short, he does not adequately consider many of the details on which this study focuses.

10

Luke's Audience, the Chief Priests, and the Motive for Jesus' Death

RICHARD J. CASSIDY

In composing his two-volume work, Luke probably had more than one prospective audience in mind. Many analyses have established that Luke was concerned with the situation of the Gentile Christians, but it has also been maintained that he was concerned to interpret salvation history for Jewish Christians and prospective Jewish converts.[1] Luke may also have been writing for educated pagan readers who had an interest in the new Christian way.[2] Indeed, Theophilus, a person mentioned in both of Luke's prefaces, may have been among this group.[3]

It is of interest to note that, even if Luke's intended audience came from only one of the above categories, questions about Jesus' death upon a Roman cross were almost certainly among the concerns of his audience. It is evident from Paul's letters that Christ crucified was a central element in the Christian proclamation.[4] In addition, there was the fact that any secular inquiries into the origins of the Christian movement would almost certainly bring to light the fact of Jesus' crucifixion.[5] Thus, either from Christian preaching or from secular sources, Luke's intended audience would have been challenged and confronted by reports about the startling circumstances of Jesus' death.

Luke may well have been responding to these concerns as he began to write. In the preface of the Gospel he states his intention of supplying an "orderly" (*kathexēs*) account and the circumstances of Jesus' death may well have been one of the areas in which he felt that better order was desirable. By drawing upon Mark and other sources available to him, he may have intended to present his readers with a report that would shed new light upon the various events leading up to Jesus' death.[6]

To suggest that this was one of Luke's purposes in writing is not to main-

146

tain that it was his exclusive or even central purpose. There were numerous other matters of concern to Luke's readers, and there were undoubtedly questions that Luke wished to treat as a result of his own interests and convictions.[7] It is thus important to respect the complexity of Luke's broader endeavor. As phrased by Paul Minear, this means to bear in mind that "in his writing Luke was responding to multiple problems with multiple 'intentions.' His conversation with his readers moved on several levels."[8]

In the sections that follow, the chief priests will be seen to emerge as the principal opponents of Jesus and Luke's description of their motives will be the ultimate concern of the analysis. However, as a preliminary step it is important to consider the responses given by Pilate and by the people who are favorable to Jesus. The issue of Luke's alleged political apologetic is also a preliminary matter to be considered briefly.

THE ROLE OF THE ROMAN GOVERNOR

While the chief priests and their allies are the ones principally responsible for bringing about Jesus' death, Luke does not exonerate the Roman governor and the Roman soldiers from their own respective involvements. At first it is not clear that Pilate has actually ordered Jesus' execution. Luke states (23:24–25): "So Pilate gave sentence that their demand should be granted . . . but Jesus he delivered up [*paradōken*] to their will." However, as the narrative moves forward and the Roman soldiers impress Simon of Cyrene to help in carrying Jesus' cross (23:25), it becomes apparent that Pilate has decreed death by crucifixion.[9]

Crucifixion is indeed the outcome when the procession reaches the place called the Skull. Jesus is crucified there along with two others in accordance with normal Roman procedures. A centurion is present supervising the other soldiers and there is a Roman inscription above Jesus' head indicating that his offense was sedition. Luke also indicates that, as Jesus hung on the cross, the Roman soldiers mocked him, challenging him to save himself (23:36–37).

After Jesus had died, Joseph of Arimathea went to Pilate to secure permission for burying Jesus (23:52). By reporting that it was necessary for him to do so, Luke again indicated that the Roman governor had control of the procedures regulating Jesus' death.

In light of these reports, one effect of Luke's narrative was to confirm for his audience that Jesus had indeed died as a consequence of a Roman decree. Previously, by one means or another, they had heard that Jesus had died on a Roman cross. Now Luke had confirmed the truth of this report and had also indicated that Pontius Pilate had been the governor in charge and that the official charge had been sedition.

In addition to reporting that these were the immediate circumstances of Jesus' death, Luke also situated these events within a broader context.[10] Luke indicated to his readers that, although the Roman governor ordered Jesus' death and although Roman soldiers executed him, it was the chief priests of

Jerusalem and their allies who had pressured Pilate into destroying him. In a very carefully written presentation, Luke left no doubt that, while Pilate had ultimately condemned him, the real explanation for Jesus' death was that the chief priests ardently desired his demise.

THE ROLE OF THE CHIEF PRIESTS

When Luke's Jerusalem narrative is analyzed with reference to the activities of the chief priests, the insights that emerge are startling. Clearly, Luke goes far beyond Mark in emphasizing the persistence with which the chief priests and their accomplices pursued Jesus and the intensity of the pressure they brought to bear upon Pilate.[11]

After reporting Jesus' protest at the temple and adding a verse to indicate that Jesus then taught daily there, Luke indicates that there was negative reaction to Jesus' intervention on the part of three groups. The reaction was so strong against him that they actually would have liked to destroy him. Luke writes (19:47–48): "The chief priests and the scribes and the principal men of the people sought to destroy him; but they did not find anything they could do, for all the people hung upon his words."

In this passage Luke indicates that "the principal men of the people" (*hoi prōtoi tou laou*) were aligned with the chief priests and the scribes in seeking for a way to destroy Jesus. Presumably the group of lay elders who comprised the third group of the Sanhedrin is the group that is designated.[12] In addition to referring to them as "the principal men," Luke also refers to these allies of the chief priests and scribes as "the elders" (*hoi presbyteroi*),[13] and "the rulers" (*hoi archontes*).[14]

From this point forward, Luke's narrative abounds with reports of steps taken by the chief priests to discredit and destroy Jesus. Immediately following this passage, Luke indicates that the chief priests and their associates challenged him publicly in three different instances. In the first instance (20:1–8), the chief priests, scribes, and elders (*presbyteroi*) demanded to know by what authority Jesus was acting. In the second case (20:20–26), they watched him and then sent spies to ask him a question about tribute, their intention being to deliver him up to the Roman governor.[15] In the third case (20:27–40), some Sadducees came to ask a duplicitous question about a woman successively married to seven brothers and life in the resurrection.[16]

Luke indicates that Jesus responded to each of these questions in such a way as to avoid being entrapped[17] and that such outcomes temporarily frustrated the efforts of the chief priests and their associates. That they still sought to be rid of Jesus is reaffirmed when Luke states (22:1–2): "Now the feast of Unleavened Bread drew near, which is called the Passover, and the chief priests and the scribes were seeking how to put him to death."[18]

Both Mark and Luke indicate that the chief priests were glad to take advantage of the opportunity presented by Judas' offer to betray Jesus. However, in Luke's account, they are more centrally involved in the actual arrest. Mark indicates that the sword-carrying crowd that accompanied Judas at the time of the arrest were sent by the chief priests, the scribes, and the elders (14:43–52). In Luke's version, the chief priests, captains of the temple, and the elders actually arrest Jesus and are directly addressed by him (22:47–53).

After the arrest, Luke reports that Jesus was taken to the high priest's house (22:54) and was mocked and beaten while held there (22:63–65). He was then brought before an assembly of elders (*to presbyterion tou laou*), an assembly which included the chief priests and the scribes (22:66–23:1).[19] Luke narrates that, after interrogating Jesus by asking him two questions, the entire assembly decided to bring him to the governor.

In Mark's Gospel the chief priests take an aggressive role in the proceedings before Pilate, accusing him of many things (15:3) and stirring up the crowd to call for the release of Barabbas (15:11), and presumably joining in the cries that Jesus be crucified (15:13–14). In Luke's account they are even more formidable in their opposition of Jesus.

First, Luke shows the chief priests formally pressing three charges against him (23:2).[20] Secondly, they boldly reiterate their case against Jesus when Pilate's initial inclination is to release him (23:5). Thirdly, they followed Jesus to Herod (23:10) and pressed their charges there.[21] Fourthly, when Pilate summons them and their allies along with the people to announce his decision that Jesus was not guilty, they react by crying out for Jesus' demise and Barabbas' release. They began to chant "crucify him, crucify him" when Pilate again expressed his desire to release him. They kept up their loud cries for Jesus' death, refusing to be swayed by Pilate's statement that he intended to release Jesus after chastising him. Luke concludes his report of this dramatic confrontation (23:13–23) by stating that, in the end, "their voices prevailed."

As noted earlier, from this point forward, Luke reports on active involvement by the Roman soldiers in carrying out the crucifixion of Jesus. Within this context, though, he does report that some of the chief priests' associates came to the site of the crucifixion to jeer at him. Luke states that as Jesus hung upon the cross "the rulers" (*hoi archontes*) scoffed at him, challenging him to save himself. As noted above, this is one of the terms that Luke has used to designate the allies of the chief priests.[22]

Within the Gospel itself, Luke includes one more report regarding the role of the chief priests in bringing about the death of Jesus. In narrating the appearance on the way to Emmaus, Luke shows the disciples describing the chief priests and their allies as having had the dominant, almost exclusive role in bringing about Jesus' death (24:20): ". . . our chief priests and rulers delivered him up to be condemned to death, and crucified him" (*hopōs te parēdōkan auton hoi archiereis kai hoi archontes hēmōn eis krima thanatou kai estaurōsan auton*).

In many respects this report serves to crown the long series of reports that Luke has given his readers concerning the role of the chief priests. Luke has confirmed to his readers that Jesus died upon a Roman cross in a crucifixion carried out by Roman soldiers at the decision of the Roman governor, but he has made it abundantly clear to them that the Jerusalem chief priests were the driving force in bringing about this outcome. So strong had they been in their desire to destroy him; so relentless had they been in pursuing this objective that the Emmaus disciples can speak in terms which suggest that the chief priests themselves crucified Jesus.[23]

In Jesus' third prediction of his passion earlier in the Gospel (18:31-33), Luke had reported a higher degree of Gentile involvement in Jesus' death. And in the Book of Acts, some of Luke's reports about Jesus' death will indicate a higher degree of Roman involvement than the Emmaus report does;[24] but, for now, at the conclusion of the Gospel, Luke seems determined that his readers not finish the book without a clear appreciation for the dominant role played by the chief priests.

THE ROLE OF THE PEOPLE

In addition to providing considerable information regarding the efforts of the chief priests against Jesus and their role in pressuring Pilate, another important characteristic of Luke's account is that it portrays a sharp distinction between the response of the chief priests and the response of a group in Jerusalem that is favorably disposed toward Jesus and his teaching. From the time of Jesus' entry into Jerusalem onwards, Luke uses the term "the people" (*ho laos*) to refer to this latter group and almost always distinguishes their response from that of the chief priests and their allies.[25]

Indeed in many of the passages considered above, Luke indicates a response on the part of the people that contrasts markedly with the response of the priests. His first presentation of the two distinct responses came when he initially reported to his readers that the chief priests were bent on Jesus' destruction. Following Jesus' protest at the temple, Luke reported that the chief priests and their allies wanted to destroy Jesus. Then, continuing, he stated that they could not do so "for all the people hung upon his words" (*ho laos gar hapas exekremato autou akouōn*).

In his next passage, Luke portrays the tension between priests and people in even stronger terms. When the priests and their allies challenge Jesus about his authority for acting in such a manner (20:1-8), Jesus asked them whether John's baptism was from God or from men. Luke states that they were afraid to answer "from God" because Jesus would ask them why they did not believe John. However, on the other hand, they were afraid to answer "from men" because "all the people will stone us" (*ho laos hapas katalithasei*). Here it is significant that Luke has specifically indicated why they fear the people, i.e., because they might be stoned.[26] Mark (11:32) only states that they were afraid of the people.

The next passage, containing the parable of the wicked tenants, is again a passage in which both the people and the chief priests play a role. While a full analysis of this important passage will be delayed until later, it is desirable here to note briefly that Luke reports a strong negative reaction on the part of the chief priests but implies a favorable reaction on the part of the people. Indeed, Luke indicates that "the scribes and the chief priests tried to lay hands on him at that very hour" and follows with the phrase, "but they feared the people" (*kai ephobēthēsan ton laon*).

Luke then reports that the priests and their allies sent spies to ask Jesus the question about Roman taxes. However, because of the character of Jesus' response they were unsuccessful in their efforts to entrap him. Including a point that Mark's version does not contain, Luke indicates that they could not shake Jesus' good standing in the sight of the people, "And they were not able in the presence of the people to catch him by what he said" (20:26).

Prior to the beginning of the passion narrative proper, Luke includes one additional passage in which he sharply distinguishes between the response of the chief priests to Jesus and that of the people. Luke states that, as Passover drew near, the chief priests and scribes were seeking how to put Jesus to death and then he adds a phrase that recalls the phrase he used in his description following the parable of the wicked tenants. Here Luke's statement is that the chief priests wished to put him to death "for they feared the people" (*ephobounto gar ton laon* [22:2]).

In describing the first part of Jesus' trial before Pilate, Luke indicates that the chief priests re-stated their case against Jesus by charging (23:5): "He stirs up the people . . . even to this place."[27] The character of this statement is such that it does not break the previous pattern of Luke's reports about the response of the people to Jesus' teaching. The priests seem to allege that Jesus is gaining some degree of favorable response from the people and indicate to Pilate that he must remedy this situation by condemning him.

However, in describing the second scene before Pilate (23:13–25), Luke seemingly portrays a change in the attitude of the people, indicating that they joined with the chief priests in calling for Jesus' crucifixion. The scene takes place after Herod has returned Jesus to Pilate. Pilate then calls together the chief priests, the rulers, and the people (*tous archiereis kai tous archontas kai ton laon*). He then proceeds to announce to them his decision only to find out that "they" refuse to accept it and call for Jesus' crucifixion. Since the people were named as comprising part of the group Pilate assembled and since there are shouts for Jesus' crucifixion from those assembled, it has been assumed by most commentators that Luke was now reporting an important shift in the allegiance of the people.

Whether or not the above passage should actually be interpreted as delineating a shift in the outlook of the people is far from certain, however.[28] Indeed, from a standpoint which conjectures that Luke had his own personal perspective on Pilate's action, there are grounds for holding that Luke is still portraying the people as favorable to Jesus. In this view Luke depicts Pilate calling the people into the proceedings at this point in order to indicate that the governor was trying to halt the forward momentum of the chief priests' efforts. In other words, what Luke is portraying here is Pilate's attempt to counter the pressure being brought by the chief priests and their allies. Having people present who were favorably disposed toward Jesus would facilitate Pilate's efforts to release him.[29]

In the verses that follow, Luke indicates that Pilate was fully unsuccessful in this tactic. Instead the priests became more adamant than ever and there was a crescendo of cries for Jesus' death. However, Luke does not specifically indicate who joins in this clamor for Jesus' death and it need not be supposed that the people actually did so.[30] Rather, Luke may have been indicating that the convictions of the chief priests and their allies were so intense that they eventually dominated the scene, sweeping away any objections from persons favorable to Jesus and causing Pilate to overturn his own decision.

Whatever the exact sense of these verses, as Luke's narrative continues, he again clearly portrays the people as favorably disposed toward Jesus. He reports that, as Jesus was led away (23:27) ". . . there followed him a great multitude of the people and of women who bewailed and lamented him." Subsequently, in his description of the crucifixion site, Luke draws a distinction between the people who stood by "watching" and the rulers who "scoffed" at Jesus (23:35). Finally, in the Emmaus passage (previously cited) Luke again carries forward the distinction between all the people (*pantos tou laou*) and the chief priests and rulers (*hoi archiereis kai hoi archontes*). The people viewed Jesus as a prophet mighty in word and deed. The chief priests and rulers delivered him up to be condemned to death and crucified him.

In summary, the general tenor of Luke's many reports about the people reveals them to be favorably disposed to Jesus' teaching and not sympathetic to the chief priests' efforts to destroy him.[31] And, apparently, Luke also wishes to communicate that the chief priests considered these people a force to reckon with. For, as indicated above, there are three separate instances in which Luke uses the word "fear" (*phobeō*) to describe the attitude of the chief priests toward this group.

THE QUESTION OF POLITICAL APOLOGETIC

Earlier in this analysis it was noted that Luke's conversation with his readers often moves on several levels. Perhaps nowhere is this observation more valid than with regard to Luke's rendering of the circumstances surrounding Jesus' crucifixion. In addition to confirming Pilate's involvement in Jesus' death, establishing the dominant role of the chief priests in bringing about his death, and indicating that Jesus had support among the people, Luke's reports also stress that Jesus was innocent in the eyes of Pilate and the Roman centurion who supervised his crucifixion.

In 23:4, at a point where there is no comparable declaration in Mark, Luke reports that Pilate explicitly stated to the chief priests and the multitudes: "I find no crime in this man." When they persisted in their accusations and mentioned that Jesus had been active in Galilee, Pilate sent him to Herod for

Herod's assessment. Upon receiving him back from Herod, Pilate then pronounced a much more extensive declaration concerning his innocence (23:14): "You brought me this man as one who was perverting the people; and after examining him before you, behold, I did not find this man guilty of any of your charges against him; neither did Herod, for he sent him back to us. Behold, nothing deserving death has been done by him." In contrast, at the comparable point in Mark, Pilate only briefly states (15:14): "Why, what evil has he done?"

As noted earlier, this is the place in Luke's account where the chief priests and their allies raised a great outcry in response to Pilate's words and called for Jesus' demise and Barabbas' release. Once again, Pilate addressed them, desiring to release Jesus (23:20). Again there was an outcry, this time with shouts for Jesus' crucifixion. Luke indicates that Pilate responded with another explicit declaration of Jesus' innocence (23:22): "Why, what evil has he done? I have found in him no crime deserving death; I will therefore chastise him and release him."

Inasmuch as Luke has gone far beyond Mark with respect to the number and magnitude of Pilate's declarations of innocence, it seems clear that he wished to emphasize for his readers that Jesus was innocent of the charges the chief priests had brought against him. This emphasis is subsequently heightened by Luke's report of the Roman centurion's declaration. In Mark 15:39, the centurion confesses that "Truly, this man was the Son of God." In Luke 23:47, by contrast, the centurion declares, "Certainly, this man was innocent."

Largely because Luke's Gospel does contain these four affirmations of Jesus' innocence, numerous commentators have concluded that Luke wished to make a "political apologetic" to Roman officials and others concerning the new Christian movement.[32] In the present context it is not possible to undertake a comprehensive discussion of this question. Nevertheless, as a point of related interest, it should be noted that there are serious reasons for denying that political apologetic was one of Luke's concerns. The presence of an innocent Jesus in Luke's account does not thereby establish the presence of political apologetic even though the two concepts have been linked in many previous analyses.

THE CHIEF PRIESTS' BACKGROUND

At this point in the present analysis, questions concerning the identity and character of the Jerusalem chief priests become extremely important. Luke has portrayed them as unrelenting opponents of Jesus; but, what else is known about them? Luke's reports indicate that they were influential before the Roman governor as well as prominent in temple affairs, but how did they acquire such influence? Before attempting to analyze Luke's Jerusalem narrative with regard to their *motive* for opposing Jesus, it is desirable to consider the various descriptions of their background and involvement which come from sources outside the gospel traditions.[33] Reports coming from Josephus, from the rabbinic writings, and from other ancient sources are important in this regard.

On the basis of these reports, it can be shown that four families dominated the office of high priest and other positions of religious and civic importance from 35 B.C. to A.D. 66. The opening for this new arrangement came with Herod the Great and it was a pattern that continued during the period of the procurators until the outbreak of the revolt.

In order to consolidate his own position, Herod ended the Hasmonean dominion over the office of high priest by appointing a priest of authentic Zadokite lineage. Because of the Hasmoneans' powerful reaction, this priest's term in office was short-lived, but Herod eventually overcame his opponents and began to appoint high priests of his choosing for limited terms in office. He allowed the next priest he appointed, a member of the Phiabi family, to serve for thirteen years, but he later gave several shorter-term appointments to members of the Boethus family.

During this period of direct rule, the Roman governors appointed priests from both of these families and from the Kamith family as well. Significantly, during the years of Jesus' lifetime, several appointments were also given to the house of Annas. Annas himself held the office from A.D. 6 to 15, and his son-in-law Caiaphas served a long term from A.D. 18 to 37. Subsequently, four of Annas' sons and one of his grandsons succeeded to this office.

After being rebuilt by Herod the Great, the Jerusalem temple became even more prominent in Jewish religious life. Since there was a steady influx of Jewish pilgrims from throughout the diaspora, and since adult male Jews made annual half-shekel contributions to the temple even if they did not undertake a pilgrimage, the economic and commercial dimensions of the temple activity also developed significantly. Thus, by reason of their high offices, the priests of these families possessed considerable economic as well as religious influence. In addition, since the reigning high priest was the president and convener of the Sanhedrin, and since former high priests and other prominent temple officials held seats on this body, these priestly families also possessed a high degree of political influence.

While these priests exercised a high degree of influence over Jewish religious and political life for many decades, it should not be thought that they held their positions without opposition from other Jewish groups. Indeed, there are several ancient sources which indicate opposition to these priests because of their exploitative practices and what is more, some of these sources indicate that, in the eyes of many of their contemporaries, these four families held the high priesthood illegitimately.

In a passage from *Jewish Antiquities* in which he is describing some of the events which occurred after the revolt against Rome had broken out, Josephus writes: "Such was the shamelessness and effrontery which possessed the high priests that they actually were so brazen as to send slaves to the threshing floor to receive the tithes that were due the priests, with the result that the poorer priests starved to death.''[34] In addition, Josephus reports that when they came to power in Jerusalem in 66, one of the Zealots' first actions was to burn the archives building in which the moneylenders' bonds were kept. Since the moneylending facility was operated in connection with the temple, this step indicates that there was at least some popular resentment against the stewardship of the chief priests in this regard.

Although the rabbinic traditions did not reach written form until much later, they frequently provide reliable information about various facets of first-century life. Without giving specific details, the following passage from the *Tosefta Menachoth* explicitly names the four priestly families previously identified and protests bitterly against their abuses: "Woe to the Boethusim; woe to their spears! Woe to the family of Annas! Woe to their serpent hissing! Woe to the family of Kanthera; woe to their pens! Woe to the family of Ishmael ben Phiabi! Woe to their fists! They are high priests; their sons are treasurers; their grandsons captains of the Temple, and their servants smite the people with their rods.''[35]

While the passage just cited represents the most explicit protest against the priestly families of this era, there are also other rabbinic passages that charge individual priests with bribery. Indeed, it is alleged in these sources that the coveted office of high priest was more than once secured through bribery.[36]

In addition to those just considered, an indictment that seems to refer to the priests who held high office during this period can also be found in *The Assumption of Moses*, a pseudo-epigraphic work written sometime during the first century. Here unnamed rulers who seek to avoid reproach by claiming sacred prerogatives are criticized as being "devourers of the goods of the poor," and "filled with lawlessness and iniquity from sunrise to sunset.''[37]

The foregoing references indicate significant criticism of the chief priests because of their exploitative practices. In and of itself, if it were widely accepted, such criticism was serious. However, when the even more basic criticism, that these families had no authentic right to even serve as high priests, was added to this first criticism, the potential for widespread popular opposition was significantly enhanced. Signs that this second more basic criticism was being made against these priests can also be found in the writings of Josephus. Josephus indicates that, in the end, the Zealots responded to this criticism by destroying the reigning high priest and installing a truly legitimate successor.[38]

Since these four families previously identified had dominated the office of high priest for a period of ninety-five years, their priestly credentials may have seemed satisfactory to many. Yet, clearly, Solomon had established the priest Zadoq as hereditary high priest initiating a Zadokite succession that lasted hundreds of years. And, clearly, though the members of the Annas, Boethus, Phiabi, and Kamith families were of priestly rank, they were not of Zadokite descent.

The question of legitimate succession was complicated by the fact that

Hasmoneans had received considerable popular support when, in a crisis situation, they had inserted themselves into the high priestly office. Yet certain segments of the populace never lost sight of the legitimate Zadokite succession being maintained in exile in Egypt and never accepted the Hasmonean legitimacy. Herod the Great cleverly assessed this situation when he was searching for a way to lessen the influence of his Hasmonean opponents. In order to break the Hasmonean hold over the high priesthood, Herod took the astute step of appointing Ananel, a Zadokite priest from Babylon, as the new high priest. Due to the residual power of the Hasmoneans he was not able to make this appointment stand, and he had to depose Ananel and appoint a Hasmonean in his stead. Subsequently, though, he had the Hasmonean (his brother-in-law!) murdered and then began to appoint priests from the Phiabi and Boethus families.

Within this context it is reasonable to presume that Herod's appointment of the Zadokite Ananel, short-lived though it was, re-kindled the convictions of the more dedicated Jews about the need for an authentic Zadokite high priestly succession. Indeed, this seems to have been one of the convictions that the Zealots themselves harbored.

As previously indicated, when the Zealots gained control of Jerusalem, they burned the archives building and executed the reigning high priest. They then instituted a lottery to choose the new high priest but only priests of the Zadokite descent were eligible for this lottery.

When these events took place, it became clear that, despite the longevity of their domination over the office and despite their influence, the high priests of these families still possessed an Achilles heel in their lack of legitimacy. As Joachim Jeremias has succinctly stated, "Riches and power the new hierarchy had in plenty, but these could in no way make up for their lack of legitimacy."[39]

LUKE'S KNOWLEDGE OF PRIESTLY MATTERS

In presenting his readers with a narrative in which the chief priests are portrayed as the central adversaries of Jesus in Jerusalem, was Luke aware of the charges against these priests that had been made in these other traditions? While the question cannot be answered with certainty, there are two factors which encourage speculation that Luke may have been personally familiar with some of these extra-gospel traditions. First, it can be established from the rest of his writing that Luke had a definite interest in various matters pertaining to the priests and priestly practices. Secondly, in terms of the Jerusalem narrative itself, it can be shown that Luke carries and emphasizes material relating to the two principal extra-gospel criticisms against the chief priests, i.e., their illegitimacy and their dishonesty.

It is well known that, after his prologue, Luke begins with a description of the angel's appearance to Zechariah announcing John the Baptist's birth. This appearance takes place in the Jerusalem temple. In describing the circumstances, Luke specifies that Zechariah is a priest "of the division of Abijah" (1:5) and includes several details about the manner in which he served "according to the customs of the priesthood" (1:9). In addition, when he describes Elizabeth, Luke indicates that she also is from a priestly family, telling his readers that she is "of the daughters of Aaron" (1:5).

Other early passages which indicate Luke's interest in temple and priestly patterns are those in which he describes the presentation of the child Jesus in the temple (2:22–38) and Jesus' subsequent teaching activity there (2:41–51). In both instances Luke shows Jesus and his parents following the prescribed temple procedures; but, in neither case, does he portray Jesus being ministered to by the chief priests or their allies from the scribes. In the first instance it is Simeon and Anna, neither of them representatives of the temple hierarchy, who bless God for the presence of Jesus. In the latter case Luke shows Jesus in discussions, not with the chief priests or the scribes, but "among the teachers" *(en mesō tōn didaskalōn).*

In giving his readers information about the political and religious context for Jesus' ministry (3:1–3), Luke includes a reference to Annas and Caiaphas as the reigning high priests. This reference suggests that he considers it important for his readers to be aware of their presence on the scene. Luke writes "in the high priesthood of Annas *and* Caiaphas," a reference correct in the broader sense if it is assumed that Annas, though no longer officially in office, still exerted a semi-official influence over the proceedings through his son-in-law.

Numerous passages in the Acts of the Apostles also testify to Luke's interest in priestly behavior. Among them is Acts 6:7. Here Luke's statement that "a great many of the priests were obedient to the faith" is interesting because it indicates that at least some priests were favorable to the Christian way even if the chief priests remained opposed to it.[40] In Acts 9:12, Luke's report on Saul's planned persecution implies that letters from high priests could have considerable influence in synagogues as far away as Damascus (see also Acts 9:14, 22:5, and 26:12). In 19:14 Luke indicates that some of the itinerant exorcists presuming to pronounce the name of Jesus over those with evil spirits were "the seven sons of a Jewish high priest named Sceva." In 23:3–5 Paul sharply rebukes the high priest and then apologizes for his words when he learns that it is the high priest.

Twice within the body of the Gospel, Luke reports cures from leprosy in which Jesus instructs those cured to go and show themselves to the priest(s). In the first instance, 5:1–16, Luke follows Mark 1:40–45 where Jesus states that the leper shall also make an offering for his cleansing "as Moses commanded, for a proof to the people." Later at 17:11–19, Luke reports a cleansing of ten lepers that is not given in Mark. In this instance Jesus simply asks them to go and show themselves to the priests.

The other priest-related passage that is in common with Mark preliminary to the Jerusalem narrative is the passage concerning the plucking of grain on the Sabbath (6:1–5). Following Mark 2:23–38, Luke reports that Jesus defended this practice by citing the case of David entering the house of God and eating the bread of the Presence "which it is not lawful for any but the priests to eat." However, in a departure from Mark, Luke omits the phrase in which Jesus states that this occurred when Abiathar was high priest. Seemingly, Luke is in accord with the general description given by Mark but has knowledge of his own about the succession of high priests which makes him reluctant to include Mark's reference to Abiathar.[41]

LUKE'S DESCRIPTIONS OF THE PRIESTS' MOTIVES

Luke's interest in and awareness of priestly matters has been amply testified to in the preceding passages. Nevertheless, nothing in any of these passages indicates that he has extra-gospel information on the issues of legitimate succession and corruption. Still, when Luke describes the character of Jesus' challenge to the chief priests in Jerusalem, these are the two areas in which Jesus' interventions come.

Before adverting to Luke's description of the demonstration that Jesus made at the temple, it is important to note that Jesus' entry into Jerusalem has a context in Luke that it does not have in Mark. Luke reports that as Jesus drew near to the city he spoke apprehensively about the city's fate (19:41–44). "Would that even today you knew the things that make for peace! But now they are hid from your eyes" are words which express a sense of forboding that the teaching offered will not be accepted.

In Luke's version Jesus' intervention at the temple has a milder character than it does in Mark's.[42] Nevertheless, the central Markan elements are preserved: Jesus drives out those who sold, and citing verses from Isaiah and Jeremiah, he charges them with having changed the temple from a house of prayer to a den of robbers.

The fact that it is those who *sold* (*tous pōloutas*) who are driven out and the fact that they are charged with thievery would have indicated to Luke's audience that Jesus was concerned with corrupt practices on the part of the unnamed persons involved in the selling that was being done. If Luke's rather sparsely detailed report caused his readers to wonder about the identity of the persons against whom Jesus' outburst was directed, the Gospel's very next lines would have informed them that not only the merchants were challenged by Jesus' intervention. There, for the first time in his narrative, Luke explicitly indicates to his readers that the chief priests and the scribes and the principal men of the people want to destroy Jesus. Luke does not specifically state that they were motivated to do so as a consequence of Jesus' protest at the temple, but this inference is almost impossible to avoid.

As noted above, Luke next reports that the chief priests and their allies challenged Jesus to tell them the authority by which he was acting. Jesus does not answer the question directly, but instead replies with his own question about John's baptism. Following Mark (12:1–2), but modifying his account significantly, Luke then portrays Jesus telling a parable that had a profound effect upon the chief priests. This parable and the verses immediately following it have extreme significance for the question of the chief priests' motives for seeking Jesus' death.

In addition to modifying Mark on several points with the parable proper, Luke also modifies or supplements Mark with respect to what precedes and follows the parable. The net effect of the modifications is to take an already powerful parable, to delineate its thrust more clearly, and to heighten its explosive impact.

Luke begins by modifying Mark to explicitly indicate that the parable was addressed to the people (*ton laon*). In the interpretation now advanced, this is a significant modification because of the favorable response that Luke elsewhere shows Jesus receiving from this group of people. In effect, then, Jesus is narrating a parable about wrongdoing to a group that has interest in the subject matter of the parable and to a group that is favorably disposed toward him.

Following C. H. Dodd and others, it is well to see most parables as having a central point.[43] In this instance the point is expressed in the answer given to the question of what the owner of the vineyard will do to the evil tenants. The answer is given by Jesus himself: "He will come and destroy these tenants and give the vineyard to others" (20:16).

It is possible to find meaning in the subordinate details of the parables[44] and in this parable the rejection and murder of the owner's son recalls Jesus' earlier predictions concerning rejection and death, most recently before his entry into Jerusalem. (In Mark, the closest prediction of rejection occurs in 10:32–36). This idea is also echoed and intensified in the modifications that Luke makes in the next verses. However, while this and other subordinate dimensions of meaning are present within the parable, it must be emphasized that the central point concerns the expulsion of the chief priests from their positions of responsibility. This interpretation is confirmed by Luke's description of the emotional outcry which took place immediately after Jesus spoke those words as well as by his descriptions of the rejoinder that Jesus made in the face of this outburst.

Relating an emotional reaction not recorded by Mark, Luke states, "When they heard this, they said, 'God forbid!' " (*akousantes de eipan mē genoito*). In treating this verse, most commentators attribute this reaction to the people, viewing them as expressing horror over the whole sequence of events or horror at the reaction of the owner. This interpretation accords well with the fact that the parable was explicitly presented to the people.

On the other hand, it may actually be the case that what Luke is describing here is the outraged reaction of the chief priests and the scribes themselves. Although he indicates that Jesus addressed the parable to the people, the chief priests, scribes, and elders were present (challenging his authority) in the verses immediately preceding, and Luke does not state that they departed. Further, when Jesus completes the parable and his additional remarks, they are portrayed as trying to lay hands on him.

The argument that they have been present for the parable and are greatly shaken by it gains additional support from an analysis of the verses that immediately follow:

> But he looked at them and said, "What then is this that is written: 'The very stone which the builders rejected has become the head of the corner?' Everyone who falls on that stone will be broken to pieces; but when it falls on anyone it will crush him" [20:17–18].

In contrast with the RSV translation, the Jerusalem Bible translation of *ho de emblepsas autois eipen* is, "But he looked hard at them and said." If such a rendering of the Greek can be granted, additional weight is given for the interpretation that Jesus is actually confronting some of those present. The sense would then be that Jesus has refused to yield ground in the face of the outburst by those offended at his parable. Rather, he fixes his gaze on them and holds fast to his position challenging them to deny the meaning of the Psalm reference he adduced.

Whether Luke is portraying Jesus speaking directly to the chief priests and scribes with the people as onlookers or speaking directly to the people with the result that the priests and scribes hear of his words later, the passage just cited (20:17–18) uses several scriptural allusions to reiterate the central point of the parable.

Following Mark, Luke reports that Jesus cited verse 22 of Psalm 118. Then, in a departure from Mark (where Jesus continues on to cite verse 23 as well), Luke reports that Jesus cited a verse whose language reflects Daniel 2:34–44 and Isaiah 8:14–15. As the passage now stands in Luke, it provides a reprise for the principal point of the parable, i.e., that the wicked tenants will be destroyed. In addition, it also makes reference to the parable's subordinate point concerning the rejection of the son. Since Luke has omitted the other Psalm verse cited by Mark, there is no elaboration upon the rejection of the cornerstone, an elaboration which shifts the meaning of the passage in Mark. Rather, in Luke's next verse, the verse reflecting Daniel, a powerful link is made between the rejection of the cornerstone and the destruction of those who reject it.

Luke concludes the dramatic sequence just described with the report that "the scribes and the chief priests tried to lay hands on him at that very hour, but they feared the people; for they perceived that he told this parable against them [*kai ezētēsan hoi grammateis kai hoi archiereis epibalein ep auton tas cheiras en autē tē hōra, kai ephobēthēsan ton laon egnōsan gar hoti pros autous eipen tēn parabolēn tautēn*]." Clearly, they have been deeply shaken by Jesus' words.[45] The intensity of their reaction is underscored by the phrase "at that very hour" (*en autē tē hōra*), a phrase not present in Mark.[46]

It should be recalled that in describing their reaction after Jesus' protest at the temple, Luke states that the scribes and chief priests were not able to proceed against Jesus because all the people hung on his words. Here in contrast, Luke reports that they did not proceed against him because they feared the people. The sense is that the people are favorably disposed to the teaching that Jesus is bringing them and would come to his aid. That the priests fear the response of the people in defense of Jesus is thus the primary meaning of *ephobēthēsan*, but there may also be the additional meaning that they feared the people because of *what* Jesus was teaching them.

As indicated above, Luke may have presented the passage describing Jesus' protest over the "robbery" at the temple and the passages just considered with some consciousness of the fact that there were other contemporary outcries against the Jerusalem chief priests. However, even if Luke were not conscious of these other criticisms and did not realize how well his own reports converged with them, he still communicated valuable information to his readers concerning the chief priests' motives. In effect, these passages represent what Luke considered it important for his readers to know concerning the chief priests' reasons for seeking to destroy Jesus. He himself may have known more about the background of the Jerusalem high priests than he indicated. However, what he told his readers was more than enough to give them a basis for understanding why the chief priests were so resolutely opposed to Jesus.

In summary, what Luke indicated to his readers was that Jesus constituted a threat to the chief priests of such a magnitude that they were convinced that he had to be destroyed. Luke described Jesus entering into the temple and calling out against those who had made it into a den of robbers. He then stated (for the first time) that the chief priests and their allies wanted to destroy Jesus. He then showed the priests trying to discredit Jesus by questioning his authority only to find that he turned and attacked them with a powerful parable. In concluding his description of this exchange, Luke told his readers that the chief priests and their allies wanted to take control of Jesus "at that very hour."

The descriptions Luke has given are thus of such a character that there was little room for mistaking the nature of Jesus' challenges to the priests. From Luke's reports it is not clear why Jesus reached the conclusion that the priests have made the temple a den of robbers, nor is it clear whether he had any other grounds for judging them to be wicked tenants, but it is evident that these were in fact the conclusions Jesus reached. It is also evident that the chief priests and their allies took Jesus' challenge to them extremely seriously and resolved to destroy him because of it.

The interpretation that Luke was concerned to explain the chief priests' sustained efforts against Jesus in terms of the threat that Jesus posed to them receives additional confirmation from the fact that, in contrast to Mark, Luke does not identify envy as a factor motivating them.[47]

In Mark's account the mention of envy as a factor motivating the chief priests occurs during Jesus' trial before Pilate. In providing his readers with a rationale for Pilate's reluctance to condemn Jesus, Mark states that Pilate knew that the chief priests were opposing Jesus out of envy (*dia pfthonon*):

"For he perceived that it was out of envy that the chief priests had delivered him up" (15:10).

Had he wished to do so, Luke could have included this note concerning the chief priests' envy in his own description of Pilate's reaction to Jesus or else made reference to it at some other place within his narrative. Seemingly, though, he was satisfied to have his readers focus upon the challenges that Jesus made to the chief priests as their basic reason for proceeding against him.

THE REACTION OF LUKE'S READERS

Even though most of them would not have been familiar with the specific characteristics of the various Jewish groups and institutions, the Gentiles among Luke's audience would still have had little difficulty in grasping that the chief priests of Jerusalem relentlessly sought Jesus' death and finally succeeded in persuading Pilate to execute him.

Regardless of how much they knew concerning the position of the chief priests in the Judaism of Jesus' day, Luke's Gentile readers would have perceived from Luke's reports that the priests wanted to destroy Jesus because he had raised serious challenges against them. Even if they did not know that the chief priests were responsible for the selling which took place at the temple, Luke's explanation of the priests' reaction to Jesus' demonstration would have made it evident that, somehow, in making such an intervention, Jesus had effectively threatened the priests. Nor would the implications of Jesus' attack upon the priests and their allies in the parable of the wicked tenants have escaped Luke's Gentile readers. Clearly Jesus was hurling several criticisms against the priests and clearly their own response was to seek to destroy him.

Luke's Jewish-Christian and Jewish readers would undoubtedly have grasped these and many more of the elements in Luke's reports concerning the circumstances of Jesus' death. They would have more easily grasped the relationship between the chief priests and the various other Jewish groups that were described in Luke's accounts, and they would have also been sensitive to many other features of Jewish life under Roman rule.

Specifically, with respect to Luke's description of the chief priests' motives, it is interesting to ask whether any of Luke's Jewish-Christian readers had any knowledge of the extra-gospel criticisms of the chief priests discussed above. If they were not aware of the issue of legitimate high priestly succession and the charges of corruption that had been levelled against these priestly families, then they probably reacted to Luke's passages much in the way that Luke's Gentile readers presumably did. However, if they were informed concerning these controversies, then how much more would they have resonated to Luke's descriptions of Jesus' challenges to the priests and their allies.

For readers sensitive to this background, how much more understandable was the extreme reaction against Jesus that Luke attributes to the chief priests. Particularly because Luke described Jesus as receiving a favorable response from the people, the more was he a threat to these priests. Clearly, that was their motive for opposing him so vigorously and relentlessly.

As indicated at the outset, whatever the exact composition of Luke's audience, it is reasonable to suppose that his readers were interested in knowing more about the circumstances of Jesus' death and the reasons why it occurred. Luke responded to his readers' concerns in terms of his own resources and perspectives by providing them with an account that sheds much light on the circumstances of Jesus' death. Whether they came to his account as presumably less knowledgeable Gentiles or as well-informed Jewish Christians or from somewhere in between, Luke's readers would have learned a great deal from reading the descriptions he set before them.

Luke's readers were also undoubtedly interested in many other questions besides those relating to the circumstances of Jesus' death and, as noted above, Luke himself certainly had many other reasons for writing. But, inasmuch as they came to Luke's account looking for a coherent explanation of the circumstances and the motives for Jesus' death, Luke's readers found what they desired within his Gospel. Indeed, they found that there was a noteworthy "order" in the account that Luke had produced. It was, though, an order which took into consideration a multiplicity of factors and nuances.

NOTES

1. Alfred R. Leaney, *A Commentary on the Gospel according to St. Luke* (New York: Harper, 1958; 2nd ed., Naperville, Ill.: Allenson, 1967), pp. 7–8. I. Howard Marshall, *The Gospel of Luke: A Commentary on the Greek Text* (Grand Rapids: Eerdmans, 1978), p. 35, states that Luke's work was intended for members of the church, but was also intended to be used evangelistically with a wide audience in view. Frederick Danker, *Luke*, Proclamation Commentaries Series (Philadelphia: Fortress Press, 1976), pp. 2–4, indicates that Luke was trying to respond to Jewish as well as Gentile misunderstanding.

2. J. O'Neill, *The Theology of Acts* (London: SPCK, 1961), pp. 168 ff.

3. W. Marx, "A New Theophilus," *EvQ* 52 (1980): 18, lists seven names that have been suggested in trying to identify Theophilus. Marx argues that King Agrippa II is a more likely candidate.

4. David W. Tiede, *Prophecy and History in Luke-Acts* (Philadelphia: Fortress Press, 1980), p. 97, focuses attention upon 1 Corinthians 1:23 where Paul states, "But we preach Christ crucified, a stumbling block to Jews and folly to Gentiles." While any form of ignominious death of the Messiah would have constituted a stumbling block for Jews, to preach a Messiah whose death had come through crucifixion would be particularly foolish in the eyes of Romans.

5. Ordinarily, news of events occurring in Judea might not have made its way into the main channels of the Empire. However, inasmuch as there were Christians in Rome at a relatively early date and inasmuch as Judea became the subject of great interest due to the campaigns of Vespasian and Titus (commemorated in public cele-

brations, coins, and Josephus' writings), there is reason to suppose that Jesus' death on a Roman cross would have circulated in at least some public circles.

6. In indicating that he was aware that others had previously given accounts and that he now wishes to present his own orderly narrative, Luke is not deprecating the efforts of his predecessors. Most recently, see R. Dillon, "Previewing Luke's Project from His Prologue (Luke 1:1-4)," *CBQ* 43 (1981): 207.

7. C. Talbert, "Shifting Sands: The Recent Study of the Gospel of Luke," *Interpreting the Gospels*, ed. J. Mays (Philadelphia: Fortress Press, 1981), pp. 197-213, provides a helpful survey of the various aspects of Luke's perspective.

8. Paul Minear, "Dear Theo: The Kerygmatic Intention and Claim of the Book of Acts," *Int* 27 (1973): 132.

9. Marshall, *The Gospel of Luke*, p. 862, indicates that Luke's readers would not have been left in uncertainty about the outcome, since crucifixion was known to be a Roman punishment carried out by soldiers. D. Flusser, "The Crucified One and the Jews," *Immanuel* 7 (1977): 27, indicates that it was not at all unusual for occupying Roman forces to demand such humiliating service from passing Jews.

10. In what follows, Luke's reports will be analyzed with reference to what they reveal about the roles played by various persons and groups in the events of Jesus' death. However, in addition to what he wished to communicate about this aspect of Jesus' death, Luke was also concerned to relate his death to the resurrection and to situate both within the larger context of salvation history. See W. Grundmann, *Das Evangelium nach Lukas* (Berlin: Evangelisch Anstalt, 1974), pp. 454-457 and F. Danker, *Luke*, pp. 110-112. See also, Tiede, *Prophecy and History*, pp. 97-125.

11. J. Tyson, "The Opposition to Jesus in the Gospel of Luke," *Perspectives in Religious Life* 5 (1978): 149, speaks of a "geographical" opposition whereby the chief priests constitute Jesus' opposition within the city of Jerusalem. J. Ziesler, "Luke and the Pharisees," *NTS* 25 (1979): 154, holds that Luke wants to show that the Pharisees are not even partly responsible for the death of Jesus.

12. Grundmann, *Das Evangelium nach Lukas*, p. 370; Marshall, *The Gospel of Luke*, p. 722. Luke also uses this term to describe the group acting with the chief priests in Acts 25:2.

13. See Luke 9:22, 20:1, 22:52, and Acts 4:5, 8, 23; 23:14, 24:1, 25:15.

14. In Luke 23:13, 24:20, and Acts 4:5, the group designated by this term is shown to be working collaboratively with the chief priests. In Luke 23:35 and Acts 3:17, 4:8, 13:27, and 23:5, *archōn* is used in such as way that it may designate the chief priests themselves.

15. While preserving the substance of Mark's account of the question regarding tribute (Mark 12:13-17), Luke does include various details that have the effect of heightening the chief priests' involvement. First, Luke adds to Mark to indicate that the chief priests were keeping Jesus under surveillance (*kai paratērēsantes*). Secondly, where Mark states that the priests sent some Pharisees and some Herodians and thus indicates that persons from both of these groups also opposed Jesus, Luke keeps the focus concentrated upon the chief priests themselves, stating that they were the ones who sent "spies" (*engkathetous*). Luke's next phrase also indicates the specific character of the plot that the chief priests had formulated. He states that their purpose was to "deliver him up to the authority and jurisdiction of the governor." In contrast, Mark merely indicates that they wanted to entrap him in his talk.

16. At this point in their reading of the Gospel, some of Luke's readers may have missed understanding that the Sadduccees who ask this question are in alliance with

the chief priests, scribes, and elders who were responsible for the preceding question. However, informed Jews and Jewish Christians among Luke's readers would have understood this connection and other readers who continued on into Acts would have subsequently arrived at it. In Acts 4:1 the chief priests are accompanied by the captains of the temple and some Sadduccees, and in Acts 5:17 Luke explicitly states that the high priest was supported by the Sadduccees.

17. For an analysis of the pattern and the content of Jesus' replies to these challenges, see R. Cassidy, *Jesus, Politics, and Society: A Study of Luke's Gospel* (Maryknoll, N.Y.: Orbis Books, 1978), pp. 56-59.

18. This report, indicating the continuance of the chief priests in their resolve, comes after Luke has reported a series of teachings and discourses by Jesus including prophecies about future destruction (20:41—21:38). In 21:5-6, Luke indicates that Jesus prophesied the destruction of the temple, and his readers may have inferred that this prophecy gave added incentive to the chief priests' efforts, but Luke does not expressly state this. Nor, in contrast with Mark, does he report it as one of the charges against Jesus at the Sanhedrin hearing. Cf. Mark 14:58.

19. The contrast between Luke's account of a less than formal Sanhedrin hearing at daybreak and Mark's much more structured evening proceeding followed by a morning consultation (Mark 14:55-65 and 15:1) are widely recognized. See Cassidy, *Jesus, Politics, and Society*, p. 64, for a fuller analysis of the hearing Luke describes.

20. The charges that the chief priests bring are essentially false but are cleverly phrased so as to have credibility, Cassidy, ibid., pp. 65-66.

21. Both the Gospel and Acts contain a goodly number of references to various members of the Herod family (Luke 1:5, 3:1, 3:19, 8:3, 9:7-9, 13:31, Acts 12:1-21, 13:1) and Luke seems interested in recording their respective responses to Jesus and the early Christians. Indeed, as indicated by Robert F. O'Toole, *Acts 26: The Christological Climax of Paul's Defense* (Rome: Biblical Institute Press, 1978), pp. 22-25, Luke seems especially concerned to show parallels between the hearing of Jesus before Pilate and Herod Antipas and that of Paul before Festus and Agrippa II in Acts 26. An additional reason why Luke may have included this passage is that the chief priests are again shown to be seeking Jesus' condemnation.

22. Inasmuch as Mark indicates that the chief priests themselves were present and that they "mocked him to one another with the scribes" (15:31), it is not clear why Luke prefers to use *hoi archtones* here. Cf. Emil Shurer, *The History of the Jewish People in the Age of Jesus Christ*, 175 B.C.-A.D. 135, 2 vols., ed. Geza Vermes and Fergus Millar (Edinburgh: T. and T. Clark, 1976; Naperville, Ill.: Allenson, vol. 1, 1973, vol. 2, 1979), vol. 2, p. 212; the author thinks that Luke may have been including the chief priests within this group when he used this term. See Note 14 above.

23. Marshall, *The Gospel of Luke*, p. 895, states the following in commenting upon this verse: "note that the Jews (sic) are themselves said to carry out the crucifixion there, although *paredōkan* contains a hint of Jesus being handed over to the Romans." Later in Acts, Luke sometimes indicates that the high priest, scribes, rulers, and elders played the central role in Jesus' death (4:10), sometimes indicates that Pilate and Herod had a prominent role (4:27), and sometimes presents the "men of Israel" having a great responsibility (2:23, 36).

In another instance (13:27-28) he also indicates that "those who live in Jerusalem and their rulers" were involved. In view of the fact that he generally uses the term *laos*, Acts 3:12-15 is particularly noteworthy. There Peter is addressed *ton laon* when he tells them that they are the ones who handed Jesus over and disowned him, who demanded the reprieve of a murderer while they killed the prince of life.

24. See preceding note and Acts 4:27, 13:28.

25. The analyses of G. Rau, "Das Volk in der lukanischen Passionsgeschichte: eine Konjektur zu Lk 23:13," *ZNW* 56 (1965): 41–51, and J. Kodell, "Luke's Use of *Laos*, 'People,' Especially in the Jerusalem Narrative (Lk. 19:28—24:53)," *CBQ* 31 (1969): 327–343, are both extremely helpful for delineating the various degrees to which Luke distinguishes the response of the group (*ho laos*) from that of the chief priests and their allies. My own position with respect to the interpretation of the troublesome use of *laos* in 23:13 is given below.

26. In Acts 5:26, when he describes how the captain of the temple and his assistants went to take the miraculously released disciples into custody, Luke indicates that they did not use force to do so "for they were afraid of being stoned by the people" (*ephobounto gar ton laon mē lithasthōsin*).

27. In 23:4 Pilate has indicated to the chief priests and the multitudes, *tous ochlous,* that he found no crime in Jesus. However, in response to Pilate's declaration, they urgently reiterated their charge. Marshall, *The Gospel of Luke,* p. 853 notes that these "multitudes" appear suddenly from nowhere and holds that Luke's sense is that the chief priests retain the leading role in responding to Pilate. See 23:48 for the other principal instance in which the multitudes appear within the Passion narrative.

28. Following P. Winter and basing his view strongly upon the overall patterns of Luke's reports concerning the people designated by this term, G. Rau, "Das Volk," p. 48, argues that Luke's original phrase has been mis-copied here. In his view the passage should read that Pilate called together "the chief priests and the rulers of the people" (*tous archiereis kai tous archontas tou laou*), rather than "the chief priests and the rulers of the people" (*tous archiereis kai tous archontas kai ton laon*), as it does now in virtually all manuscripts. Marshall, *The Gospel of Luke*, p. 858, emphasizes that this suggestion lacks textual support.

29. A. Plummer, *A Critical and Exegetical Commentary on the Gospel According to Saint Luke* (Edinburgh: T. and T. Clark, 1922), p. 524, provides support for this interpretation when he states: "Pilate is taking the matter in hand summoning not only the hierarchy whose bitterness against Jesus he knew, but the populace, whom he hoped to find more kindly disposed, and able to influence their rulers." While Marshall, *The Gospel of Luke*, p. 858, is inclined to Grundmann's view that the *laos* are present to serve as witnesses to Pilate's statement of Jesus' innocence, he does hold that Pilate is looking for a way to take the heat out of the situation.

30. Marshall, *The Gospel of Luke,* p. 860. Marshall notes that Luke omits Mark's report (15:11) that the crowd, stirred up by the chief priests, called out for Barabbas' release.

31. As indicated in Note 23 above, the most noteworthy exception to this pattern is Acts 3:12–15.

32. For an interpretation of how Conzelmann views Luke relating political apologetic and eschatology, see Cassidy, *Jesus, Politics, and Society*, pp. 7–8. The argument against Conzelmann's position is made on pp. 128–130.

33. The presentation that follows relies heavily upon the analysis of the chief priests' background given in Cassidy, *Jesus, Politics, and Society*, pp. 114–121.

34. *Ant.* XX. 8.8.

35. Pesachim f. 57,1. *Tosefta Menachoth.* Cited in F. Farrer, *The Herods* (New York: Herrick, 1898), p. 117.

36. See P. Gaechter, "The Hatred of the House of Annas," *TS* 8 (1947): 7. Gaechter references several texts given by Strack and Billerbeck (*Kommentar zum Neuen Testament*).

37. *The Assumption of Moses* (London: Black, 1897) 7:3–10.

38. *War* IV.3.8.

39. Joachim Jeremias, *Jerusalem at the Time of Jesus*, trans. F. Cave and C. Cave (Philadelphia: Fortress Press, 1969), p. 198.

40. Although Zechariah and now these "ordinary" priests are portrayed in a favorable way, Luke's Good Samaritan parable (10:29–37) portrays both a Levite and a priest negatively.

41. According to 1 Samuel 21:1 and 22:20, Abiathar was not high priest at the time this incident occurred. Various explanations have been advanced to explain why most texts of Mark seem to suggest that he was. Luke seems to have been well enough informed about the subject to recognize the difficulty posed by Mark's reference.

42. Mark 11:15–17 portrays Jesus driving out those who bought as well as those who sold, indicates that he overturned the tables of the moneychangers and the seats of those who sold pigeons, and specifically states that he would not allow anyone to carry anything through the temple. The protest that Luke describes is much milder; but, interestingly, it is directed only against those who sold, not those who bought.

43. C. H. Dodd, *The Parables of the Kingdom* (New York: Scribner's, 1961), pp. 7–9; Joachim Jeremias, *The Parables of Jesus* (New York: Scribner's, 1963), p. 19.

44. J. D. Derrett, "The Parable of the Wicked Vinedressers," *Law in the New Testament* (London: Darton, Longman, and Todd, 1970), pp. 286–312, examines several of the other dimensions of meaning, particularly the meaning connected with Palestinian legal procedures, that are present in this parable.

45. Dodd, *The Parables of the Kingdom*, p. 11, and Jeremias, *Parables of Jesus*, p. 21, both express the view that the parables of the Gospels were frequently intended to engender a strong reaction in those who heard them. Jeremias states: "They correct, reprove, attack. For the greater part, though not exclusively, the parables are weapons of warfare. Every one of them calls for immediate response." As indicated by the analysis presented above, this judgment has particular application in regard to this parable.

46. By specifically naming the scribes and the chief priests and by indicating that they tried to take hold of him at that hour, Luke reports a stronger reaction than Mark does. In 12:12, after Jesus has concluded the parable and the Psalm citation, Mark has only "and they tried to arrest him."

47. In Acts 5:17–18, Luke does indicate that the high priest and his supporters were "filled with jealousy" (*eplēsthēsan zēlou*), when they arrested the apostles and put them in jail.

Biographical Notes

Editors

Richard J. Cassidy is a graduate of the Gregorian University in Rome (S.T.L.) and the Graduate Theological Union in Berkeley (Ph.D.). A priest of the Detroit archdiocese, Fr. Cassidy is presently directing the Archdiocesan Office for Justice and Peace and teaching New Testament ethics and moral theology at St. John's Provincial Seminary.

Philip J. Scharper has served as an editor of *Commonweal,* American editor of Sheed and Ward and is the founding editor of Orbis Books. He has received seven honorary degrees and numerous awards for his contribution to religious publishing. With his wife he has authored more than thirty nationally televised religious documentaries, which have received twenty international and national awards, including several Emmys.

Contributors

Frederick W. Danker is Professor of Exegetical Theology at Christ Seminary-Seminex in St. Louis. He has co-edited *A Greek-English Lexicon of the Greek New Testament and Other Christian Literature* and is the author of several other books including *Jesus in the New Age According to St. Luke* and the Proclamation Commentary on Luke. His most recent publication (1982) is entitled, *Benefactor: Epigraphic Study of a Graeco-Roman and New Testament Semantic Field.*

J. Duncan M. Derrett has served as Wilde Lecturer in Natural and Comparative Religion at Oxford University and, until his recent retirement, as Professor of Oriental Law at the University of London. He has published *Law in the New Testament* and several other studies on the legal and social background to the New Testament texts. His most recent work (1982) is *The Anastasis: the Resurrection of Jesus as a Historical Event.*

J. Massyngbaerde Ford, a native of England, did her graduate work at Oxford. In the United States she has given the Schaff Lectures (Pittsburgh), the E. T. Earle Lectures (Berkeley), and held the Bernard Hanley Chair at Santa Clara University. Dr. Ford is the author of, among other works, *Trilogy on Wisdom and Celibacy* and *The Pentecostal Experience.* She has edited *Revelation* in the Anchor Bible Series and is presently serving on the Theology Faculty of Notre Dame University.

168

Robert F. O'Toole, S.J., received his doctorate in Sacred Scripture from the Pontifical Biblical Institute in Rome. He is the author of *Acts 26: The Christological Climax of Paul's Defense* and numerous articles on other themes in Luke-Acts. He presently serves as the chairperson of the Department of Theological Studies at St. Louis University and is a convener for the Catholic Biblical Association's task forces on Luke and Acts.

Quentin Quesnell received his doctorate in Sacred Scripture from the Pontifical Biblical Institute in Rome. He has published several books on New Testament subjects including *The Gospel in the Church: a Catechetical Commentary on the Lectionary (Cycle C: the Creed),* published this year. He has served as vice-president of the Catholic Biblical Association and is currently Lecturer in Religion and Biblical Literature at Smith College.

Daryl Schmidt is a graduate of the Associated Mennonite Biblical Seminaries (M. Div.) and the Graduate Theological Union (Ph.D.). He is the author of *Hellenistic Greek Grammar and Noam Chomsky* and currently teaches in the Department of Religion Studies at Texas Christian University.

Willard M. Swartley received his doctorate from Princeton and is now director of the Institute of Mennonite Studies and Professor of New Testament at the Associated Mennonite Biblical Seminaries, Elkhart, Indiana. He is the author of *Mark: The Way for All Nations* (1979) and is currently at work on *Case Issues in Biblical Interpretation: Slavery, Sabbath, War, and Women,* a book scheduled for publication in 1983.

Charles H. Talbert received his doctoral degree from Vanderbilt University and is currently Professor of Religion at Wake Forest University. He has authored a number of New Testament studies and in 1978 edited the collection *Perspectives on Luke-Acts.* He is currently serving as chairperson of the Society of Biblical Literature's Luke-Acts Seminar and will publish his own commentary on Luke's Gospel later this year.

E. Jane Via has followed her doctorate in theology from Marquette University with a degree in law from the University of San Diego. She currently teaches Biblical Studies at the University of San Diego and combines her interests in the Bible and law with interests in Jungian psychology and feminism.

Index of Names and Subjects

Index of Scriptural References

OLD TESTAMENT

NEW TESTAMENT

Prepublication Statements on *Political Issues in Luke-Acts*

"One might be tempted to think that all that can be said about Luke's attitude to social and political issues has already been said in the numerous works that have been published in recent years, but this book manages to bring together a set of essays which offer new insights into the problem. The contributors represent varying outlooks in New Testament study, so that the book offers a continuation of the current debate rather than a set of agreed conclusions. Nevertheless, the measure of agreement is significant. While Luke envisaged that Christians would live in a non-violent manner and develop a new social order among themselves which would serve as an example to others, their way of life could bring them into conflict with the state and the religious authorities, and they had to be prepared, like their Master, to pay the price for their loyalty to the gospel.

"If we shall not succeed in understanding Luke without paying attention to this aspect of his teaching, it is equally true that we shall not succeed in living as Christians today without taking into account Luke's teaching on these issues. The editors of this symposium deserve our thanks for bringing together this series of useful essays which no student of the social teaching in the New Testament and of Luke's writings in particular ought to miss."

I. Howard Marshall, Professor of New Testament Exegesis,
University of Aberdeen

"The beginnings of Christianity did not take place in a political vacuum. This is evident from all the New Testament writings, but especially in those of Luke, who does more than any other New Testament author to relate his story to the wider world. Although Jesus refused to take the Zealot line, his teaching and activity impinged on sensitive areas of contemporary Palestinian policy—especially in relation to the Roman administration, the Herodian dynasty, and the Jewish establishment. When his message was carried farther afield by his followers, it was bound to attract the attention of the Roman authorities in one province after another, and before long in Rome itself. Luke shows discretion as he documents the gospel's interaction with the secular and religious powers of his day, but the careful reader of Luke-Acts can see at how many points the gospel presented a challenge to those powers.

"Various phases of this challenge are discussed in some detail by the contributors to this symposium, and in consequence much light is thrown on Luke's purpose in writing. Where their arguments do not carry total conviction, they nevertheless provoke serious thought about the meaning of the texts which are handled. Many of the contributions bear witness to the stimulus provided by Dr. Cassidy's own recent work: *Jesus, Politics, and Society.* I am happy to commend this new volume of studies to the serious attention of students and teachers of the New Testament and early Christian history."

F. F. Bruce, Rylands Professor of Biblical Criticism and Exegesis,
University of Manchester

"These lively, provocative and well-informed essays center around the thesis of Dr. Richard J. Cassidy, in his *Jesus, Politics, and Society,* in which he challenges the notion that Luke-Acts was written as a political apologetic. As editor of the essays, he is to be commended for including studies which take issue with his own point of view, on both political and methodological grounds. The result is a stimulating debate, as though one were participating in a discussion, at once learned and relevant, on the exegetical issue of Lucan redaction, and of course on the moral question of Jesus' attitude toward civil authority. On both scores, this is an important contribution to scholarly studies, as well as to the study of the Bible in the church."

Howard Clark Kee, William Goodwin Aurelio Professor of Biblical Studies and Director of the Graduate Division of Religious Studies, Boston University

"Richard Cassidy's *Jesus, Politics, and Society* has proved to be a catalyst, at times a direct stimulus, for renewed investigation of the political dimension of the writings of Luke, in contrast to the 'quietist Jesus' interpretation which seemed to be the outcome of Conzelmann's work. Here we have ten studies which sharply probe aspects of the political Luke and/or Luke's political Jesus, including a study by Cassidy himself as well as studies which take him to task on various counts. Conzelmann finds some qualified support among these essays, too, but in the main there is new ground broken, moving not toward a new consensus on Luke-Acts, but toward a multi-faceted exploration of a complex author.

"One impression left by the book is that some of our methods in Gospel-study may be less valuable as tools than we have supposed, in view of their inadequacy to resolve fairly simple issues in interpretation; if this impression is correct, we may be summoned to new methods—or the putting of new and better questions. All told, *Political Issues in Luke-Acts* is an extremely valuable showcase of the most current research in Luke-Acts and its societal concerns."

Edward C. Hobbs, Chairman of Department of Religion and Professor of Religion, Wellesley College; Visiting Professor of New Testament, Harvard University

"Four years ago Richard Cassidy's *Jesus, Politics, and Society: A Study of Luke's Gospel* focused on the political issues at stake in Jesus' ministry; and the book specifically addressed the question of whose responsibility it was, humanly regarded, that led Jesus to the cross. The thesis that the Jewish priestly leaders were held to be blameworthy in Luke's view has provoked discussion *pro* and *con*. And the wider concerns of Luke's Gospel as reflecting political *Tendenz* were brought to the fore thereby.

"It is good to have some of these reactions, both positive and negative, brought together in *Political Issues in Luke-Acts* since Cassidy's position is shown to be applicable to Acts and yet to need some refinement. But its overall cogency is still very plausible."

Ralph P. Martin, Professor of New Testament, Fuller Theological Seminary